THE PRACTICAL HOMESTEAD

THE PRACTICAL HOMESTEAD

THE BACKYARD HANDBOOK FOR GROWING FOOD, RAISING ANIMALS & NURTURING YOUR LAND

PAUL HEINEY

DK'S BESTSELLING CLASSIC *COUNTRY LIFE*, NOW AVAILABLE IN PAPERBACK

Discover more at
www.dk.com

London, New York, Melbourne,
Munich, and Delhi

Project Editor Edward Bunting
Art Editor Robert Purnell
US Editor Irene Pavitt
Design Assistant Simonne Dearing
Assistant Editor Lynda Warrington
DTP Designer Matthew Greenfield
Picture Researchers Melissa Albany, Sarah Moule
Artwork Visualizer Paul Bates
Production Managers Ruth Charlton, Meryl Silbert,
Patricia Harrington
Managing Art Editor Steve Knowlden
Managing Editor Ian Whitelaw

Illustrators Maltings Partnership, Peter Morter, Murray
Zannoni, John Woodcock, Chris Orr, Sarah Young

Outdoor photography Peter Anderson

Studio photography Clive Streeter

First published in the United States as *Country Life*
by Dorling Kindersley Ltd, 1998

This edition first published 2010
Published in the United States by
DK Publishing
375 Hudson Street
New York, New York 10014
10 11 12   10 9 8 7 6 5 4 3 2 1
177792—07/2010

ISBN 978-0-7566-6213-4

DK books are available at special discounts when purchased in
bulk for sales promotions, premiums, fund-raising, or educational
use. For details, contact: DK Publishing Special Markets,
375 Hudson Street, New York, New York 10014 or
SpecialSales@dk.com.

Reproduced by GRB Editrice, Verona, Italy
Printed and bound in China by Toppan

Discover more at
www.dk.com

CONTENTS

HOME FARMING 6

ANIMAL HUSBANDRY 38

FRUITS OF THE EARTH 88

WIDER HORIZONS 112

FOOD FROM THE FIELDS 128

HOME COMFORTS 164

HOME FARMING

HOME FARMING STARTS WITH A DREAM, and it takes many steps to change the dream into a reality. This is a book for those who want to turn their fields, plots, or gardens – real or imagined – into working home farms. It is also a source of

information for those who are already farming, whatever the acreage. Some of the steps you have to take will seem huge,

but you need be afraid of none of them, for each brings you closer to that deep satisfaction that can come only from living and working on the land.

WHAT IS HOME FARMING?

HAY FROM THE STACK
There is deep satisfaction in watching the progress of any crop – from sowing the seed to storing and using the harvest.

HOME FARMING IS first and foremost an adventure of the mind and body, every step of which takes us closer to the land, which is where home farmers believe they truly belong. Sitting discontentedly in an office, we dream of open spaces, broad skies, and the rich fruits of our own harvest. This is when the call of the land overwhelms us. Would it not be, we wonder, far better to earn a simple living working the land by the strength of our hands and bodies than to be paid a high wage for a softer, but less satisfying, life? Surely a life working in the open air would be a better one?

There are plenty of other attractions, too: the country is a better place for the children to grow up in; the pace of life there is slower and allows time for deeper reflection; many people prefer to have their routines dictated by natural forces rather than artificial ones; and many wish to grow their own pure food. All these things inspire the home farmer's dream.

LIVING BETTER OFF THE LAND

Food production today is a huge, mechanized industry. But it was not always so and does not have to be. From the time of the earliest settlements, people all over the world have used the land around their homes to grow crops and raise animals for the family's use. Through history, their houses have been farm workshops, accommodating the diverse businesses of dairying and preserving, pickling and brewing, milling and baking, all these crafts being carried out on a domestic scale.

It can still be done. The wisdom of those centuries is still available for us to use. What I call "home farming" is a celebration of that wisdom; it is interesting, fun, wholesome, and gentle on the earth's resources.

The pitchfork – a symbol of the "hands-on" approach

It is no ambition of mine to overturn the sophisticated empires of modern food production. We live in an urban age, in which few people can hope to be wholly "self-sufficient." This book is about how, in the midst of modernity, we can add a measure of home farming to our lives and enjoy living and eating better.

HOME FARM – HOMEMADE
One of the delights of home farming is looking forward to your food with an anticipatory smile and a clear conscience.

If you are interested in a healthier life, you will be interested in *organic* farming. This is both a practice and a philosophy. In terms of practice, your soil will be free from pesticides, herbicides, and other chemicals. Your livestock will be fed naturally and live in conditions that suit their needs. As for a philosophy, you will seek ways to work with nature, not against it.

With an acre or two of land, you can keep animals and reap a harvest; with a backyard or even window boxes, you can grow food; and anyone with a kitchen can pickle and preserve. And nothing makes a house quite so homelike as an element – however small – of home farming!

CHALLENGE OF THE LAND

ALTHOUGH THE REWARDS of home farming are huge, the effort involved can be enormous; before you decide to take it up, you should be aware of the hard work and determination needed to run a farm of any size. There are moments of heartbreak when crops fail or animals die, and times of exhaustion after harvesting, digging, or shearing. At times you doubt if it is worth it, but the next day brings new rewards and presents new challenges. You learn to look forward, never backward.

THE LAY OF THE LAND

THE HOME
When choosing a farm, don't forget that the house is an important consideration. Do not buy just on the strength of the land – make sure the house is one you will be happy in.

Somewhere, there is a farm that is just right for you. It might be on the fringes of a village or town, at the back of a house, amid rolling meadows, close to a forest, or high in the hills. There is hardly a limit to the places in which a home farm of some kind can be established, given ingenuity and vision. So do not think that because vast fields are beyond your grasp, you can never be a farmer. Home farming is not burdened with the same preoccupations as modern farming, and so there are places that home farmers will delight in, but others would shun. The trick is in spotting them. This does not mean that you are a completely free agent in the matter of the crops you grow and the animals you keep; farmers and growers will have defined the limits after centuries of trial and error. But as a home farmer less driven by commercial concerns, you have more freedom than most, and you should take every advantage your land has to offer.

GETTING AN OVERVIEW

Whether farming in a backyard or a barnyard, before embarking on any firm plans take a good look around you; glance over the garden walls or hedges and see what everyone else is up to. Learning to read the lay of the land is one of the first steps in becoming a home farmer. Experienced farmers are able to take one

FROM COAST TO LOWLANDS

Included in this view are four kinds of landscape in which conditions are suitable for farming: the coastal lowlands, the urban fringe, the low plain of a river valley, and the gently rolling lowlands.

COASTAL GRAZING MARSH
There are two forms of this highly distinctive landscape: saltwater and (shown here) freshwater.

BACKYARD FARM
If you live in or near a town, but wish to be involved in farming, rent a plot of land or start some other form of backyard farm near your home.

Coastal marshes have good, rich grazing

Where town meets country is often a place to find a corner for a home farm

look at a field or plot and tell you that it's fit for nothing but sheep, just right for potatoes, too exposed for soft fruit, or too rocky to be worked with horses. But, of course, what they mean is that the most *profitable* use of the land is that which they recommend. You can keep sheep or cattle anywhere you like, short of on a rocky ledge; but there is a danger of the rewards not being as great as they would have been had you chosen something better suited to the location. In short, the secret of successful farming depends on what you want to be successful at.

There are four basic factors to consider when you are assessing a piece of land: climate, water, soil, and exposure. It is the interaction of these that determines what you will be able to achieve in any spot you may choose. There is very little you can do to cheat them, so work with them. Farming should not be a fight.

> *Learning to read the lay of the land is one of the first steps in becoming a home farmer.*

FINDING OUT ABOUT THE CLIMATE

The prevailing wind; the likelihood of snow, frost, and fog; the annual rainfall; and the highest and lowest temperatures are all of vital concern. Does spring come late, or dare you contemplate planning an early lambing? Is autumn dry enough for you to work the soil before the land becomes too wet or too frozen?

Is the rainfall reliable enough to guarantee lush grass, or sufficient to swell vegetables that need rain to ripen? It is a widely accepted view that world climate is changing, and so, as well as consulting the official opinion, ask neighbors for their experiences of recent years. In fact, in all matters relating to the land, those

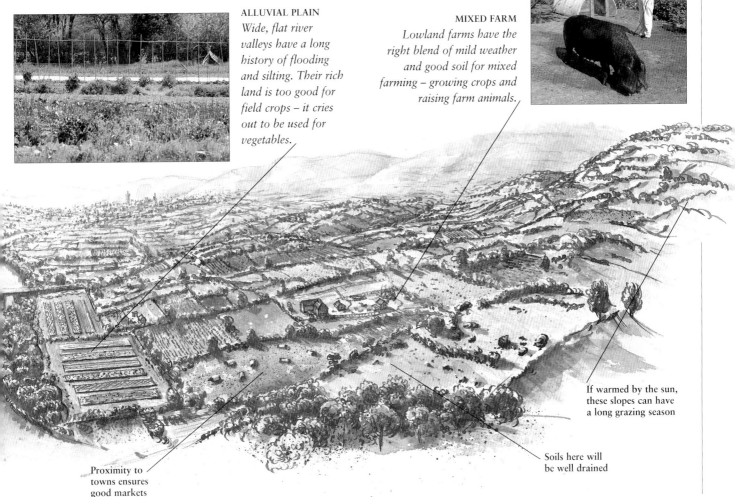

ALLUVIAL PLAIN
Wide, flat river valleys have a long history of flooding and silting. Their rich land is too good for field crops – it cries out to be used for vegetables.

MIXED FARM
Lowland farms have the right blend of mild weather and good soil for mixed farming – growing crops and raising farm animals.

If warmed by the sun, these slopes can have a long grazing season

Soils here will be well drained

Proximity to towns ensures good markets

around you are the best sources of knowledge. Your neighbors may well have worked farms hereabouts for generations, and the store of wisdom they have built up will be invaluable. If you are lucky, they will share it with you. For this and many other reasons, you should always approach neighboring farmers in a spirit of learning, recognizing that you are the novice and they the professionals. A little humility opens a lot of doors.

> **66** *On most farms, the richer the soil, the greater the value of the crop that can be grown.* **99**

WHERE WILL THE WATER COME FROM?

Water is a commodity of which you never seem to have the right amount in the correct place because on most farms there are many conflicting interests. It never rains when you want the grass to thicken, but waits until the hay is cut and drying, and then it pours. This happens to be the time when potatoes need it most, but that is little consolation.

There is, however, one thing that is worse than having to put up with showers at the wrong time: outright absence of water. If your farm is prone to drought, it is up to you to ensure that adequate supplies of water are available from wells, boreholes, or rivers. But before you make plans to take water from such sources, remember that you cannot assume that any water is yours for the taking.

Although a river may enhance the landscape in summer, what threat might it pose in winter when the water is high as a result of heavy rain? Coastal farmers need to be aware that flooding by salt water can ruin land for a generation.

FOOTHILL FARM
Farms situated in the foothills generally have good soils and are well drained, but are too steep for a tractor to plow; so a mixture of cattle and sheep is ideal.

FOOTHILL FRUIT FARM
In countries with a Mediterranean climate, the foothills are a source of tree fruit – apples (as here), citrus, apricots, peaches.

FOOTHILLS AND UPLANDS
There are two main farming environments in this view: foothills, where conditions are right for mixed arable and livestock farming; and uplands, which are used mainly for grazing, and which extend to the altitude limit for farming.

On dark sides of valleys, the growing season will be shorter

Soils will get thinner with altitude

WHAT SORT OF SOIL DO YOU HAVE?

On most farms, the richer the soil, the greater the value of the crop that can be grown. So if you have a rich, peaty loam, it would be a waste to graze low-value sheep when you have the perfect conditions in which to grow vegetables. On the other hand, upland fields with thin layers of stony soil over rock are difficult to cultivate, and are best left to grass for stock to graze.

You must also think about how the soil will behave at different times of the year. Light, sandy soil will be a joy to work in the spring, when it is still crumbly after the winter rains, but when the sun has baked it dry, it can be as hard as rock and may even break the plow.

WHICH WAY DOES THE LAND SLOPE?

Crops will grow only in the right temperatures, with a sufficient intensity of light and with enough water. A plot sloping steeply away from the sun (north or south, depending on the hemisphere) supports little more than sheep grazing. Land that slopes toward the sun is warmer, although the intensity of the summer sun may make it uncomfortable for livestock and too dry for grass or crops to grow. As a rule of thumb, if you are taking up backyard farming, get all the sun you can.

HILL SHEEP FARMING
Soils are thin, over rock, and spring comes late. Hill sheep thrive here, but be prepared for the labor of bringing winter feed out to your stock.

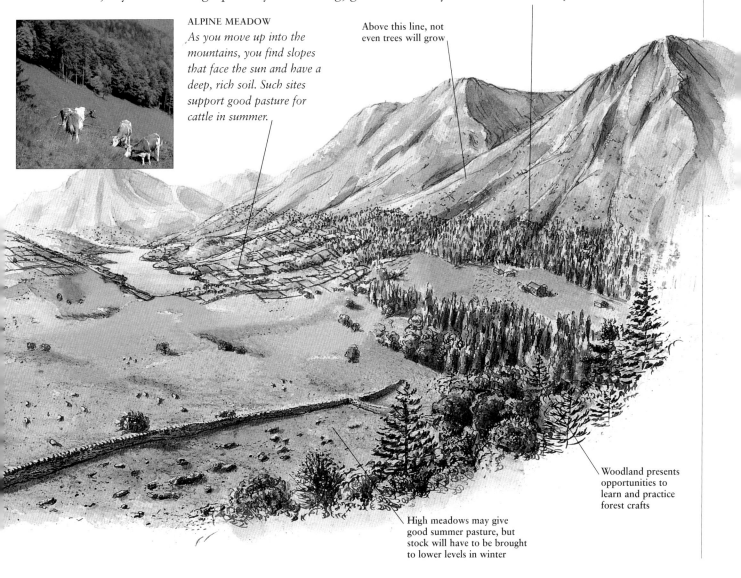

ALPINE MEADOW
As you move up into the mountains, you find slopes that face the sun and have a deep, rich soil. Such sites support good pasture for cattle in summer.

Above this line, not even trees will grow

Woodland presents opportunities to learn and practice forest crafts

High meadows may give good summer pasture, but stock will have to be brought to lower levels in winter

Garden farm

CAN A GARDEN ever be a farm? Yes, of course it can. Take a look over a few walls and see how tiny plots are put to productive use, packed with as tempting a range of fresh foods as any supermarket. That's how I started – by growing a tiny area of wildflower meadow in the depths of inner London! It can be done, but the smaller the plot, the greater the cunning required. On a large farm, the odd unused corner doesn't matter, but the garden farmer uses every space and, constrained only by a care for the environment, squeezes the last drop of value from the land.

SELF-CATERERS
Pigs can forage in woods that are otherwise unused: a natural sort of place for pigs to be.

PLANNING THE GARDEN FARM

The best use of a small area will require meticulous planning to make sure that at every stage of the year the land is bringing you some reward. Even leaving an area fallow, possibly planting a green manure (see p. 137), must be part of a grand plan to ensure that, despite the intensive nature of your farming, the land is not paying the price. It is all too easy to allow a garden to become over-exploited so that after a while the soil is exhausted, and you have no farm at all. Start by deciding not only what you are going to grow, but how you intend to rotate the crops to prevent buildups of diseases or pests (see p. 97).

Wherever your garden, whatever the climate, there are things that you cannot manage without. You will need a proper compost area and (if the climate is cool) some cold frames, a greenhouse, or a polytunnel. Well-made fencing is also essential, to exclude urban rabbits and

foxes, and the possibly well-meaning, but disruptive, cats and dogs. Good fences will also help to prevent young chicks or ducklings from going astray.

Look also at what lies outside the garden. A patch of derelict land may provide a home for a rooting pig (with the owner's and neighbors' consent), and woodland edges will offer you free fruits and berries, all of which can be considered part of your farm, without your having to do much about it.

WHAT TO GROW

Are you growing for yourself only, or also for others? This is where gardening differs from farming; if sales and profit come into it, then the cropping list you arrive at will be based on some research that suggests you are able to fill a gap in the range offered by your local stores. This is not as difficult as it seems. If you are growing organically, that in itself will endear you to potential customers.

Others will be happy with food that is freshly picked. They may, as ingrained supermarket shoppers, be amazed at the taste of truly garden-fresh food. If your interest is self-sufficient production, then it simply depends on what you want to eat and how ingenious a rotation plan you can put together (see p. 97).

GARDEN LIVESTOCK

On this scale, livestock is almost out of the question, but not quite. It takes only the tiniest space to house a hive of thousands of bees, and although some of your neighbors might object at first, any reservations usually melt away at being offered a jar or two of the honey.

A few chickens are possible too, if you have room to offer them occasional fresh pecking. But noisy roosters do not make for neighborhood harmony and are best shunned. Another poultry option, even if your only water supply is city water, is to keep ducks or geese.

THE SMALLEST LIVESTOCK
A well-kept hive will supply your household all year round, with perhaps a share for neighbors.

HEALTHY HARVEST
A guarantee of hand-produced, carefully grown foodstuffs is sure to tempt the customer.

WOODPILE
If wood is your fuel, plan your garden farm to include areas for drying and storing the logs.

FOOD FOR FREE
Food grows wild on bushes and in fields, supplementing what you can grow on your patch.

100-FOOT FARM

There is no doubt that this is a farm, despite its diminutive size – 100 × 50 ft (30 × 15 m). Maximum use has been made of every inch. Don't forget the sign saying what you have for sale!

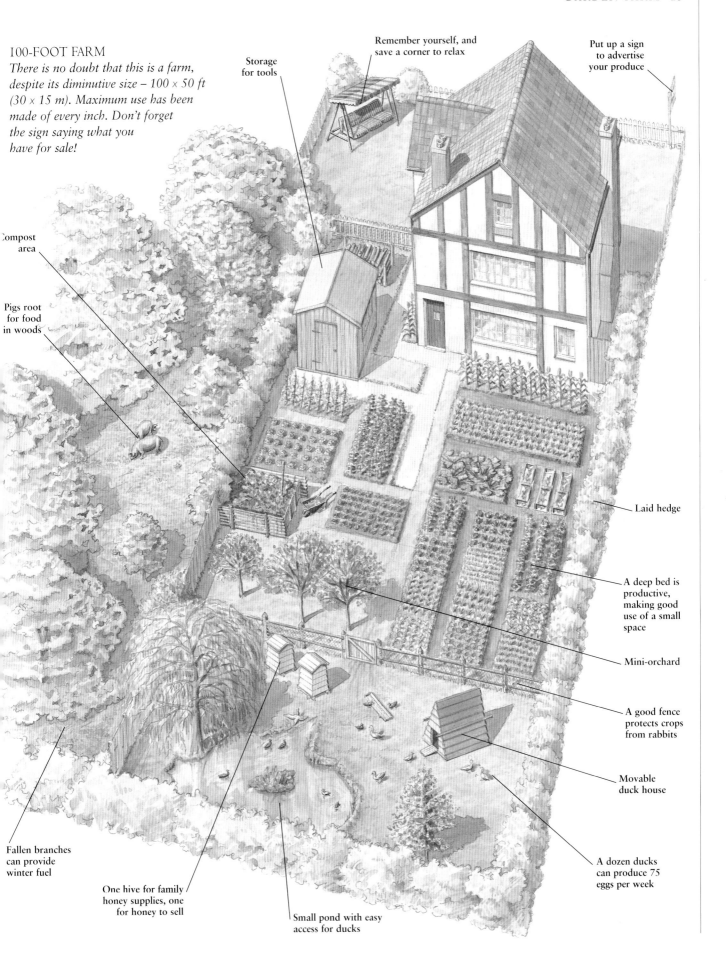

Remember yourself, and save a corner to relax

Put up a sign to advertise your produce

Storage for tools

Compost area

Pigs root for food in woods

Laid hedge

A deep bed is productive, making good use of a small space

Mini-orchard

A good fence protects crops from rabbits

Movable duck house

A dozen ducks can produce 75 eggs per week

Fallen branches can provide winter fuel

One hive for family honey supplies, one for honey to sell

Small pond with easy access for ducks

Small home farm

POSSIBILITIES OPEN UP once you have a farm of this extent. You can start to think both about keeping livestock and about growing fodder crops to feed them in winter. The area you are able to devote to vegetables should give you considerable surpluses to sell, and you will have room for a polytunnel or two, expanding your range of vegetable crops.

Managing an area of land of this size is almost a full-time job, but if you plan it out carefully, you will still have time for other things. This makes it a useful size of holding to have if you are trying to balance a farming life alongside part-time paid employment. But remember that the workload will vary with the seasons – you may need help (or a very tolerant employer) at certain times of the year.

GOAT AT LARGE
Goats are useful for clearing areas of weeds, some of which they will eat in preference to grass. This is the smallest size of holding on which it is possible to keep a goat.

CHOICE OF VEGETABLES

Your main crop on a plot this size will be vegetables. You might choose to specialize in high-value, out-of-season produce, which may have to be grown under cover, or decide on lower-value, easy-to-grow garden vegetables, such as potatoes, cabbages, and salad crops, or you might want to grow some of each. But avoid the temptation to grow a little bit of everything, or you will find that you have no time to tend to any of your crops properly.

To decide which type of vegetables will suit you better, you will have to assess the soil (see p. 132), the climate, and your level of skill, and take a guess at what will sell best in your area.

If you are able to keep animals, they may help mop up surpluses of produce. If you have ragged cabbages that are too caterpillar-eaten to sell, a goat or a pig will be more than pleased to clear them up for you. This is an alternative recycling system to your compost pile.

ANIMAL HUSBANDRY

With ½ acre (0.2 ha), you have enough land to keep animals, but make sure that they will fit in with your lifestyle or your farm will soon become a burden. Keeping livestock will present you with daily chores. For example, keeping pigs will mean you have to feed and muck out daily. Goats will also need milking every day. These jobs cannot be put off just because you are unwell or do not feel like doing them.

You will also need to think carefully when deciding what type of animals you wish to keep – some require more care than others. For example, pigs are great creatures of habit and look forward to their meals at fixed times. They do not understand that meetings will keep you late at the office. In contrast, ducks seem happy to be kept waiting.

It might be tempting to have a wide range of different animals, but farms are not zoos. Do not look on your stock as pets, or if you do, admit it, and don't complain about the extra work.

FODDER CROPS

You could also use a part of your land to grow fodder crops for your livestock. Although this is too small an area to make hay worthwhile, both corn and alfalfa could be grown here – alfalfa is particularly useful because it can provide three crops a year. You may be able to manage all this without using any machinery – but only just.

POULTRY CHORES
Regular cleaning of the poultry yard is important to prevent parasites and diseases.

ONION HARVEST
If you find a good market for a crop you enjoy growing, you are well on the way to success.

PICKING APPLES
Fruit trees provide a crop at the end of the growing season, when there is less work in other areas.

MANURE PILE
If it is to sustain the fertility of a holding of this size, the manure pile must be properly managed.

HALF-ACRE FARM

Small though it is – ½ acre (0.2 ha) – this plot has room for far more diversity than a garden farm (see p. 14). All stock will need to be securely fenced: a pig, for example, could devastate a plot like this in one glorious night.

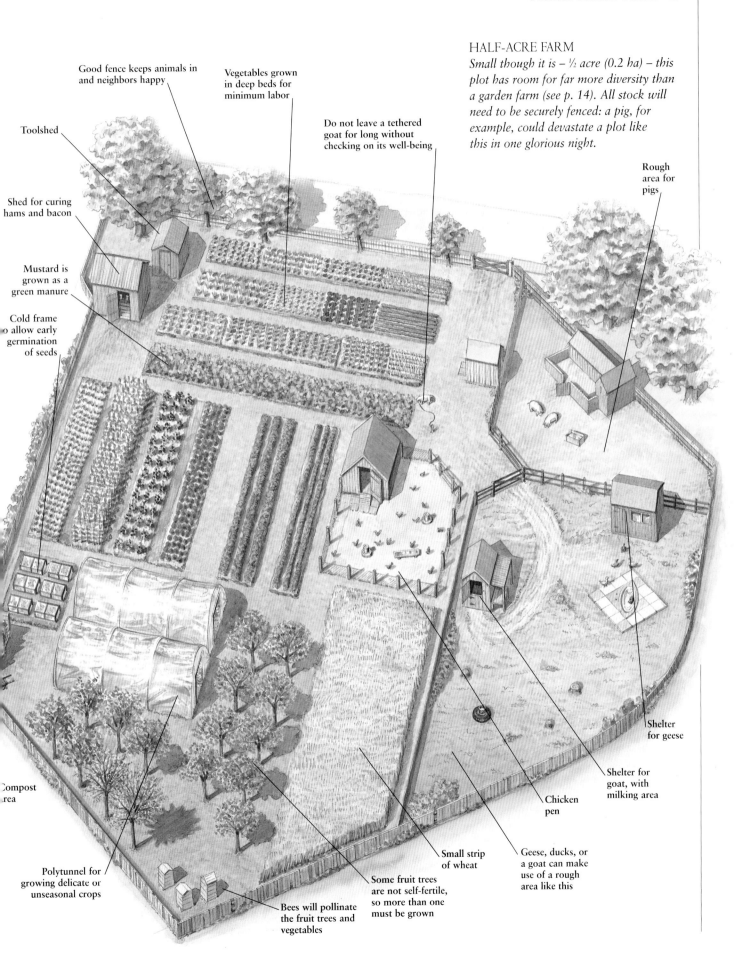

Good fence keeps animals in and neighbors happy

Vegetables grown in deep beds for minimum labor

Do not leave a tethered goat for long without checking on its well-being

Toolshed

Rough area for pigs

Shed for curing hams and bacon

Mustard is grown as a green manure

Cold frame to allow early germination of seeds

Compost area

Polytunnel for growing delicate or unseasonal crops

Bees will pollinate the fruit trees and vegetables

Some fruit trees are not self-fertile, so more than one must be grown

Small strip of wheat

Chicken pen

Geese, ducks, or a goat can make use of a rough area like this

Shelter for goat, with milking area

Shelter for geese

Medium home farm

ON A HOLDING OF THIS SIZE, farming is going to be the major activity in your life. If you like the idea of self-sufficiency, this farm is capable of supplying all your own food and even a surplus to sell. This is, of course, a more demanding farm; it can accommodate a selection of the larger types of livestock – a cow, a small flock of sheep, and a couple of pigs – and with them comes the added labor. It remains, however, well within the grasp of one hard-working person to run a farm like this.

The medium home farm brings with it responsibilities that smaller holdings do not. Your walls and fences require tending to keep them stockproof, but walls are also an important haven for wildlife and you have a duty as a responsible farmer to ensure that all the animals on your land – invited and uninvited – are treated with respect.

PLANNING THE FARM

Design the farm to suit the kind of life you want to lead there. Just because you have room to keep a cow does not mean you *have* to. The happiest home farmers are those for whom the farm is a comfortable extension of themselves; for them the burden of the labor is outweighed by the satisfaction.

A farm of any size needs diversity if it is to operate in a sustainable way, and on this size of farm real diversity is a practical proposition. I would argue that it is essential to keep some form of livestock, if only because of the organic fertilizer they produce.

But diversity does not mean a little bit of everything; it takes careful thought to integrate your dreams and desires with the demands of the farm, bearing

in mind that there are only 24 hours in the day. And whatever your farming plans, more land means more work, and so this is where you take the leap from using only hand tools and wheelbarrows to requiring some form of help.

Although some jobs can be done just by setting more pairs of hands to them, there are limits to what can be achieved in this way. The next decision is horse versus tractor; and after that, whether to rent machinery (and hire people to run it) for the mechanical tasks.

If you make the latter choice, you have no machinery to buy or repair. All you have to do is make a telephone call, and then pay the bill. But there is something unsatisfactory about it, and you may feel that anything coming between you and your land is unwelcome.

THREE-ACRE FARM
If you have this much land (roughly 3 acres/1.2 ha), you are going to have to work out plans for rotations of crops and livestock. This is the smallest size of farm on which you can realistically talk about working "fields." Remember that fields have edges and trees, and you farm not only what you plant, but everything that grows on your land.

This strip belongs to a neighbor, who may rent it to you

This much wheat will feed a family for a year

Small flock of sheep kept for wool rather than meat

HAND SOWING
Sowing by hand works. Fields are still small enough for manual labor to achieve most tasks.

WATER MEADOW
This is a type of field that is flooded in winter and provides lush grazing in other seasons.

WHEAT HARVEST
If growing wheat only for your own bread, harvesting by hand is the cheapest option.

MILKING TIME
If you have animals, the secret of good husbandry is getting into a routine and sticking to it.

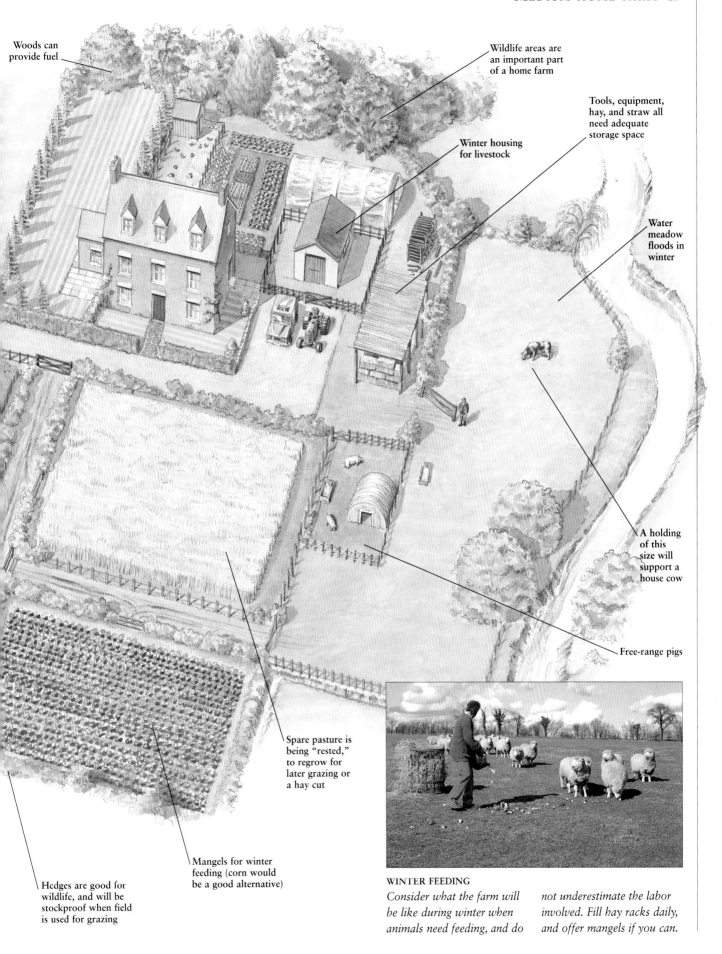

Woods can provide fuel

Wildlife areas are an important part of a home farm

Tools, equipment, hay, and straw all need adequate storage space

Winter housing for livestock

Water meadow floods in winter

A holding of this size will support a house cow

Free-range pigs

Spare pasture is being "rested," to regrow for later grazing or a hay cut

Mangels for winter feeding (corn would be a good alternative)

Hedges are good for wildlife, and will be stockproof when field is used for grazing

WINTER FEEDING

Consider what the farm will be like during winter when animals need feeding, and do not underestimate the labor involved. Fill hay racks daily, and offer mangels if you can.

Larger home farm

TAKE EVERYTHING THAT HAS BEEN SAID about smaller farms, add to it a hefty measure of management and even greater commitment, and you have the recipe for successfully running a larger home farm. But you are now out of the realms where you have a free choice of what to grow, and are more confined by climate and terrain; on a field scale, individual plants or plots cannot be protected from extremes of weather, and you have to grow what will do best on your land. Do it with crops that are in demand, and there is a living to be made from a farm of this size.

PLANNING THE FARM

A farm of this size is a big commitment and is too large to be worked by one person alone. If you are just starting out, try to find an experienced helper and make use of his or her knowledge as well as muscle power.

Mechanical help is definitely needed, and a variety of implements, from a plow to a hay mower, will have to be obtained. A pair of versatile horses or a small tractor would fit in well.

LARGER LIVESTOCK

You will have enough space to keep a fair number of sheep and goats, and even a modest herd of cows. If you live in a region where the climate is cool, you will have to bring the cows indoors during the cold weather.

A dozen cows might not seem a lot when they are out at pasture in summer, but you may change your mind in the winter when you have to start carting enough food to satisfy them all. If you are lucky enough to live in a warm climate, you may be able to avoid this chore in all but the coldest of winters.

Think carefully before deciding on the mix of animals you want to keep. They will, of course, have to suit the area and climate in which you farm, but bear in mind that you will be selling most of what you produce, so research the local demands. There may be a market for more unusual produce, such as ostrich eggs or meat, in your area. But do not be in a hurry to specialize too much – this is still a home farm.

COTTAGE INDUSTRY

If your farm does not occupy you every minute, you could consider starting a profit-making enterprise. A small dairy could produce enough butter, cheese, and yogurt to sell. You might keep Angora goats or rabbits and spin the wool yourself. Or perhaps you would prefer to brew wine from your own grapes or cider from your own apples.

Field of hay

Cereals grown for own bread-making and animal feed

Sunflower seeds can be pressed for oil

Each cow needs plenty of space, as grazing is poor in the warm climate

Meadow may become parched in summer

OLIVE HARVEST
Olives will grow and ripen only in hotter climates. They are then picked and pressed for their oil.

FLEECE FROM GOATS
Goats do well in warm climates. Angora goats can be kept for their wool, known as mohair.

GRAPE PICKING
Grapes grown in the right soil and climate, and lots of practice, are needed to make good wines.

RICE FIELD
With a warm climate and a field that you can flood and drain, you could grow rice successfully.

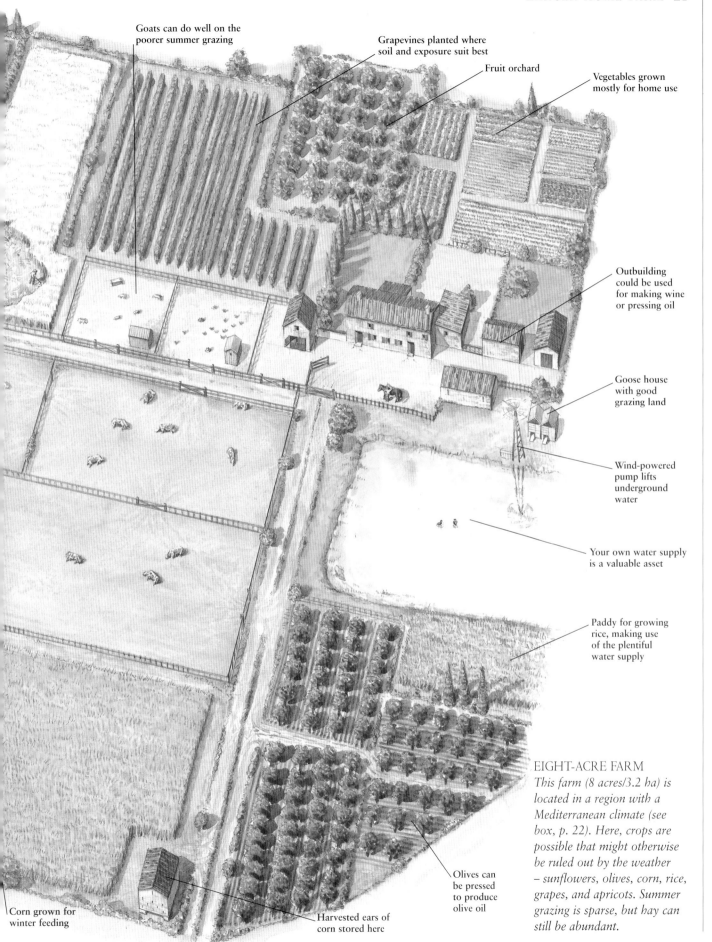

Goats can do well on the poorer summer grazing

Grapevines planted where soil and exposure suit best

Fruit orchard

Vegetables grown mostly for home use

Outbuilding could be used for making wine or pressing oil

Goose house with good grazing land

Wind-powered pump lifts underground water

Your own water supply is a valuable asset

Paddy for growing rice, making use of the plentiful water supply

EIGHT-ACRE FARM
This farm (8 acres/3.2 ha) is located in a region with a Mediterranean climate (see box, p. 22). Here, crops are possible that might otherwise be ruled out by the weather – sunflowers, olives, corn, rice, grapes, and apricots. Summer grazing is sparse, but hay can still be abundant.

Olives can be pressed to produce olive oil

Corn grown for winter feeding

Harvested ears of corn stored here

THE FARMING YEAR

EARLY AUTUMN
Spread manure on the fields before plowing. If you have any fieldwork of this kind, get it finished before winter, when the soil will become too sticky.

THERE IS NO TELLING when the farming year starts, because it never stops. Work carries on seamlessly through the seasons as the year spins by. The secret of managing the farming year is never to be taken by surprise. Have a clear picture of what demands the farm will make on you *next* month, not now. That way, you will not find yourself in the position of being late with last month's jobs, overloaded with the current month's, and shocked by the sudden arrival of next month's, all at the same time. Having said that, I have never managed to get it right. I had a flock of sheep that lambed in very early spring. No sooner were three weeks of broken sleep over than spring plowing and sowing began.

There is always the temptation to think that soon there will be a break or that there's a quiet time ahead. But it never arrives – instead, the next job appears over the horizon. Farming is a dizzying experience. Be prepared for a bumpy ride.

The *cool temperate* climate, in which northern Europeans, Americans of the northern states, and the majority of Canadians live, demonstrates a vivid range of farming conditions, including possibly severe cold, fierce summer heat, drought, and deluges of rainfall, so let us take it as our main example.

AUTUMN AND WINTER

Most farmers calculate that the year begins just as late summer turns to autumn. Cereals have been harvested, and stubble is ready for plowing. The kitchen garden will have lost its summer gloss, and you will need to be more cunning to keep the produce coming. Animals, too, sense the approach of winter as the grass becomes less lush and the daylight hours are curtailed. If you have surplus stock and do not want the work of feeding them in the winter, now is the time to sell.

With the exception of root crops, which are still growing, you should now have an idea of how much homegrown fodder you have for the winter, and so can start to make calculations. Farming is like the greeting-card industry – you

EARLY WINTER
The ram has to be raddled (see p. 56) and put to the flock to secure a crop of spring lambs.

FARMING IN SUNNIER CLIMATES

A COMPLETELY DIFFERENT farming year exists in the Mediterranean climatic zone, which is distributed in many parts of the world and consists of such areas as southern Europe and parts of southern California. In the southern hemisphere, it occurs in the areas surrounding such centers as Adelaide and Perth in Australia, and Cape Town in South Africa.

In this zone, frosts are rare and summers long and hot. Annual rainfall is usually less than in temperate countries, and is concentrated in the winter. Farmers have to cope with uncertain water supplies that may not last through summer. On the other hand, this is a climate in which you can grow oranges and grapes, and winemaking will be high on the home farmer's agenda. Melons grow without a glasshouse or other special provision, and figs ripen fully.

FEEDING HORSES IN MIDWINTER
All livestock need additional feed. In cold, wet climates,
horses and cattle are often brought in from the fields and kept
in sheltered, strawed yards for the worst months.

LATE WINTER
Livestock are still being fed. It is time to get out the mangels you stored in autumn: they can be chopped with a special cutter to make succulent fodder for sheep.

are always thinking months ahead. The first frost of autumn always seems to be a turning point. It is a reminder that if you still haven't harvested your potatoes or your more tender roots, such as mangels, then you might have left it too late. If you plan to make any late sowings of garden vegetables or to sow winter cereals, the weather and soil together are going to determine when you can do it. Too much rain, and the sodden land will be spoiled by working it; too much frost, and it will be too hard for you even to start.

As winter draws on, there comes a day when the meadows give out and the livestock have to be fed. You may have been supplementing their feed with a little freshly cut corn since late summer, but now they must be fed their full ration. If you have the sort of land that will be spoiled by the trampling of feet in winter, livestock, especially cattle, need to be brought into strawed yards for the winter.

The work is beginning to pile up, and the days are getting colder and shorter. Troughs freeze, and water has to be carted. If your plowing is not finished, you must wait for the thaw. If your ram has been with the ewes, the flock will need careful feeding to produce a good crop of lambs. You will have firewood to chop, gates to mend while your meadows are empty, ditches to clear, and equipment to check. You will be looking at your hay supply, wondering whether it will last, and anxiously awaiting the first signs of spring.

SPRINGTIME ON THE FARM

The welcome change from winter to spring brings warmth, newborn lambs, and chicks. And for the home farmer, a mad dash to get seeds sown while conditions are right. But lambing is starting; the pasture needs harrowing to clear out the dead, matted grass; and fertilizer, if used, has to be applied. This is also the best time of year for producing fine tilth in field and garden, after the winter frosts have done their work and reduced clods to crumble. Spring vegetables and late cereals are sown now too, and there are next winter's root crops to think about.

As the days lengthen and the temperature climbs, the grass starts to grow once again. That means livestock can leave the yards and return to the pastures. But the flourishing grass also means that haymaking is not far away. All the time, the clock is ticking: if you don't make a start now on digging out that yard where the animals have overwintered, the time the manure spends in the pile will be reduced and it will be that much poorer. And lambing is not even finished yet!

EARLY SPRING
The whole farm bursts into life, and so do you. The many jobs to do include plowing, creating good tilth, planting potatoes (shown here), and sowing late cereals.

SUMMER – OVER ALL TOO SOON

Make hay while the sun shines, if you can fit it in with everything else. Some legumes can be cut for hay three times a year and, in wet summers, much time can be spent getting grass dry enough to cart or bale.

Animals need watching in hot weather, when parasites can be a problem. In farm or garden, weeds will get the better of you if you are not swiping them with a hoe every spare minute as they appear. The cereal harvest must be planned for, and the equipment serviced. The finest field of wheat is useless if you cannot cut it because the machine you want to use is broken.

It is a time when farmers get hot and bothered, horses suffer from flies, and long days make for tired homecomings. And when the harvest is gathered, and you think at last you can put your feet up, you will find that the days are getting shorter, the plowing is not finished, and the meadows are looking bare . . .

LATE SPRING

Sprouted seeds need attention. Here, beans that were sown in a polytunnel or in cold frames are being planted out. Weeds can get a hold on the farm at this time if you are not careful.

HIGH SUMMER

Summer means harvest, and this is the high spot in the farming year. This is the most productive season in the kitchen and fruit gardens too.

PEOPLE POWER

PATIENT WORK
Sowing cereal crops by hand is a slow, quiet job. You might save time with a tractor and a seed drill, but this way saves money – and the environment.

OF ALL THE THINGS on the farm, you are the most valuable. Everything else is allowed to break down, snap, or perhaps have an off day, but not you. Rest days are for employees, but on your farm there is probably only you, and you *have* to be there. So conserve yourself, just as you would your land. Learn when to call it a day and finish a job tomorrow. We have all fallen into the trap of working every daylight hour, ending up too exhausted to derive any of the pleasures that we know can be had from home farming.

Of course, you could pay money to people, and let them take the responsibility off your shoulders, but that is not why you took up farming in the first place. It is your intention to get the hands-on experience of working the land, not to manage other people. Granted, you will probably get weary often enough, and frustrated when seemingly simple jobs develop an unexpected complexity: this is part of the way of life. Farming, thankfully, has an uncanny way of obliterating all the bad days and letting only the glorious ones survive in your memory.

PEOPLE ON THE LAND

By far the greatest part of your effort will come in working the land. This is where you will learn the feel of the wooden handle of a pitchfork, hoe, or spade. And you will be surprised how attached you become to your hand tools. I have made hay with farmhands who have carried their own pitchforks for 30 years and could contemplate using no other; it would feel as strange to them as to a violinist picking up the wrong bow. I used to mock such silliness, but now I find I have my favorites, and you will develop yours too.

Some techniques take many years of practice to perfect, and you will see that, throughout this book, I describe techniques that can be mastered only after a long life on the land. But this does not mean that a reasonable degree of competence does not come quickly. The forking of hay or the chopping of weeds would seem

HUMAN VERSUS MACHINE POWER

	Turning land	*Sowing cereals*	*Harvesting cereals*	*Threshing grain*	*Cutting hay*
Human power	One fit person digging 1 acre (0.4 ha) of land with a spade, to a depth of 10 in (25 cm), will take between 14 and 21 days. It is very good for fitness!	One fit person could sow seed on 1½ acres (0.6 ha) an hour by broadcast sowing.	It will take a day for a fit, well-practiced person to cut 1 acre (0.4 ha) with a scythe.	Two people flailing grain will thresh 56 lb (25 kg) of wheat in a day.	A skilled scyther can expect to cut 1 acre (0.4 ha) in a day. With a sickle, you can cut approximately half this area.
Simple machinery	A single-furrow plow drawn by two fit horses will be able to plow 1 acre (0.4 ha) a day.	A seed drill pulled by two horses and worked by two people can sow 1¼ acres (0.5 ha) in an hour. The drill is slower than hand sowing, but it saves on seed and achieves a better rate of germination.	A binder can harvest 1½ acres (0.6 ha) an hour; a small combine harvester completes about 6 acres (2.4 ha) an hour.	A threshing machine can thresh as much as 15 tons a day, but it is costly to run: it needs 14 people to operate it. A combine harvester removes the need for this labor and harvests and winnows as well.	A small horse-drawn mower will cut 1 acre (0.4 ha) an hour.

WORKING IN THE HAY FIELD
Turning hay with a pitchfork is slower than using a machine – but the comradeship of working together has a value too.

HOEING SEEDLINGS IN A DEEP BED
No mechanical device can weed vegetable beds as accurately or as thoroughly as an experienced person swinging a hoe.

HARVESTING WHEAT BY HAND
This is hard work, and the cut wheat still has to be bundled and tied. But it works, and it's cheaper than a combine harvester!

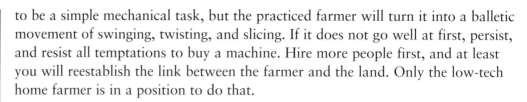

BLACKSMITHING
Things will break, and you will have to repair them. Having a basic knowledge of skills like blacksmithing is as important in farming as working the land.

to be a simple mechanical task, but the practiced farmer will turn it into a balletic movement of swinging, twisting, and slicing. If it does not go well at first, persist, and resist all temptations to buy a machine. Hire more people first, and at least you will reestablish the link between the farmer and the land. Only the low-tech home farmer is in a position to do that.

IN THE FARMYARD

Farming is only one of the many skills you need. At times you will be blacksmith, plumber, builder, carpenter, and mechanic. You do not have to be particularly good at any of these things – if you don't believe me, look around any farm – but you must be able to take a hammer, pipe wrench, or chisel and make a reasonable stab at any job. It is too expensive to pick up the phone every time something goes wrong. Anyway, there is satisfaction to be had in mending a sty that a pig has just demolished, or hammering back into shape the bent coulter of a plow. And again, it is all down to you and your two – often blistered – hands.

CARING FOR LIVESTOCK

Handling farm animals is as much a matter of exerting the mind as exercising the body. Good livestock farmers develop levels of communication with animals that you cannot begin to comprehend, until you start to develop them yourself. And they *will* come, with time. It took me a couple of years to find the secret. Take the task of moving sheep, for example: eventually I could spot all the possible things that could go wrong in getting them safely from one place to another. That was because I had learned to think like a sheep, and then it became easy.

Other livestock skills are manual: shearing (see p. 60), drenching (p. 57), foot trimming (p. 64), milking cows (p. 76), feeding pigs (p. 69), and helping calves to be born (p. 78). All these have to be learned, but with them comes the bonus of understanding your farm animals better, which brings a happier farming life.

MAKING YOURSELF AT HOME

It is easy to forget that without a home, there can be no home farm. When I was buying a farm, I remember saying, "This is the right place for us!" having viewed only the fields and barns, without even setting foot inside the house. But at the end of an exhausting day, when the rain pours or the snow settles and darkness falls, it becomes the most important place on the farm. Think of it as your stable or sty, where you go to wallow when the work is done.

You will find that home and farm become indivisible. If you are daunted by that thought, don't be, because it is when you get the fruits of the farm back to the kitchen that you start to reap the rewards for your efforts. I have met farmers who grow vast acreages of potatoes and have never tasted them; instead, they buy from the supermarket. That is not the home farmer's way. Preserving fruit, curing hams, grinding grains for making bread, and collecting eggs and inventing things to do with them – all these will occupy you when you are not on the land. If you have a cow, then cheese and butter will also be on your list.

In more senses than one, there is always plenty on the home farmer's plate. That is when you should remember that you are the most important item on the farm and if you break down, so does the rest. Don't be tempted to take on more than you can manage. It is a real danger.

SHEEP SHEARING
Livestock skills and handling take time to learn. Your first shearing will be slow, and not much fun for the sheep.

THATCHING
A straw thatch (see p. 45) is an excellent roof for sheltering livestock and is cheap. With practice, you will be able to master the basic principles of simple thatch work.

HOME SPINNING
Half the pleasure lies in making use of your own produce. Here, raw wool from a fleece is being carded prior to spinning (see p. 61).

MAKING A WATTLE HURDLE
If you can master the craft of hurdle making, then you have a cheap and extremely flexible way of confining your sheep and goats.

Hedging

THERE IS NO BETTER WAY of confining livestock than with a properly laid hedge. As well as forming an impenetrable barrier, it provides stock with shade from the sun and shelter from cold winds and rain. It will also act as a windbreak for crops and may even provide a welcome addition to the larder in the form of nuts or blackberries.

But a farm needs hedges for another reason – a good hedge acts as a haven for wildlife. You might be totally unaware of the wildlife thriving on your farm, but it is there, nesting in the hedges, scuttling through the long grass, and feeding off the fruits that a mixed hedgerow provides. Hedges are living things, and it is only through the farmer's efforts that they stay healthy. When you realize that some of them are quite old, you learn to treat them with respect. They were there long before you.

COPPICING

COPPICING MAY LOOK cruel, but cutting a hedge right down to the ground and letting it regrow is often the only way to restore a hedge in poor condition. It will look very sick at first, but this is what you will see after three years.

HEDGE STRUCTURE

A GOOD HEDGE is dense, with no gaps, especially near the base, which is wide and gives the hedge an A-shaped cross section. It takes a lot of work to lay a hedge initially and care for it in the early years, but do it well and the established hedge will form an excellent barrier and require a minimum of maintenance.

QUICK ESCAPE ROUTE
This hedge has been left unmanaged and has developed gaps all along its base. It will need extensive work to make it stockproof.

SOLID STRUCTURE
This hedge has been well looked after. It is a thick, effective barrier and contains a rich variety of species, which will attract wildlife.

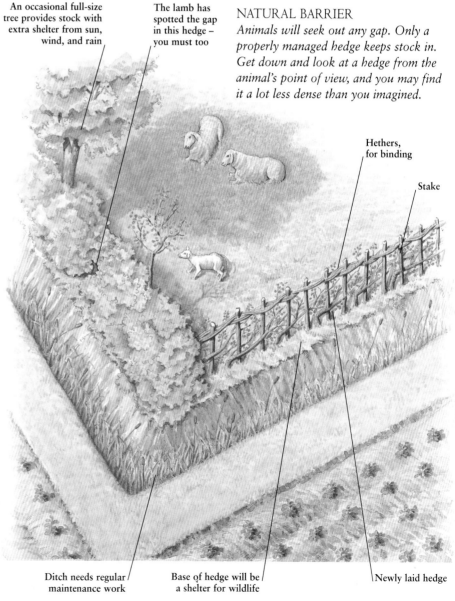

An occasional full-size tree provides stock with extra shelter from sun, wind, and rain

The lamb has spotted the gap in this hedge – you must too

NATURAL BARRIER
Animals will seek out any gap. Only a properly managed hedge keeps stock in. Get down and look at a hedge from the animal's point of view, and you may find it a lot less dense than you imagined.

Hethers, for binding

Stake

Ditch needs regular maintenance work

Base of hedge will be a shelter for wildlife

Newly laid hedge

HEDGE LAYING

THIS IS A GREAT SKILL, and you need plenty of practice to become proficient. It calls for an understanding of the way a hedge grows and of how far it can be bent to your will. Note that this craftsman works according to his local style. There may be a different style in your area, but despite variations like this, hedging is the same basic craft.

You will need a billhook, an ax, a bow saw, a mallet, and tools for sharpening. Keep your billhook razor-sharp (see p. 36). Wear a pair of strong leather gloves and old, close-fitting clothes for safety when working with sharp cutting edges. Expect progress to be slow on your early attempts.

NEGLECTED HEDGE
A view of the hedge before work started: it had not been trimmed for at least five years, nor had it been laid within living memory.

MATERIALS YOU NEED
Stakes should be ash or hazel, 2 in (5 cm) thick; hethers (some say ethers or edders) can be hazel or willow, 10 ft (3 m) long.

1 CUTTING *Thin the hedge and keep only young stems. Make a cut (leaving a "hinge") in each stem you keep, aiming to make it fall in the line of the hedge.*

2 LAYING *Bring the stem down gently, helping it to fall in the right direction. Take care not to twist it too much, or you will cut the flow of sap and it will die.*

3 STAKING *Start staking once the first few stems have been laid. Push each stake in between the laid stems and drive it home. Weave the flexible ends of the* stems through the stakes, angling the ends out into the field to stop stock from pushing or leaning on the hedge. Continue along, alternately laying and staking.

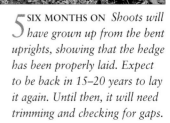

Hethers stop growing hedge from pushing stakes out of line

4 HETHERING *Weave hethers in to bind the hedge; knock them down to final height with a mallet; trim hedge and stakes.*

5 SIX MONTHS ON *Shoots will have grown up from the bent uprights, showing that the hedge has been properly laid. Expect to be back in 15–20 years to lay it again. Until then, it will need trimming and checking for gaps.*

Gates and fencing

PERFECTLY HUNG GATES are like old slippers – they fit well and are a pleasure to use. Fences, too, can put you at ease if they are taut, upright, and secure. But a gate that gives no satisfying "clunk" as it is closed is depressing, and a fence that sags as if it lacked the will to survive is not a cheering sight. Livestock can sense when boundaries are not secure, and they will not be slow to take advantage.

Gateposts and fenceposts must be very firm, and to achieve this you have to excavate the holes properly. Remember to plan enough time if you have to do this task manually. Give thanks if you can use that most wonderful of inventions, the tractor-driven auger.

THE PROPERLY FENCED FIELD

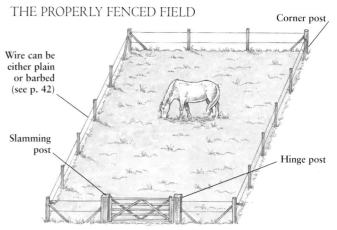

Corner post

Wire can be either plain or barbed (see p. 42)

Slamming post

Hinge post

THE KEY TO SECURITY
Strength is the secret of success with a fenced field. Strong corner posts and two heavy gate posts, all properly dug in, make for a secure field that will contain the most determined animal.

GATES

EVEN A SMALL gate is heavy, so the post from which it hangs (the hinge post) should be substantial. Treated lumber is best, as untreated wood will rot. A 3-ft (90-cm) hole might seem very deep, but it will not be too much; it may have to be deeper in light soils, which are more likely to give.

Decide which way the gate is to open. Most gates open *into* fields – the animals find it harder to pull a loose gate open than to push it.

1 **HINGE POST** *Having dug the post hole by hand or machine, drive the post in and press the loose soil back in. Check that it is vertical, using a level.*

2 **TOP HINGE PIN** *Drill a hole in the post for the top hinge pin, and hammer it home. This is the hinge pin to adjust if you want the gate to be self-closing.*

3 **BOTTOM HINGE PIN** *Drive the lower hinge pin into the post. Make sure it is the right distance below the top pin, so both pins share the gate's weight.*

4 **HANGING THE GATE** *Fit the hinges (attached to the gate) over the hinge pins. If the gate does not hang straight, you can make adjustments to the top pin. If you have not already done so, now put in the slamming post (the post against which the gate closes – see above). It, too, should be a thick post, as it will take a fair amount of strain.*

Hinge pin is attached to the hinge post

Hinge is attached to the gate

CORNER POSTS

CORNER POSTS HAVE to be set deeply in the ground and braced in every direction in which the post is likely to be strained. A brace is a slanting support strut, often fixed into place by its own small post. Without braces the corner post will, over time, slowly creep out of the ground and the fence will sag. The only remedy will be to take the whole thing down and start again. Rocks and stones pressed in around the base of the post will help to prevent movement.

1 **THE HOLE** *Dig the hole with a spade or with a mechanical auger. Then (as shown) use a narrow spade to bring out the last of the loose soil.*

2 **THE POST** *Drive in the post and press a few rocks in around its base. Shovel the soil back into the hole, tamping it down hard to consolidate it.*

Using a post driver gives a firmer post

3 **FIXING THE BRACE** *Cut a notch in the post to take the top end of the brace; dig a shallow hole to take the lower end; fix in place with a stake.*

4 **FINISHED CORNER** *Properly braced, a corner post will not yield to normal strains. Try it. If it moves, start again.*

STRAINING FENCE WIRES

IT IS THE TIGHTNESS of the wire that contains livestock, and that can be achieved only by proper fixing and straining. Use a wire strainer – you will not get the wire tight enough by hand. A spinning jenny is a rotary dispenser for wire; load it with enough wire for the fence you are making, and unwind it as you use it. If you try to work with wire still in the coil it comes in, you will find that it unwinds itself and gets kinked, and you cannot pull it straight again without weakening it.

1 **FIXING** *Use staples to attach the loose end of the wire to a post; twist to secure. Unreel wire from the spinning jenny and lay it out along the fence.*

2 **STRAINING** *Cut the newly laid-out wire free from the spinning jenny, pull it around the post, tighten it with the strainer, and staple it into place.*

3 **JOB DONE** *Wires should be tight and parallel. Three may be enough for cattle; you might need five for sheep. Retighten every couple of years.*

TOOLS FOR FENCING

KEEP A FENCING kit together, ready for quick use. Besides the specialized equipment shown here, you will need a hammer, fencing staples, and a pair of pliers with which to cut wire and remove staples.

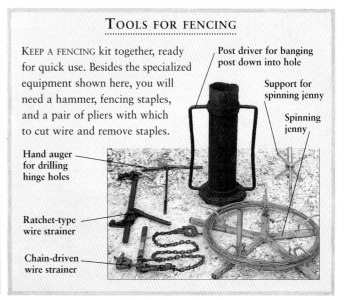

Post driver for banging post down into hole

Support for spinning jenny

Spinning jenny

Hand auger for drilling hinge holes

Ratchet-type wire strainer

Chain-driven wire strainer

Blacksmithing

NEVER UNDERESTIMATE THE NUMBER of things that can break on a farm. Even substantial pieces of metalwork succumb to the rigors of farming use, and sooner or later you will find yourself with a twisted tine on a fork, a bent coulter on a plow, or a broken harrow spike. Try your hand at the skill of the blacksmith. You may not become good at it, but you can learn enough to get yourself out of trouble whenever an urgent farm task needs finishing and the tool is out of action.

The easiest metal to work is wrought iron. Get some, and practice on it. However, these days most metal objects on a farm are made of mild steel, which is harder to work, and you will need perseverance to get the knack of using it. You will need a coal forge to heat the metal (modern forges are on wheels) as well as good coal, an anvil, a ball peen hammer or two, pairs of tongs, a cold chisel, and a vise to hold your work. It is crucial to heat the metal to the correct temperature for the task at hand; you will learn to judge the temperature from the color of the metal.

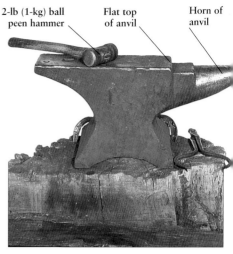

2-lb (1-kg) ball peen hammer   Flat top of anvil   Horn of anvil

THE ANVIL
Judge an anvil by its "ring" when struck. It should sound like a bell. If it sounds flat or muffled, this may indicate that the anvil is cracked or that the metal is too soft.

USING THE HORN OF THE ANVIL

THE HORN, OR BEAK, of the anvil is the right location on which to create curves, bends, or rings in your piece of metal. On this page, an experienced blacksmith is shown at work. If you are a beginner, it will not be as easy as he makes it look, for these operations are hard to perform accurately; but do not let this put you off: you *will* succeed. One useful tip: when you start acquiring blacksmithing equipment, have an expert "set" the anvil – fix it at the right height and distance from the forge and fasten it to the floor.

MAKING A WIDE CURVE
Do not hit the metal where it is directly supported by the horn, or you will simply dent it. Strike your metal a short way off the anvil, so that the metal is forced to bend around the horn. For this kind of work, you should heat the metal to a bright red heat. You will have to reheat it as soon as it starts to cool.

MAKING A TIGHT CURVE
Forging rings that are perfectly circular, and of the size intended, takes months or years to learn. Again, heat the metal to a bright red heat, and expect to reheat it several times. Start by making a wide curve in the rod on one of the anvil's rounded corners, then tighten the bend on the narrow tip of the horn, closing the ring.

USING THE ANVIL TOP AND EDGES

THE FOUR OPERATIONS shown here are easier than using the anvil horn or forge welding, so let these be your first. They are close to the heart of home farming: squaring off to match the rest of what you are repairing; sharpening the points of a harrow; cutting bars to forge replacement parts; and punching holes for bolts. Blacksmiths will tell you that the hammer does half the work for them. Watch the way they allow it to bounce off the work, and get two blows for the price of one.

SQUARING OFF
Bring the rod to an orange heat and place it on the anvil. Hit and rotate through 90°, hit and spin it another 90°, and work around the piece. As it loses its orange heat, heat it again in the fire.

CUTTING
You can cut metal either hot or cold. To cut cold, nick it with a cold chisel and break it over the edge of the anvil. To cut it hot, bring it to an orange heat, place it over a wedge (left), and then hammer until it is cut through.

PUNCHING A HOLE
A bright yellow heat is needed for punching. The benefit of punching is that nothing is taken away, and the grain of the metal flows around the hole, making it stronger than a drilled hole.

SHARPENING
Bring to a white heat: the metal will become plastic. Set the tip at an angle to the flat anvil top and hammer it to a point. The first time you do this, do not attempt the diamond shape, as shown.

FORGE WELDING

WELDING IN A FORGE is not easy and takes practice. Electric and oxyacetylene welding are more common, but involve costly equipment. If the weld you need is a matter of life and death, then find yourself a welder. But if you can afford to get it wrong, have a go with your own forge and hammers.

A successful weld is a perfect fusion of the two pieces, and you should not be able to see the join. High temperatures are required, so the fire must be very hot.

1 PLACING *Heat the two ends to a yellow heat. Fix one rod in a clamp. Position the other so that the hot ends meet, with a 2 in (5 cm) overlap. Hammer them together and reheat.*

2 FUSING *Work all around the join with quick blows, to hammer out the double thickness. Put some flux (a compoud that reduces the buildup of scale) on the metal, reheat it, and repeat.*

3 FINISHED WELD *You may need to reheat again, before giving a final hammering to smooth out the weld. This is how it should look in the end: you cannot see the join.*

Blades and sharpening

NO CRAFTSMAN OR -WOMAN will pick up a bladed tool and start to work without first checking that it is sharp. If it is, then the work will be done both swiftly and cleanly. If not, he or she will sharpen it: a blunt tool is hard to control and therefore dangerous, and it takes more time and effort to use than a properly maintained tool.

Learn how to sharpen tools correctly and to use the right equipment. Examine, too, the way the blades of different tools are formed. One of the first things you will notice is that blades are all either single-beveled (like the blades of sheep shears) or double-beveled (like an ax blade). This affects how they work and how they are sharpened.

EQUIPMENT FOR SHARPENING BLADES

BESIDES THE general-purpose sharpeners shown here, you may be able to buy custom-made sharpening stones or steels for the specific blades you have. Contact the manufacturer or supplier. Stones ("rubs") are made from a hard carbon compound. Sharpening steels are made from specially toughened steel.

OIL AND OILSTONE
These are used particularly for sharpening planes and chisels.

COARSE FILE
Smooth badly nicked blades with a rough file before honing to give a sharp edge.

SHARPENING STONES
A sharpening stone, or rub, should live in your pocket when doing a job that needs a sharp blade.

Disks can be changed to suit different metals

ELECTRIC GRINDER
Very effective, but if used without care, it can harm the hardness, or "temper," of a blade.

TYPES OF CUTTING EDGE

THE EDGE OF ANY cutting blade will be either single- or double-beveled. The blade of a single-beveled tool has one flat face, while the other face is ground at an angle, creating a bevel. On a double-beveled blade, both faces are ground at an angle, and the two ground surfaces meet.

On both types of blade, the angle of the bevel depends on the tool and its intended use. An ax needs to be broad to part wood fibers, but a sickle needs only the finest of blades to cut down cereals and grasses.

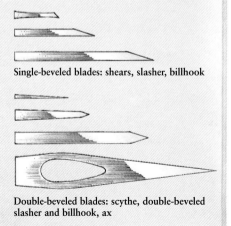

Single-beveled blades: shears, slasher, billhook

Double-beveled blades: scythe, double-beveled slasher and billhook, ax

SINGLE-BEVELED BLADES

THESE INCLUDE TOOLS that work like a pair of scissors, such as sheep shears and hay knives, and some cutting tools, like billhooks and slashers. But beware: some billhooks and slashers have double-beveled edges. And there are two-edged billhooks, with one of each type!

BILLHOOK
Often used for trimming hedges. The hook helps you to drag the work toward you.

A good hook has a balanced feel

SHEEP SHEARS
Both left- and right-handed sheep shears are available.

SHARPENING A BILLHOOK

WITH SINGLE-BEVELED tools, such as the billhook shown below, the flat face of the blade must not be rounded over. Instead, the bevel must be honed down to meet it. Billhook blades are made of hard steel and will keep an edge longer than most other blades.

FINE SHARPENING
Here a sharpening stone is being used to keep an edge on a billhook. Regular sharpening improves both the blade and your technique. Always rub the stone against the blade, not the other way around.

Slasher blade has a profile similar to that of a billhook

HAY-MOWING KNIFE
This is a toothed knife that moves horizontally between fixed teeth on a hay mower (see p. 158). Sharpen it with a hard file, kept at a constant angle and an even pressure.

Sharpen all around each tooth, top side only

5-ft (1.5-m) wooden handle

SLASHER
This is used for clearing overgrown areas. It is quite a crude tool, and the more effort you put into swinging it, the better the result. There is not a lot of subtlety about a slasher.

DOUBLE-BEVELED BLADES

TOOLS WITH A double-beveled blade include axes, scythes, sickles, and some types of billhook and slasher. The two bevels of a double-beveled blade must be ground equally when sharpening, to make sure that the blade does not become lopsided.

POCKET KNIFE
Think of this as a safety device. You may have to cut the harness of a horse in trouble or the fleece of a trapped sheep.

SICKLE
The wide hook enables you to gather grass as you slice through it. Sickles quickly lose their edge.

Scythe handle, or snaith

SCYTHE
Tune your scythe to suit yourself. It has three adjustments – both handles and the pitch of the blade. Adjust so that the blade is parallel to the ground when working.

AX
If working mainly with hard wood, file the bevels until they are at a wide angle; for soft wood, file them to an acute angle.

"Grass nail" stops blade from flexing while cutting

SHARPENING AN AX

AN AX WORKS by removing a chip each time it strikes the wood. If the cutting edge is too rounded in profile, and strikes the wood at an angle, one of the bevels will make contact before the edge of the blade does, and the ax will bounce off. If you sharpen an ax to too fine an edge, it will cut the wood, but will stick fast in it.

1 USING A COARSE FILE *Stand the ax with its handle on the ground, and hold its head against your leg. If the edge is chipped, you can use a rough file to remove pitted areas.*

2 FINE FINISHING *A less coarse file will give the final bevels. Make sure you sharpen both bevels of the ax blade equally. When you think the blade is sharp, try the ax. If it bounces off or sticks, file it again.*

SHARPENING A SCYTHE

WEAR GLOVES the first time you sharpen a scythe – I bear scars from early attempts.

To sharpen a scythe, use the same basic method as for a carving knife. Sharpen with a stone as soon as you feel the scythe begin to drag. The thin stalks of grass will bend away from the blade if not cut cleanly, so the scythe has to be razor-sharp all the time.

1 TOP SURFACE *Start with the top surface. Hold the stone at 15° to the blade, and slide it forcefully along toward the tip. Keep the stone at a constant angle for the length of the blade.*

2 BOTTOM SURFACE *Place the stone under the blade and, again holding it at 15° to the blade, slide it down toward the tip. Then work alternately down the top and bottom surfaces; you will get quite quick at this.*

ANIMAL HUSBANDRY

THE FIRST RULE for anyone to follow in keeping animals is this: do not try to farm any kind of animal that you do not like. Working with animals requires an understanding

that will not come unless, somewhere within you, there is a concern for their welfare beyond that needed to ensure a good profit. Home farmers always care

about nature. They can end up so close to their animals that the relationship is like a family one, almost a marriage. That is why animal "husbandry" describes the craft so well.

THE FARMYARD TURKEY
You can choose from a huge range of poultry. Turkeys can provide a seasonal income.

WHICH ANIMAL?

W HO AM I TO TELL you which animals you should keep? I might just as well try to dictate which partner you should choose. When you are choosing livestock, you are, in effect, selecting animals with which you are going to spend a significant portion of your life; you are setting out on a relationship. When commercial considerations come first, things are much easier; you assess the market, balance the costs with the profits, and arrive at a money-making conclusion. But if profit is not the sole ambition, which it rarely is for the home farmer, then a whole new set of questions arises and you must have the answers before you purchase your stock. The heart should not entirely rule the head, but your "feel" for the animals must be a factor in your eventual choice. Decide first which animals you have an affinity for, then consider the work and

YOUR CHOICE OF ANIMALS

	Chicken	*Duck/Goose*	*Rabbit*
Advantages	Pleasant to have around. Eggs and meat in return for little work.	Hardier and less prone to infection than chickens. A duck also has a longer laying career than a chicken. Geese are good grazers, efficient at removing weeds from pastures.	Cheap, easy to handle. Quiet animals.
Disadvantages	Hardly any. Smelly if kept on the same patch of land for too long.	Ducks especially are waterfowl. You need a pond, ideally, or a good area of water. Geese are noisy and stronger than they look.	A low-value enterprise. *Healthy dandelions!*
Special needs of livestock	Protection from foxes and vermin. Somewhere dark and high to roost at night. Shelter from extreme weather.	Both ducks and geese need shelter at night and from extremes of weather, both hot and cold. Both need protection from foxes and vermin.	Protection from weather, foxes, and vermin. Dry, draft-free accommodation needed.
Labor required	Daily feeding and egg collecting, confining at night, shelter cleaning. *Hen's egg*	Ducks: confining at night, taking eggs, cleaning shelter. Geese: collecting eggs, cleaning shelter.	Feeding, regular inspection, hutch cleaning.
Special skills needed by farmer	Killing your own chickens, catching escaped hens, clipping wings to discourage flying. Putting up high fencing if you do not clip wings.	Normal poultry keeper's skills. *Duck house*	Recognizing signs of *Rabbit hutch* good and bad health in stock. Possibly killing your own rabbits.
Diseases	Worms can be a problem if the chickens are kept on the same area for long periods of time. Lice and mites need to be controlled.	Ducks: few health problems; hardier than hens. Geese: few problems; young birds can contract gizzard worm if kept on overused grass.	Generally free from disease, but rabbits can catch colds. Ears need checking regularly for mites. Claw trimming also required.
Making money	Eggs can be sold at the farm gate. Home-fed chickens are too good to part with – eat them yourself.	Ducks: meat and eggs. Geese: a sought-after meat; eggs are large but can be hard to sell.	Good, low-fat meat. Some demand for rabbit skins.

costs involved in keeping them, and decide how they would fit in on your farm. Think also of the animals, and of how natural a life you can offer them. Will they be able to exercise their instincts? Satisfy yourself that, on your farm, any animal you keep will be content with what you can offer it, and only then go shopping.

HAPPY ENDINGS

Don't forget to think ahead to what will happen to these animals in the end. Few farm animals die natural deaths; they are usually killed for food. That is simply what they were bred to provide, and apart from those that yield fleece, milk, or eggs, they are of little value otherwise. If you can't contemplate sending stock you have reared to the butcher, or are unable to ensure that your animals will have a relatively dignified death free from pain and fear, then you should not own them in the first place. Farm animals do not make good pets. If you can't kill them, get a dog or a cat and grow vegetables. It makes you no less a farmer.

LLAMAS ON YOUR FARM?
Llamas and alpacas can be expensive to buy, but their fleeces can fetch a good price.

Sheep	Goat	Pig	Cow
Excellent grazers, maintaining pastures in good condition. Provide lambs, wool, and possibly milk. Certain breeds can fatten well on small amounts of feed. Hardy.	A low-tech, hardy animal suited to most climates. Provides meat and milk, and certain breeds have valuable fleeces.	Cheap to feed. Will get fat on what other animals waste. Good provider of pork, ham, sausages, bacon. Good company – you can tell your troubles to a pig.	Gentle animals, self-feeding for half the year, providing calves, and milk for you to drink or turn into butter, cheese, ice cream, and yogurt.
Regular attention required by ewes and lambs. Prone to many diseases. Famed escapologists.	If not well confined or tethered, they will cut a destructive swath through a vegetable garden in no time.	Will wreck decent grass if allowed to turn it over with their powerful snouts.	Large animals. A certain amount of strength is needed when they have to be caught and handled.
A good shepherd to keep them out of trouble.	Good pasture not necessary. Goats will browse scrubby land, often preferring weeds to good grass. Protection needed from extreme weather.	Shelter at farrowing; otherwise hardy animals.  *Pig sty*	Cows need good grass in summer if they are to yield strong calves and plentiful milk. Shelter from cold winds and rain is required in winter.
Continual. Watching for pest attack in the summer, careful observation at lambing.	Twice-daily milking. Otherwise similar to shepherding.  *Milking a goat*	Daily feeding. Regular mucking out if kept in sty.	Twice-daily attention if milking; otherwise, a daily inspection when at grass. Careful watching needed when planning to put cows to the bull.
Understanding of the subtle ways of sheep. Shearing, foot trimming, lambing.  *Hoof-paring knife*	Milking, shearing, foot trimming, kidding.	Moving pigs around a farm is an acquired skill. You will need to be fast on your feet if you ever hope to catch a reluctant pig.	*Hand milking* Milking, handling cattle, helping with calving.
Blowfly strike, foot rot, and countless other diseases, the first symptom of which is often death.	Goats need high levels of minerals. Deficiencies can cause serious problems. Internal parasites should be controlled.	Not many. Watch for mastitis after farrowing; otherwise, healthy, well-fed pigs will need little veterinary attention.	Mastitis when milking, mineral deficiencies when feeding calves, foot problems if heavy with milk.
Totally at the mercy of the markets. Making cheese from sheep's milk may be a profitable enterprise.	Milk, cheese, and yogurt sell if well made. Check local dairying and food regulations (see p. 172).	Home-cured hams and bacon are greatly sought after, as is pork from breeds that have a finer flavor.	Good returns from dairy produce. Profit on calves and fattened stock dependent on markets.

Confining your livestock

ALL ANIMALS WILL WANDER, given a chance. Do not imagine that your sheep will fail to discover that one gap in the wall you forgot to plug, or that the pig will not detect that the electric fence battery is dead. Once escaped, an animal can clear a vegetable garden before you have even noticed it is missing. Properly constructed and maintained walls and fences are your guarantee of a quieter life and a good night's sleep. And what they say is true: good fences make good neighbors.

MAKING PLANS

Fencing is expensive – if you are starting from scratch, money and labor will be needed in quantity. And fences matter, both for keeping animals in and for keeping them out: growing vegetables in country where rabbits thrive is a waste of time without a secure, rabbit-proof fence. It all costs.

But the cost of letting animals escape is even higher, and the secret of confining your livestock is to match the fence to the animal and to the farm.

It is not simply a matter of strength. A flimsy electric wire will contain a bull, but not a chicken. What you must do is understand how the animals plot their escape, then outwit them. If your pig can get its snout under the fence and lift it, that was no barrier in the first place. One strand of barbed wire at ground level will defeat this breakout. Plan your fences to cover all eventualities, or one

day you will find that the cow has to be moved to a plot fenced with chicken wire, or the hens have to live in a field with only a thin hedge to contain them.

PLANTING HEDGES

If you are a lover of hedges, and this would be understandable because apart from being useful they are virtual nature reserves, start planning and planting when you first move to your farm.

If you plant a hedge now, in five years it will have grown enough to be laid (see p. 31), and then you will have both a stockproof barrier and a healthy wildlife community. You can, of course, renovate an old hedge, although this is more laborious than laying one that you have planted and tended yourself.

CHOICE OF WOODEN FENCES

The commonest types of wooden fence are a post-and-rail fence and one made from woven wattle hurdles. On its own, a post-and-rail fence is a costly form of decoration – I have never seen any value in it. Horses and cattle like to get their heads over the top rail and rub, which soon makes the fence lean over and it will not be a pretty sight for long.

Wattle hurdles, neat and new, are a joy to the eye, and they provide very good shelter and confinement for lambs or poultry. But weaving them is skilled work, and, as they are made of untreated wood, they have a limited life.

Whatever wood you want for your fencing, choose a durable one. Wood preservatives are effective but toxic, so a naturally durable wood is better. Oak will outlast most farmers, if you can afford it. There are alternatives to oak if this is too expensive or unobtainable, and these include chestnut and larch.

WIRE FENCES

These are the cheapest kind of fencing and are quick to erect. They are at their most effective when put up for horses and cows. Details of construction are given on page 33. You can use either plain or barbed wire, although welfare considerations clearly favor plain wire.

What makes a wire fence secure is the tightness of the wire, nothing else. So if, for any reason, the wire becomes slack, animals will soon learn that their heads fit through, and before long the rest of them will follow. I find that only the idlest of sheep do not attempt to get through a plain wire fence.

Escapes, however, are only part of the problem: much worse is the danger that your animals can become tangled and hurt in the attempt.

USE OF BARBED WIRE

Use barbed wire as a reinforcement, in combination with other materials. There is no doubt that it enhances security, but this comes at a price. Even when it is not slack, horses and cows sometimes harm themselves by rubbing against it. Cow hide is tough, but you do see the scars left on cows by this kind of injury.

A sagging barbed-wire fence is a real menace, especially if it is so loose that it catches the legs of animals as they walk innocently alongside the fence, without even contemplating a breakout.

SAFETY WITH BARBED WIRE
Workers erect a fence enclosing farmland alongside a canal (left). Livestock will be kept off the barbed wire by a hedge (right).

DRY STONE WALLS

A DRY STONE WALL may be centuries old and can be considered as much a part of the landscape as are the fields and trees. Designed to enclose sheep or cattle, it can be very effective if properly looked after. Maintenance is a skilled task that takes time to learn. Expect to have to rebuild a wall at least once a century.

WIRE-MESH FENCES

FOR CONFINING SMALLER stock, such as pigs, sheep, goats, rabbits, and poultry, wire mesh is the first choice. Pig mesh is the strongest. Sheep mesh is much lighter, which helps if you are planning strip grazing and the fence has to be moved. Mesh is not suitable for horses – they have an expensive habit of putting their feet through it, which may cause them injury and often removes a shoe.

Chicken and rabbit netting is thinly made, with very small mesh; because the wire is so light, it will snap if put under any pressure, and so this type of mesh fence will not contain sheep.

LARGE MESH
A fence like this will keep goats and sheep secure. To contain pigs, a heavier gauge of mesh will probably be needed.·

FINE MESH
Chickens will be safe behind this, but bury the bottom at least 12 in (30 cm) deep to prevent vermin from entering the run.

ELECTRIC FENCES

AN ELECTRIC FENCE is flexible and cheap to install, and the animals will quickly learn to respect it. Temporary electric fences are very useful for restricting grazing to a small area of a field.

Problems arise when the voltage on the wire drops as a result of a power failure or because grass has grown up around the wire. When wet, grass will ground the current, leaving a section of the fence without electricity. Animals will occasionally test a fence and may discover that it is not working. They might spot it before you do.

Movable fences are made with nylon strings containing strands of electric wire; permanent ones have solid wire.

MOVABLE ELECTRIC FENCE
A single electrified wire will contain cattle or horses. You can use a movable fence to stop cows from grazing a whole field at once. As each strip is grazed, move the fence on.

PERMANENT ELECTRIC FENCE
This is easier to build than other permanent fences because it relies on an electric shock, instead of the strength of the wire, to confine the stock. A good fence for almost all stock.

COMBINATIONS

TO GET THE BEST of both worlds, have a bit of each. Most of the fences around my fields have mesh along the bottom and electrified wire along the top. The mesh keeps sheep in, and the electrified wire prevents cattle from getting their heads over the top of the fence and leaning on it, or horses from getting too close and putting their feet in the mesh.

To contain poultry, I would need to use finer mesh along the bottom, while for pigs I would have to put in a strand of barbed wire at ground level, to deter digging snouts. If you really try, you can make your fences virtually escape-proof, but the ultimate constraint is cost.

SECURE BOUNDARY FENCE
This will keep almost any animal in. Fine mesh to contain poultry is attached to strong posts and rails. The electric wire across the top prevents cattle and horses from rubbing.

POULTRY PEN DIVIDER
This is a mesh fence reinforced with an old door and some corrugated sheet. These give shade and shelter, and neighboring roosters won't try to fight if they can't see each other.

Simple shelters

HOUSING ANIMALS IS no big deal. They will not know whether you have made their house out of expensive building materials, and copied fancy designs, or paid little for something that will last for years.

An animal shelter is needed for three things. It has to protect your animals from the elements, stop them from escaping, and make it as easy as possible for you to do your work with the animals. If you can achieve all three of these for a little money, why spend a lot? The skills involved in putting up a shelter are not advanced ones and include simple design, carpentry, and thatching. If you take to these, why not graduate to making your own poultry housing (see pp. 48–49) or converting an outhouse for goats (p. 64).

MOVABLE RABBIT CAGE
Costing hardly anything to build, this cage can be moved daily to give the rabbits fresh grazing. It is quick to repair. The design is very basic: for access, you just tilt it up and reach inside.

TEMPORARY HOUSING FOR PIGS

PIGS ARE NATURALLY outdoor animals, and if they lived truly in the wild they would make shelters for themselves by digging holes under trees. The modern domesticated pig needs a little more, but not much. If you can keep it dry and free from drafts, then that is all it asks. If you are in a situation where you have to put up temporary housing, here is an ideal way to do it cheaply. This humble-looking structure made of straw bales and wooden stakes is easy to take down, or even rebuild if that powerful snout decides to be a little destructive.

1 DECIDING THE LAYOUT
Use tightly bound bales of straw and lay out a pig shelter of the desired size.

If building for a young litter, remember that pigs double in size in the first ten weeks of life.

2 DRIVING STAKES *Fencing stakes will hold the bales in position and prevent a lumbering pig from knocking them over.*

Fencing stake   Tightly packed bale of straw

3 BUILDING WALLS *Make these two bales high, with stakes inside and outside. Pigs tend to pull at the straw, so bales may need protecting with wire mesh.*

4 ROOFING *Anything will do for a roof. If not fastened, weigh it down, or the wind will take it. If you expect rain, slope the roof to allow runoff.*

LAMBING SHELTER

UNLESS YOU ARE lambing in the mildest conditions, both ewes and lambs will need shelter from cold winds and rain, which account for more lambing deaths than any other single cause. A lambing shelter must be easy to assemble and disassemble so that it can be moved where needed. It must also be quick to clean – each ewe will be in it for only a couple of days, and as one leaves, the next will already be waiting to come in.

Woven wattle hurdles make good shelters because they allow fresh air to circulate while excluding wind and rain.

1 DRIVING STAKES *Form the corners of the shelter by driving stakes firmly into the ground. Place them so that the shelter has its back to the prevailing wind.*

2 HOLDING THE HURDLES IN PLACE *Bind and tie the hurdles to the stakes with twine to form three sides of the shelter. It will have to withstand all kinds of weather.*

3 FINAL STAGES *Wattle hurdles on three sides make a good structure. A metal hurdle or two across the front will contain the sheep and allow you to keep an eye on them; a wattle hurdle laid across the top will keep off the worst of the rain (right).*

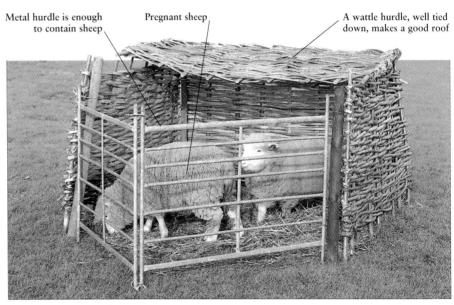

Metal hurdle is enough to contain sheep

Pregnant sheep

A wattle hurdle, well tied down, makes a good roof

SIMPLE THATCHING

IT IS WORTH thatching your animal shelters only if you have grown your own straw and cut it without using a combine harvester. Combines smash the straw, and it will not make a decent roof.

Straw is a good roofing material; it is waterproof and provides good insulation. At the same time, it is not completely airtight, allowing a very gradual flow of air, which is good for animal health. I knew an old farmer who swore that to get good leather, cattle must be kept under straw and not tiles.

1 DRAWING THE STRAW *Take large handfuls of straw, sort it into a neat sheaf, and tie it to the roof using string. Wire mesh makes a good base on which to build a simple roof like this.*

2 RAKING *Rake the roof lightly to remove any loose straw. This makes the roof look tidier and also encourages rain to run down the slope of the roof instead of dripping through it.*

3 TRIMMING *Now trim the edge. You do this for two reasons: first, for pride, and second, to prevent the animals beneath from raising their heads and eating their own roof!*

HOME FARM POULTRY

FARMYARD CLEANER
The guinea fowl is a useful bird on a poultry farm. Besides providing meat and eggs, it pecks up disease-carrying ticks.

POULTRY KEEPING CAN BE as large or as small an affair as you wish it to be. If you want to go down the road of commercialism, there are good profits to be made from poultry and eggs produced in a nonintensive way. But if you like birds for their beauty and their company, there is no reason why you should not keep them for these considerations alone. The work you do, too, can be a lot or a little, depending on how much you wish to achieve with your birds.

Most poultry will get by provided they are fed and sheltered, but you cannot stint on the basic necessities. You have a duty to protect your poultry from foxes. One determined fox will destroy a sizable flock of poultry before you have even had a chance to get out of bed to see what the row is about.

I used to give my chickens the freedom of the barn during the day. I was never quite sure where they all were, or where the broody hen might disappear to, but it was fun pulling hay from a dark corner of the barn and finding the piercing eyes of that broody hen peering at me, as she wondered why she had been disturbed.

POULTRY FOR PLEASURE

Do not be selfish about keeping poultry. If you are going to get pleasure from having them, make sure they get some pleasure out of life too. Give them as much room as you can. Ducks and geese are water-loving birds, and no self-respecting home farmer would thwart their natural desire to get on the water. You do not need a vast lake or flowing river, but you do have to provide low troughs, at least deep enough for your ducks or geese to dip their heads and satisfy their instinct

GEESE

Geese make good burglar alarms, but ganders can be aggressive. A noisy but friendly goose is ideal. Don't keep one goose – keep two. A goose and a gander form a pair that lasts for life. The bird shown here is an Embden cross.

DUCKS

Choose breeds for either eggs or meat, as few ducks are good for both. For eggs, choose a breed, like the Khaki Campbell shown, that rarely goes broody. (A broody bird is one that hides her eggs to hatch them. You never see them!)

Short, scissor-like bill used for grazing

Spiral pattern in neck plumage

Large wings provide tremendous power of flight

Large breast muscles

Webbed feet with four strong claws

Geese shed down feathers from the breast and belly to line their nests

Wide, flat bill used for sieving food particles from water

Broad body with large breast muscles

Slender, flexible neck

Powerful wings

Waterproof plumage

Webbed feet with four strong claws

to splash and wash their feathers. Of the two species, ducks are the more aquatic in that they spend more of their time actually swimming, but access to water is equally vital to both.

Allow your geese and hens the fun of foraging, and in return they will tidy up your fields beautifully, working their way across stubble left by cereals and feeding themselves on discarded corn and weed seeds.

POULTRY FOR PROFIT

Modern, intensive poultry rearing is perceived as being such a disgusting business that free-range meat and eggs from a home farm are highly sought after.

This opens up possibilities for you to make some money in return for your efforts. However, you get nothing for free, and profit from poultry comes only from a lot of hard work. As you enlarge your flock, expect to spend more time feeding careful rations and making regular inspections for disease and parasites. Housing will have to be cleaned regularly, and thought will have to be given to the efficient use of the space you have and the eventual killing of the birds.

Selling poultry meat can be tied up in complex health regulations, and you must be certain you comply before starting. Getting on the right side of the law can be more trouble and effort than keeping the animals. Another complication is the fact that for some operations, timing is everything – turkeys ready for killing a week *after* Thanksgiving or Christmas might as well be left to scratch around the farm.

FREE-RANGE CHICKENS
These chickens can scratch the earth for food or help themselves from feeders. The housing is secure, water is provided, and the spacious run is fenced – truly free-range.

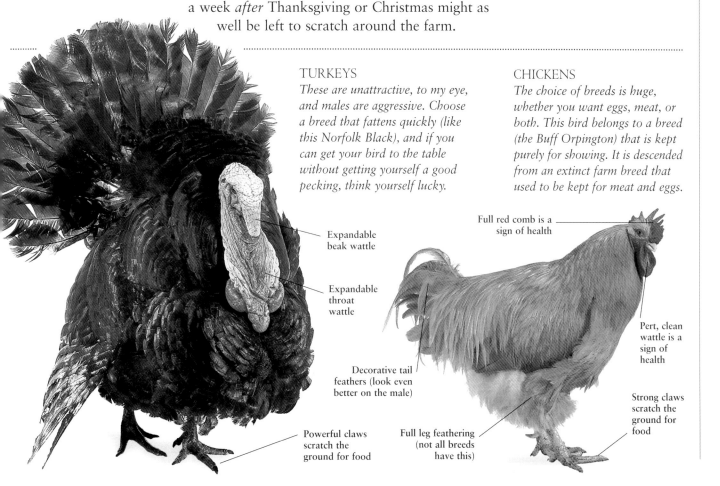

TURKEYS
These are unattractive, to my eye, and males are aggressive. Choose a breed that fattens quickly (like this Norfolk Black), and if you can get your bird to the table without getting yourself a good pecking, think yourself lucky.

CHICKENS
The choice of breeds is huge, whether you want eggs, meat, or both. This bird belongs to a breed (the Buff Orpington) that is kept purely for showing. It is descended from an extinct farm breed that used to be kept for meat and eggs.

Expandable beak wattle

Expandable throat wattle

Powerful claws scratch the ground for food

Full red comb is a sign of health

Decorative tail feathers (look even better on the male)

Full leg feathering (not all breeds have this)

Pert, clean wattle is a sign of health

Strong claws scratch the ground for food

Keeping chickens

NO CHICKENS – NO FARMYARD. It is no kind of farm that does not have a hen or two scratching about in the yard or a rooster sitting on a gatepost crowing, although you will need to confine them at night if foxes are around. Chickens are easy to keep; they feed on what other animals waste, plus a basic grain ration that you must provide. In return they provide daily eggs for you and your family, and it is always easy to find customers to buy free-range eggs if you decide you want to sell them.

All year round, chickens need dry, warm housing

Nesting box

Outside access for egg collection

No need for a rooster if you don't want chicks

FOLD UNIT

This combined grazing run and shelter is easy to carry to a fresh grazing site, which helps avoid the buildup of parasites in the ground. The unit's hinged sides can be lifted up for access.

CHICKEN RUN
You will need a strong, draft-proof, vermin-proof house, a secure fence, and a box from which to collect the eggs. Give the birds plenty of space in which to roam.

CHICKEN BREEDS FOR THE SMALLHOLDER

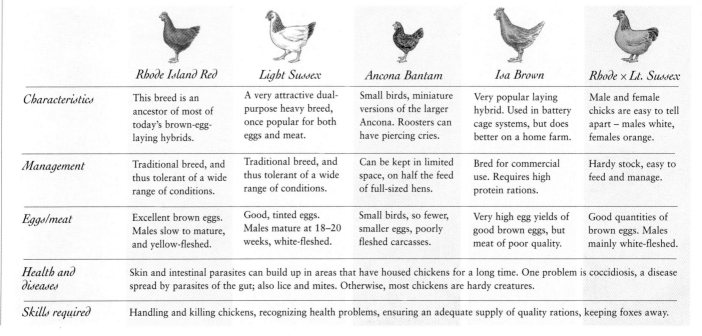

	Rhode Island Red	*Light Sussex*	*Ancona Bantam*	*Isa Brown*	*Rhode × Lt. Sussex*
Characteristics	This breed is an ancestor of most of today's brown-egg-laying hybrids.	A very attractive dual-purpose heavy breed, once popular for both eggs and meat.	Small birds, miniature versions of the larger Ancona. Roosters can have piercing cries.	Very popular laying hybrid. Used in battery cage systems, but does better on a home farm.	Male and female chicks are easy to tell apart – males white, females orange.
Management	Traditional breed, and thus tolerant of a wide range of conditions.	Traditional breed, and thus tolerant of a wide range of conditions.	Can be kept in limited space, on half the feed of full-sized hens.	Bred for commercial use. Requires high protein rations.	Hardy stock, easy to feed and manage.
Eggs/meat	Excellent brown eggs. Males slow to mature, and yellow-fleshed.	Good, tinted eggs. Males mature at 18–20 weeks, white-fleshed.	Small birds, so fewer, smaller eggs, poorly fleshed carcasses.	Very high egg yields of good brown eggs, but meat of poor quality.	Good quantities of brown eggs. Males mainly white-fleshed.
Health and diseases	Skin and intestinal parasites can build up in areas that have housed chickens for a long time. One problem is coccidiosis, a disease spread by parasites of the gut; also lice and mites. Otherwise, most chickens are hardy creatures.				
Skills required	Handling and killing chickens, recognizing health problems, ensuring an adequate supply of quality rations, keeping foxes away.				

Sow grass mixtures specially blended for poultry (see p. 154)

Ball cock ensures water is topped up as the birds drink

Burying the base of the fence deters vermin

(see p. 154)

A VARIETY OF HENS' EGGS

THE BROWN EGGS at the far right are from a Rhode Island Red hen, and are similar to those laid by the Isa Brown and Rhode × Light Sussex. The buff egg (second left, top) is from a Light Sussex. The very white egg is from a rare breed, known as the Spanish. The four tiny eggs are from a small breed called the Silkie.

COLLECTING THE EGGS
An outside door to the nesting boxes allows easy egg collection.

ENCLOSING AND PROTECTING
As well as being stockproof, this fence provides shade and shelter.

FIXTURES

THE HEN ASKS two things of her house – somewhere to lay her eggs, and a perch on which to roost at night and exercise her natural instinct to get up high, away from predators. The one thing that *you* need is easy access to get at the freshly laid eggs. This could be via an outside door to avoid disturbing the hens. Nest boxes must be warm, dry, cozy, and clean. Wood shavings (from untreated wood) make the best lining.

Stone doorstep stops chickens from trampling ground to mud

Hedge gives shade in hot weather and shelter from wind

FRONT DOOR
This is known as the pop hole. It slides up and down to open and close. For safety, the birds must be shut in at night, even if they have the run of the farm by day.

FOOD AND DRINK

VERMIN WILL BE attracted to the chickens' feed, so store it beyond the reach of rats and mice. For a good daily supply of fresh eggs, layers must have a ready supply of layers' meal or pellets.

Feed grain, but only in the afternoon and no more than 1 oz (25 g) per bird. In this way, birds will also feed on unsalted kitchen scraps and garden waste, bugs and grubs, and fresh greens, including winter kale (see p. 162).

(see p. 162)

STEP-ON FEEDER
The lid of the trough is lifted by the pressure of the bird's foot, so that the feed is kept dry and safe when birds are not feeding.

HANGING FEEDER
Usually suspended with the base just above the level of a chicken's back, this feeder is waste-free and caters to up to 25 laying hens.

WATER ON DEMAND
An automatic trough ensures a supply of fresh water. Relocate it from time to time, to stop muddy patches from forming.

Keeping ducks

DUCKS ARE EASY and versatile animals to keep. You can raise them for their meat or for their eggs, but the best reason is for their humor. I have always found ducks to be endlessly cheerful and entertaining to watch, while making few demands on the farmer. There are meat breeds and there are egg breeds (see table below), but, in contrast to chickens, a truly dual-purpose breed is hard to find. If you choose a meat breed, be warned – ducks make good pets.

Handle for moving house

Walkway

Outside access for egg collecti

The pond edge is a good place for ducks to forage

Fence to keep out predators

DUCK RUN
The run should be large enough to stop the land from becoming stale and to give sufficient variety for the ducks to be able to find food for themselves. Give them as much room as you can spare, but you should always allow at least 15 sq yd (12.5 sq m) per bird.

ROOM WITH A VIEW
This simple, effective duck house provides shelter for up to four ducks. The house is light and can be moved to fresh grazing every day, but, unless space is limited, free-range is better.

DUCK BREEDS FOR THE SMALLHOLDER

	Khaki Campbell	Indian Runner	Aylesbury	Pekin	Muscovy/Barbary
Characteristics	Found throughout the world. The best breed for eggs.	An ancestor of the Khaki Campbell. Unusual upright stance.	Pure white plumage, pinkish white beak, and yellow legs; popular duck bred for the table.	Beak is bright orange, feet reddish orange. More talkative than other breeds.	Known as the Muscovy in English-speaking countries, elsewhere as the Barbary.
Management	Careful management needed for highest production. Hardy.	A hardy duck. Runs, rather than waddles, and is a good forager.	Not hardy; normally it is crossed with the Pekin for extra vigor.	A hardy duck that grows very fast.	Makes a good mother and will hatch eggs other than its own.
Eggs/meat	Excellent breed for egg production. Over 300 eggs a year.	Second only to the Khaki Campbell in egg production.	First-class table bird. Creamy white flesh. White eggs.	Most numerous meat breed, despite high fat content of the meat.	Popular breed in France, where flesh is sold as "duck steaks."
Health and diseases	Ducks are prone to fewer diseases than hens and are generally easier to keep. Worms need to be controlled, and lack of hygiene may cause leg weakness and foot sores. Fortunately, coccidiosis (see p. 48) does not occur in ducks or geese.				
Skills required	Building duck shelter, making water available, management of hatching, rearing and sexing of ducklings, recognizing ill health.				

Ducks like a variety of wild grass and weeds in which to forage

Drainage water helps fill pond

Clay lining on pond bed and bank

Ducks like a gentle slope to walk into pond

Fine mesh stops ducklings from going astray

A RANGE OF DUCK EGGS

EGGS FROM THREE traditional duck breeds are shown here: the one on the left is from a Khaki Campbell, a prolific egg layer; the center egg is from a Buff Orpington, a dual-purpose egg and meat breed; and the large egg on the right is from a Rouen duck, which is a meat breed.

FOOD AND DRINK

DUCKS THAT ARE laying or being fattened up for market will need extra feeding, on top of the food they forage for themselves and the basic ration of grain that all ducks require. Make a mash from ground grains (corn, barley, or oats) and a little fish meal or other protein boost. Feed enough for the ducks to take 20 minutes or so to eat; there is no need to be too scientific.

WATER BOWL
Ducks must have fresh drinking water. Place the bowl on a piece of mesh to protect the grass.

FEED TROUGH
If you have a large flock, make sure there is enough space at the trough for each bird to get a fair feed without getting trampled.

FIXTURES AND FITTINGS

LET YOUR DUCKS be a part of the landscape, while at the same time protecting them from foxes and vermin. The housing needs to be draft- and predator-proof and have a nest box for the ducks to lay their eggs in.

Although you do not have to provide a pond, you will have happier ducks if you do. The birds are also more likely to mate if swimming water is available. A pond must be lined, or the water will drain away – a layer of clay is a good natural lining.

DUCK POND
A duck's dream come true. The birds feed on water weeds, snails, and insects. Divert land drains to maintain water level (right).

IDEAL HOME
You can open this duck house for thorough cleaning. When closed, it is a cozy home in which a duck can lay or sit on eggs. All the doors have firm catches for securing at night.

Keeping geese

IT IS TIME FOR THE GOOSE to have a revival. For some reason, it is deeply out of fashion, and it is rare to turn up at a farm of any size these days to have your arrival heralded by the frightening honking of a flock of geese. But geese fit in well on a home farm, for they are good at being self-sufficient, and if grass and other grazing is in plentiful supply, then for long periods of the year they will need no extra feeding. If you have stubble on fields where cereals have been grown and harvested, there would be nothing better than to set a flock of geese to work, eagerly clearing the land of fallen grain and weeds. Geese are naturally suited to home farming because of the modesty of their demands. Goose housing can be as simple or elaborate as you want it to be.

GOOSE EGGS

AT ALMOST HALF a pound (200 g), the eggs you get from your geese are bigger than you could believe possible. The laying season can start in midwinter and continue until midsummer. A single goose may lay up to 80 eggs, some breeds even more. Best for omelettes – large ones!

Wire mesh provides ventilation

Fencing mainly to keep out foxes and vermin

Outside egg collection

Paving stones protect ground from trampling

Drain stopped with a bath plug

Triangular bath makes an adequate pond

Proper drainage is essential

Humane fox trap

Drinking trough and city water

Run is adequate as a home, but additional grazing will be needed in a nearby field

GOOSE RUN

Geese are grazing animals and prefer room to roam, so do not confine them for the entire year, but only when grazing is poor. Shut them in at night to protect them from hunting predators.

FOOD AND DRINK

LET YOUR GEESE eat grass and weeds, even winter kale and roots alongside sheep. But if you have no other feed, then cereals (whole grains) and chopped greens will serve them well. The greens you feed them might be winter kale, cabbage leaves, or bolted lettuces; the birds are not fussy feeders. To fatten them really quickly, feed barley and wheat in equal amounts, twice a day.

OPEN PASTURE
This is the way geese prefer to feed, but confining them in a small area will damage the grass.

FEED TROUGH
Feed is trampled and wasted if not placed in a trough. Move it around to keep pasture sweet.

WATER TROUGH
Geese need water deep enough to dip their heads. A pond is ideal, but they can use a trough.

POP HOLE AND WALKWAY
Foxes are ruthless; you may have to use a shuttered house like this to confine geese at night.

UPRIGHT NEST BOX
Leave the open side facing such a way as to shelter the sitting goose from wind, rain, and sun.

INFORMAL NEST BOX
This old crate has been stuffed with straw and put in a corner where tin sheeting gives shelter.

FIXTURES AND FITTINGS

THE PRIME consideration in making goose housing is to ensure protection from foxes and other vermin; simple shelter is all the geese ask for. If you have other poultry on the farm, then a goose will be just as happy in a hen hut as in anything else. You need not go to a lot of trouble. A laying goose needs a house in which she can keep dry and feel safe with her eggs; she does not demand a palace.

GOOSE BREEDS FOR THE SMALLHOLDER

	Embden	Toulouse	Pilgrim	American Buff	Chinese Brown
Characteristics	Large, white bird. German. First-class carcass.	The British Toulouse (kept internationally) is larger than the French Toulouse.	Geese are light gray, ganders white. Brought to the United States by the Pilgrims.	Medium-size bird. Buff feathers.	Related to wild geese. Looks rather like a swan.
Management	Hardy goose that thrives in all parts of the world.	Sometimes crossed with the Embden.	An easygoing, farmyard goose. Can be sexed at a day old.	An easygoing farmyard goose.	Suffers from the cold, so needs good winter protection.
Eggs/meat	Largest carcass of all the geese.	Goose (not gander) as heavy as Embden.	Medium-size carcass.	Medium-size carcass.	Best breed of all for egg laying.
Health and diseases	Generally hardy birds, good grazers and foragers. As with all poultry, intestinal worms must be controlled. If insufficient water is provided for the geese to bathe in, skin parasites can sometimes be a problem.				
Skills required	Some courage is needed to face an angry gander. Provision of housing and grazing, basic poultry rearer's veterinary skills.				

HOME FARM SHEEP

A FLOCK OF YOUR OWN
It pays to learn a few tricks of shepherding. Sheep will follow an ordinary bucket, if you train them to associate it with food.

THE SHEEP IS AN ANIMAL with a rare talent for being endearing one moment, but frustrating to the point of madness the next. Having kept a flock for a number of years, I am always amazed at the way sheep can appear to be a placid part of a peaceful landscape, and yet within moments have you tearing at your hair in frustration. Something seems to get into them and make them refuse outright to go in the direction you intend, or to go anywhere at all.

But sheep can be forgiven all their transgressions – almost – for they are very good providers from the home farmer's point of view. They will live on far poorer land than that needed to support cattle; they give wool and meat, and offspring every year; and some breeds can even be milked as well.

BECOMING A SHEPHERD

This takes time. You have to work with sheep until you can think like a sheep. I was given a piece of advice by an old shepherd from the Scottish Borders: "Sheep are not stupid, they just need time." Imagine a flock of sheep grazing a field and suddenly you, the shepherd, charge through the gate and head toward them. They will scatter. Some will flock together again, but some will charge off wildly. Stupid? No, you were. Now just stand there and see what happens. Likely as not they will look at you, calm down, and eventually nosiness will get the better of them. Very soon they will be yours to do with as you wish. They just needed time. Sheep quickly sense impatience and react accordingly. Keeping your cool,

A running nose can be a sign of infection

Clear eye

A glowing, unblemished fleece is a sign of health

Clean tail area indicates freedom from internal problems

Check for a full set of lower teeth (sheep have no upper teeth, just hardened gums)

Ewe needs a good-sized udder

There should be no sign of lameness

GOOD POINTS
Learn the look of a healthy sheep, and it will be easy to spot the sick ones. Eyes must be bright, the fleece should be glowing, the nose must be clean, and the sheep should have a good set of teeth for grazing. Limping sheep may not take much to put them right. Shown here is a fine example of a Suffolk ewe.

and thereby getting the sheep on your side, is the secret of successful shepherding. You will also learn to control individuals. For a variety of shepherding tasks, such as shearing, foot trimming, and veterinary care, it is necessary to position and immobilize an animal exactly where you want it (see right).

THE RIGHT SHEEP FOR YOUR FARM

I could not begin to list all the breeds of sheep that have been developed worldwide to suit the needs of different climates, terrains, or markets. But among them will be the right sheep for you. It is important to have a clear idea of what you require. If your sheep are simply to act as lawn mowers, choose a breed you like the look of. But when it comes to the more serious matters of wool and meat, you will have to choose more carefully.

Some breeds of sheep have been developed for commercial reasons; they may always produce twins, fatten quickly, or have a carcass that is sought after by the meat trade. There is nothing wrong in choosing one of these breeds, but make sure that you understand the down side as well as the up. It is all very well to be guaranteed twins at every birth, but not if each lamb demands the shepherd's full attention. Some breeds of sheep are designed for rugged places, and if you have a warm, lush lowland farm they will be like fish out of water.

HOLDING A SHEEP
Place your right hand on the ewe's rump; use your left to grip the throat wool. Roll her over and bend her head back.

CASTING A SHEEP
Start as for holding (left), but as you roll the animal, move your legs into the position shown, so she ends up resting on them.

SHEEP BREEDS FOR THE SMALLHOLDER

	Suffolk	*Welsh Mountain*	*Mule*	*Jacob*	*Milk Sheep*
Characteristics	Black-faced, heavy sheep found all over the world. Meat sheep with a lean carcass.	A small sheep, bred to survive harsh upland winters. Not highly productive sheep.	Popular the world over. Prolific and easy lambing, producing a lean carcass suited to current market needs.	A primitive breed of sheep with a distinctive brown and white spotted fleece.	Sheep's milk is much richer than cow's or goat's. Not usually prolific lambers, but good milkers.
Management	Lowland sheep, unsuitable for upland districts. Good winter feeding needed.	Noted escapologists. Essentially a hill sheep, but also found on lowland farms where grazing is not too rich.	Best suited to systems where good grazing and careful feeding result in fast-growing and profitable lambs.	A lean, rugged animal, native to upland areas. Both sexes are horned; not everyone likes this.	Careful feeding and regular milking needed for maximum production. A heavy commitment.
Fleece	Not the highest quality wool. Used in hosiery, tweeds, and flannel.	Fleece varies in quality; may contain coarse red fibers (kemp), but is generally white.	Bred for meat, and so fleece not of highest quality. Sometimes used in carpet making.	Fleece much in demand for home-craft spinning.	Fleece not a consideration.
Health and diseases	Sheep are prone to more diseases than you can possibly imagine. Regular attention needs to be given to worm control, the condition of the feet, and parasite control in summer.				
Skills required	Ability to assist ewes at lambing, trimming feet, worming, shearing, gathering the flock, and other skills associated with controlling the sheep, such as casting. Shepherding skills come with practice – and patience.				

Shepherd's calendar

DECIDE WHEN YOU WANT your lambing to take place, and plan your shepherding year from there. It is tempting to lamb as early in the year as nature allows, so that your lambs are fat and ready for market when prices are highest. But that often falls at the tail end of winter, and tending a heavily pregnant flock in snow, fog, and frost is no fun at all. Newborn lambs don't like bad weather either. If you are keeping sheep to provide meat or wool for your own use, lamb when meadows are warm and the nutritious spring grass is full of vigor, and save yourself a lot of work and heartache. Highly commercial farmers bring their flocks indoors in the depths of winter, shear the ewes to fit as many as possible into the barn, and medicate against the diseases of intensification. This is not the way of the home farmer. Follow the traditional shepherding calendar and make life easier, for you and your flock.

Crooks help to control the flock

PREGNANT
This ewe has been marked by the crayon in the raddle, showing she has been mated. The color of the crayon is changed regularly to show roughly when each ewe was covered.

AUTUMN
Get the ewes and ram ready for tupping (mating) by feeding cereals if grass is poor. Tupping should be 146 days (average gestation period) ahead of the date you want lambs. Raddle the ram and put him with the flock. Keep feeding the flock, and watch for crayon marks appearing to make sure the ram is working hard.

TRIMMING FEET
Overgrown feet must be trimmed or they may become infected. During mating, the ram makes full use of his hind legs – if his feet are not in good condition, he may be less willing to perform.

RADDLING THE RAM
The raddle is a harness, fitted to the ram, that holds a crayon to mark each ewe as she is mated.

SUMMER
Watch for blowfly strike, which can kill lambs and make life miserable for ewes. Pastures should be providing good grazing, and lambs should be growing quickly on mother's milk and fresh grass. Move flock regularly to prevent a buildup of worms in the grass. Check udders for damage or infection, and watch for bloat (see right).

DIPPING SHEEP

SHEEP ARE DIPPED to kill pests in their fleece; this is generally done once a year, in late summer, after shearing. In some countries, dipping is a legal requirement. There are many brands of sheep dip, and again, you may be required by law to use a particular brand – check. If you have a large flock of sheep, it is probably worth building a concrete pit, with entry and exit ramps, for dipping. If you have only a few sheep, you can use a zinc bath, but it will take two of you to hold the sheep in it.

The body and legs must be dipped for a minute; make sure that the head is dipped too, even if for a shorter time.

LAMBS AT PASTURE
Lambs can be weaned at four months old and given fresh pasture. Put ewes on barer meadows to dry off their milk.

SHEARING
Shearing takes place before the height of summer when the fleece "rises" naturally from the sheep's skin (see p. 60). Choose fine, settled weather.

WINTER FEEDING

Each ewe in your flock will need 500 lb (225 kg) of hay in an average winter. Only in the harshest conditions will concentrates be needed. Once a ewe has conceived, her diet can be reduced to a maintenance level so that she is not too fat to lamb easily. Don't forget to break the ice on the water troughs.

WINTER

Feed hay through the winter, but don't feed cereals, or ewes will be too fat at lambing. Provide some protection from the worst of the winter weather for lowland flocks, and bring upland sheep down from the hills. In late winter, the ewes will need building up again in preparation for lambing, so feed cereals for 30 days before lambing starts.

SPRING

Heavily pregnant ewes are unable to regain their feet if they get rolled onto their backs: they cannot be visited too often. Check that you have a full lambing kit ready and build a lambing shelter (see p. 44). Check fences and gates. Expect to spend long hours with the flock once lambing starts. Feed roots or kale after lambing to stimulate milk flow.

DAGGING
Remove the soiled fleece from the sheep's rear – it attracts blowflies.

DRENCHING
Sheep are drenched with medicine to kill worms straight after lambing.

DEALING WITH BLOAT
If a sheep stuffs itself on rich food, the resulting gases can cause bloat. It is a killer. Treat with a dose of cooking oil, and then stand back.

TRADITIONAL REMEDIES

SHEEP NEED SALT to thrive. Spread unprocessed salt on meadows at a rate of 110 lb/acre (125 kg/ha).

Internal worms make for poor sheep, and often a deep, rough cough. Worms are one of your greatest enemies and are best controlled by strict pasture management. If that fails, add a mixture of finely chopped garlic and molasses to the regular feed.

Garlic and molasses feed supplement

Foot rot causes great pain. The feet become inflamed and smell vile. A sheep grazing on its knees is a sure sign. Wash and pare at the hoof until you reach the infected area. Dress it with a mixture of ½ lb (230 g) of pine tar and 3 oz (85 g) of salt. Foot rot is caught from wet, infected pastures. Clean pastures by leaving them empty for three weeks.

Blowfly maggots hatch from eggs laid in the fleece of the sheep. They burrow into the flesh and, if left uninterrupted, will eat a sheep alive. Telltale signs are rapid tail movements, biting of the fleece in the infected area, and large,

Painting feet with pine tar

damp, smelly patches. Remove the damp fleece, scrape away as many maggots as possible, and then dress with sheep dip or powdered derris. Treat any wounds with pine tar.

SPRING LAMBS
Lambs are bursting with life, especially when the spring sunshine hits their backs. Once they are taking plenty of milk and some supplementary feed, they soon start to put on weight. When the grass starts to grow, they will grow with it.

Lambing

STRONG, HEALTHY LAMBS are a result of the care and attention given to their mothers over a long period, not just during the last few days of gestation. Ewes must be fit, but not fat, or you will have lambing problems; feeding during pregnancy is a vital concern.

Once you are sure a ewe is pregnant (when no further raddle crayon marks are left by the ram), she can be left to feed off stubble to keep her in lean condition. Give her extra feed for eight weeks before lambing, increasing the ration steadily as lambing approaches. Feed her cereals (oats are best), good hay, and minerals. Make sure you are healthy too – you are soon going to be busy around the clock.

SPRING LAMBS
Nature planned the sheep's life cycle so that lambs are born in spring when feed is plentiful.

Ewes of most breeds cannot be got into lamb in late spring or summer. Play it nature's way.

MAKING PREPARATIONS

THERE WILL BE premature lambs, so be ready. Three weeks before the first lamb is due is not too early to start building shelters. The weather at lambing will determine how much shelter you will need. If it is going to be wet, windy, or frosty, then you will need some kind of shelter indoors. The chief enemy of a newborn lamb is a cold, damp wind.

X-shaped wall of straw bales provides shelter whichever way the wind blows

FIELD SHELTERS
If you are lambing in late spring, you may need no more than a wattle hurdle shelter (see p. 44) or a simple wall of straw bales.

Interlocking hurdles

INDOOR LAMBING
Divide your lambing shed into specific areas – for ewes not yet lambed, for those with newborn lambs, and for those with lambs that are several days old and ready to be turned back onto the meadows. Build a sick bay, too, for orphan lambs that may need fostering or hand feeding. The shed must be deeply littered with straw and shielded from driving rain, but not too enclosed.

Supply of fresh drinking water

THE LAMBING PROCESS

JUST BEFORE THE BIRTH, the ewe will lie down, with her head pointing skyward, and groan as she strains. A water bag will appear, followed by the lamb's nose and front feet. Imagine the pose a diver adopts – that is how the lamb should be positioned. Once the shoulders have emerged, the rest of the lamb will slither easily on to the ground. Quickly take the lamb to the ewe's head so she can smell and clean it. Clear the lamb's nose and mouth if they are covered in mucus.

LAMBING KIT

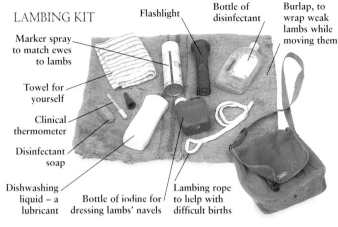

- Flashlight
- Bottle of disinfectant
- Burlap, to wrap weak lambs while moving them
- Marker spray to match ewes to lambs
- Towel for yourself
- Clinical thermometer
- Disinfectant soap
- Dishwashing liquid – a lubricant
- Bottle of iodine for dressing lambs' navels
- Lambing rope to help with difficult births

READY FOR USE
Buy a canvas bag, and dedicate it to lambing. Never be parted from it. Fill it with the items shown, and keep it under the bed at night. A good book about lambing is a must, as well as warm clothes that allow enough freedom of movement.

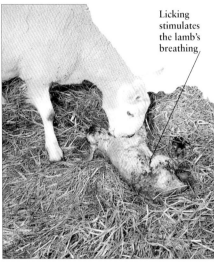

- Licking stimulates the lamb's breathing

LICKING INTO SHAPE
Once the lamb is born, leave mother and baby alone for about an hour. Don't bother them. By the time you come back, the ewe will have cleaned the lamb and it should be struggling to its legs and hunting for the teat.

- Infrared lamp provides warmth

FIRST MILK
Check on the lambs after an hour. They must suckle within the first couple of hours, and the first milk is vital. It is known as colostrum and is high in the antibodies the lambs need to protect them from disease.

IF THINGS GO WRONG

IF EVERY LAMBING goes easily, you are lucky. Nine times out of ten it will, but when things go wrong you have vital choices to make – and quickly. Once you have intervened there is no going back, so do not start unless you can finish.

When you first start out, either get to know a local shepherd whom you can call in an emergency (a good option because you will learn from him) or call out a vet when problems occur. A training course is a good start.

Pregnant women should not help at lambing time because of the danger of cross-infection by animal diseases that can damage the human embryo.

ORPHAN LAMB
If a ewe dies, you can either foster her lamb onto a ewe with a single lamb or feed it by bottle. You can buy formulated lamb milk, but lambs need regular feeding at a time when you will be busy. Try fostering if you can.

ACTING AS MIDWIFE
Some ewes will need help, but don't expect them to be grateful. Be firm and purposeful, but be gentle with your hands.

Wool

NO ONE HAS YET come up with a more versatile clothing material than that which grows on sheep. You may be tempted by all sorts of modern, weather-deflecting garments, but you will always return to wool – it is unbeatable. Not only does it expand when wet, closing up to keep out the wind, but it also has the property of giving off heat as it dries.

However, it is a big step from sheep to garment. The sheep has to be sheared successfully; the fleece has to be cleaned, carded, and spun to make a ball of wool; and even then, the knitting lies ahead of you. With the dozens of kinds of wool from sheep alone, leaving aside Angora goats (see p. 63), rabbits (p. 84), and llamas (pp. 41, 86), anyone who takes up home spinning and knitting is in for a great deal of variety.

These last two jobs I have always been happy to delegate, but I am equally content to wrap the end product around me on icy mornings. If you decide to try these crafts, do not make the mistake of using a fleece from a ram, unless you want every ewe in the county chasing you.

SHEEP SHEARS

SHEARS, HAND OR ELECTRIC, work like scissors and need to be kept ruthlessly sharp. Cheap shears will not keep their edge. Left- and right-handed versions are made – you will not get anywhere if you use the wrong one.

Simple hand shears   Double-sprung shears   Electric clippers

SHEARING

SHEARING SHEEP WOULD be easy if the sheep lay still, but they don't. Holding them is half the battle – if you win that, you can go on to master the clipping.

Shear as spring turns to summer, but wait for the "rise." This is when the fleece lifts from the sheep's back prior to a natural shedding, and it results in a greasier layer of wool appearing between the fleece and the skin. It is through this layer that the shears should pass. Sharpen the shears before you start.

1 HOLDING *Choose a level spot; the more comfortable the sheep, the happier she will be. To get her to lie down, hold her by the muzzle or under the neck, and by the fleece at the rump. Twist her around, and she should drop to a sitting position (see p. 55).*

2 FIRST SIDE *Kneel down, with the sheep across your knee. If the sheep's head is firmly held under your arm, she will not be able to move. If the belly wool is matted and filthy, clip it away and discard it. Then clip along the side of the sheep, right up the neck wool, down to the leg, and as high as the spine.*

Trim up the side of the sheep as far as the backbone

3 TURNING *Having removed the fleece from one side of the sheep, turn her over to remove the other half. You will inevitably nick the sheep with the shears during your early attempts. Have a tub of pine tar, and a short thin stick, standing by. A dab of tar will stop the bleeding and prevent infection.*

Grip the sheep firmly by the muzzle or under the neck

A firm grip on the sheep's head will stop her from struggling

The cut fleece will fall away in one piece as you turn her – with practice

SHEEP BREEDS AND THEIR FLEECES

	Suffolk	Lincoln Longwool	Cheviot	Merino	Jacob
Classification	Shortwool; lowland down.	Longwool and luster; lowland.	Mountain and hill.	Fine wool.	Medium wool.
Distribution	A British breed, now found all over the world.	Originated in north of England, now kept all over the world.	Originated in south of Scotland. Found all over the world.	Originally Spanish, now kept worldwide, mostly in Australia.	Originated in Mesopotamia. Now found worldwide.
Fleece weight	5½–6½ lb (2.5–3 kg)	15½–22 lb (7–10 kg)	4½–5½ lb (2–2.5 kg)	Up to 35¼ lb (16 kg)	4½–5½ lb (2–2.5 kg)
Fleece quality	High-quality wool with fine fibers.	Heavy, lustrous fleece with long staples.	Medium to fine wool, has natural crispness.	The finest-quality wool available.	Good, with brown and white patches.
Comments	Commonly used to sire cross-bred lambs. Wool used worldwide to make hosiery, hand-knitting yarns, tweeds, flannel, and dress fabrics.	Has been used in many countries to improve native breeds. Wool is popular with spinners and weavers.	Wool is usually used for making blankets, rugs, and outdoor clothing.	The wool is used by the clothing industry in top-quality flannel and dress fabrics. Merino wool accounts for about 40% of the world's wool crop.	Popular with spinners and weavers as an undyed, naturally marked wool. Not in use commercially.

4 SECOND SIDE *Now shear the second side, again clipping all the way from the neck wool down to the legs, but this time working down from the spine. When finished, you should be left with an entire fleece.*

Keep a firm hold on the sheep at all times

5 ROLLING UP *Let the sheep go free – a great moment. The fleece must be rolled for storage. Lay it out flat, fold the sides in to the middle, and roll it up into a bundle. Grab the neck wool, twist it into a rope, and wrap it around the fleece. Tuck in the loose end. Store fleeces in sacks where rats and mice cannot make winter homes in them.*

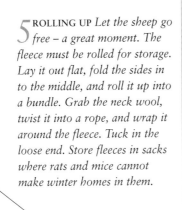

Twisted rope of neck wool is used to secure fleece for storage

HOME SPINNING

IN THE PROCESS of spinning you are drawing out fibers of the fleece and twisting them into a thread. To understand the principles, try it by hand. Take a lump of fleece, pull it apart with your fingers until the fibers are parallel (usually done by carding), then twist. You have just spun wool.

1 CARDING *Combing out, or carding, the fleece removes tangles and aligns the fibers of the wool ready for spinning.*

2 SPINNING *To produce wool in any quantity, you will need to use a spinning wheel. There is a lot to this craft, and it is best to learn it from an experienced teacher.*

HOME FARM GOATS

ANGLO-NUBIAN GOAT
This breed was established in the 19th century from Indian and Egyptian stock. Coat colors range from black or brown to almost white.

ONE IN SEVEN of the world's grazing and browsing animals is a goat, and many of the world's goats are on small, self-sustaining farms in places where other animals would not be productive. Such farms may have poor pasture, and given that five goats will live off the same area as one cow, you can see why the meat- and milk-providing goat is highly prized. Goats do not demand a lot of comfort out of life, which is why they are found all the way from high mountains to desert communities. The best grass is no good for them; they need bush and scrub to nibble at, or weeds to chew, and are ruthless in pursuit of their favorite grazing, which can be any garden plant, including rosebushes!

BUYING A GOAT

Goats are survivors. This makes them hardier creatures than sheep, but it also means they have troublesome, instinctive habits. When buying, clearly the basic health of the goat needs to be determined, but you should also ask when she last kidded, how many kids she had – some have one, while others will bear up to four – and whether it was an easy birth.

You also need to know what is going on between the goat's ears. Some are formidable jumpers, clearing any fence you can afford to build; others will be crawlers and squeezers, finding the slightest gap in a fence and working at it until they have made their escape. And can you milk her? What use is a goat otherwise, except perhaps for its fleece or hide? Ask to see the goat being milked,

WELL-APPOINTED GOAT

Unless you are a show enthusiast, do not dwell too long on the appearance of your goat; other things are far more important. A good milk goat has a deep, barrel-like abdomen; this indicates that she has a large rumen (the first of her four stomachs), providing plenty of room for bulky foods. A good udder is rounded, not drooping, and it should be soft and pliable. This goat is a Toggenburg.

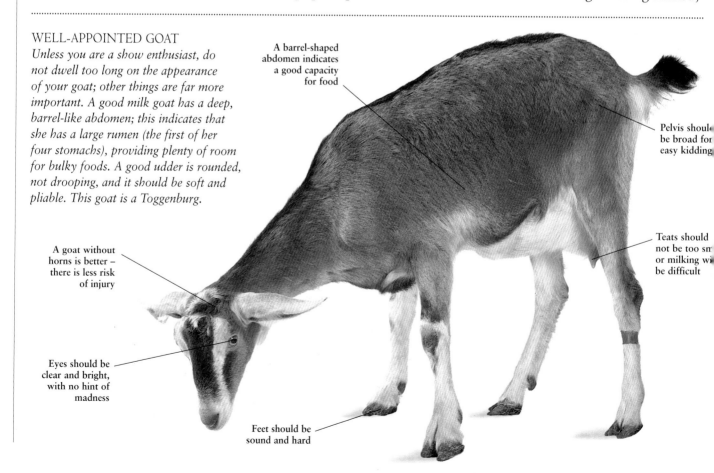

A barrel-shaped abdomen indicates a good capacity for food

Pelvis shoul be broad for easy kidding

Teats should not be too sm or milking wi be difficult

A goat without horns is better – there is less risk of injury

Eyes should be clear and bright, with no hint of madness

Feet should be sound and hard

and reach for her udder yourself – if you detect the slightest hint of a struggle, buy a different goat. You should also remember that goats are not solitary creatures; they need to have companions. However, they are not very fussy; a sheep, a donkey, a cow, a pony, or another goat – any of these will do.

GOATS FOR MILK

The vast majority of goats are kept for their milk. This is nutritious, and a useful substitute for cows' milk, which gives some people an allergic reaction.

A nanny goat may give 6 pints (3.5 liters) of milk a day, and if she has a kid it will take about a third of this. A very young nanny may give half this amount. Either way, if you need 2½ pints (1.5 liters) a day for your own family, there is little left over. If, on the other hand, you do have a surplus, remember the pigs.

If you want goats that produce enough milk not only to feed their kids but also for your own use (to make dairy produce and to provide a surplus to sell), then you are going to have to develop a small herd. With more goats, you need a more specialized setup, including a properly constructed milking area and a dairy in which to cool and store milk and make cheeses (see p. 174), ice cream, and yogurt (see p. 173). Take into account the extra demands, for space and food, that a herd of goats will make on your farm. And then there is the need to meet dairying and food regulations, which apply as soon as you sell produce.

WOOL-PRODUCING GOATS
The fleece of Angora goats is used to produce mohair. It can be valuable and provide a good business for the small farmer. You might shear twice a year.

GOAT BREEDS FOR THE SMALLHOLDER

	Toggenburg	Anglo-Nubian	African Pygmy	Saanen	Angora
Characteristics	Swiss in origin. A small, compact animal. Brown in color, with white markings.	British breed, with distinctive Roman nose and lop ears. An aristocratic-looking goat.	Generally kept as pets in areas other than their countries of origin. Popular as show animals.	White coat, pricked ears, and generally large in size. Short and fine coats. Swiss in origin.	Originally from Asia Minor. Prized for their fine, soft fleece, known as mohair.
Management	All goats like company, and a goat kept alone can become troublesome. Goats can handle low temperatures but, if housed, they need to be kept out of moisture and drafts.				
Milk	Can be a good, economical provider of milk.	Milk yield can be higher than that of some Swiss breeds. Butterfat levels are higher, so milk is good for making cheese.	Will provide a small amount of milk after kidding, but are more difficult to milk than larger breeds.	Improvement by breeding has led to excellent udder shapes and increased milk yields. Good goat for milk production.	Good milkers, but normally reared to produce their valuable fleece.
Health and diseases	Goats are prone to gut diseases similar to those of sheep, and may need protection by vaccination. Worming should be carried out regularly, as should delousing and hoof trimming.				
Skills required	Giving assistance at the birth of kids, rearing orphan kids, milking, handling adult goats including males, hoof trimming, injecting with wormers or other preparations, recognizing signs of ill health.				

Keeping a goat

GOATS HAVE ALWAYS FITTED well into small-scale-farming enterprises. In the warmer, more tropical areas of the world, they traditionally have a place at the very heart of the small farm because they are capable of producing a good supply of milk on far less feed than is demanded by a cow. On larger farms, their habit of preferring weeds to grass allows them to use a forgotten corner other animals would shun. One thing goats do not like is rain, so provide a shelter to which they can go if the weather turns wet when they are out in the fields.

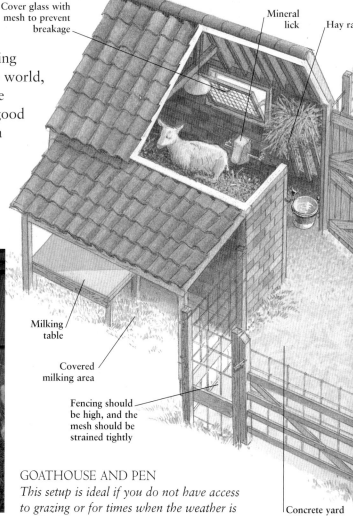

Cover glass with mesh to prevent breakage

Mineral lick

Hay ra

Milking table

Covered milking area

Fencing should be high, and the mesh should be strained tightly

Concrete yard will be easy to keep clean

IDEAL GOATHOUSE
A good goathouse will have to be a compromise between the goat's demand for freedom and the farmer's need to contain it. Goats will do well in a wide range of temperatures, but they do not enjoy drafts. Milking goats are often kept in individual pens. If you use this system, give each goat fresh drinking water.

GOATHOUSE AND PEN
This setup is ideal if you do not have access to grazing or for times when the weather is too bad for your goats to go out in the fields. The goats have some freedom, fresh green food, and a spacious scrambling area to help prevent boredom. A hard floor makes for easier cleaning and reduces the frequency of foot trimming!

GOAT CARE

GOATS ARE NATURALLY healthy animals, and with a bit of luck they will need little in the way of veterinary attention. However, their feet will need trimming regularly to prevent lameness, unless they are allowed to scramble over rocky or stony ground. You should find an experienced goatherd or shepherd to teach you how it is done.

You may never have to administer a drug by injection, but if you do, you must know how to use a needle safely and exactly where to put it. Get expert advice the first time you attempt it, and if in doubt, leave it to the professionals.

GIVING AN INJECTION
This is how some antibiotics and worming drugs are given. Make sure that you get a secure grip on the goat, or you might break the needle off – or the struggling goat might cause you to administer the dose to yourself.

FOOT TRIMMING
If you already have tools for trimming the feet of sheep, these will also do for goats. Use either a sharp knife or foot trimmers. The objective is to trim until you have a flat foot on which the goat stands comfortably.

Pile of bedding

Large, sawed-up logs and piled-up bales of straw make a good scrambling area

Browse rack is used to provide green food such as cut branches

Water bucket held in old tire to prevent spillage

GOAT-PROOF FENCE
Goats will seek out any opportunity to escape. Fences need to be strong and high to guarantee confinement.

FIXTURES AND FITTINGS

GOATS WILL TRAMPLE feed and waste it, given half a chance. Hay racks with bars stop them from pulling out too much hay at once. They have powerful necks and heads, so you will have to bolt food troughs to the wall to prevent them from being knocked over. Don't forget to secure the water bucket!

ACCESS TO MINERALS
Install a lick to make sure that your goat gets enough minerals.

SECURE DOOR
This billy has an eye on the herd, but cannot reach the catches. A bar stops him from jumping out.

DOORSTEP DRINKER
This goat can get all the water she wants with no danger of fouling or upsetting the bucket.

HAY RACK
Hay provides vital roughage for goats kept indoors and must be available at all times.

EATING OUT
Rough scrubland provides good grazing for goats, but they also like roses and ornamental trees!

FOOD AND DRINK

GOATS ARE BROWSERS and will enjoy a nibble at shrubs or scrub plants far more than a field of grass. Let them, but give a ration of grain and hay as well. If you are milking, they will need extra feed in the form of concentrates, such as flaked corn, rolled oats, or crushed beans.

However, do not assume that goats are not fussy eaters; they may have a taste for weeds, but will not eat poor-quality concentrates or hay.

HOME FARM PIGS

PIGS HAVE BEEN FAITHFUL servants to small-scale farmers for generations. They are found at the heart of many peasant cultures, for very good reasons. Not only is the pig a hardy animal, but it will grow fat on the waste from your home and farm, and on food that it forages for itself. Its meat, too, is extremely versatile, suitable either for preserving as hams or bacon, or for being made into sausages and salamis. The pig is a generous animal, giving up to 20 piglets a year, and if set to work clearing overgrown or abandoned ground, will steadily and unfailingly work its way through the thickest undergrowth, tossing aside weeds with its powerful snout. A pig is an impressive creature, and a good friend.

THE FARMER'S BEST FRIEND
The pig is an intelligent and versatile animal, earning its place on a small farm for both its meat and its friendship.

THINGS YOU SHOULD KNOW ABOUT PIGS

Do not fall into the trap of thinking that pigs are filthy and stupid. Two perfectly reasonable and healthy things account for their grubby image: the way they dig their snouts into soil, searching for grubs and worms; and the way they wallow in mud when there is a danger that strong sun will burn their skin. As for personal habits, pigs are scrupulously clean. Given a choice, they dung well away from where they sleep, and some of my pigs have kept their sties so clean that it would be no hardship to spend a night with them. There is nothing filthy about pigs.

They have bright minds too. A sow will organize her home by moving straw around with her snout to make a safe bed for her piglets. She will teach them to suckle, and scold them too. Pigs are also very good timekeepers: if you are in the

THE PERFECT PIG
Do not worry about looks unless you are interested in pedigree pigs. Instead, buy a pig with a good, easygoing temperament. Some breeds have been bred to suit the needs of commercial farmers, but older breeds (like the Saddleback, shown) often fit in better on a small farm.

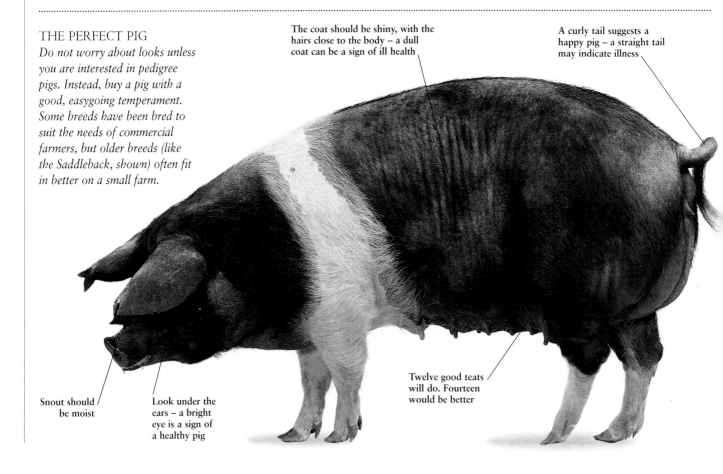

The coat should be shiny, with the hairs close to the body – a dull coat can be a sign of ill health

A curly tail suggests a happy pig – a straight tail may indicate illness

Snout should be moist

Look under the ears – a bright eye is a sign of a healthy pig

Twelve good teats will do. Fourteen would be better

habit of feeding your pigs by the clock, do not be as much as five minutes late unless you want a mutiny on your hands. I once had a sow who could tell the time better than any alarm clock, and if the morning feed was late, the whole district knew about it.

CHOOSING A BREED OF PIG

If your sole objective in keeping pigs is to make good profits out of them, there is little advice I can offer. There are pigs bred to the latest specifications of the food manufacturers; but they will be odd animals, looking like dogs, bred long and lean to produce a high proportion of bacon slices. Some are hardly able to support the length of their own bodies. Do not be tempted by these industrially designed creatures.

Choose a breed you will be happy with. As with all farm animals, if you can look on them first thing in the morning and be pleased to see them, then they are the right breed for you. The older and less developed the breed, the hardier it will be. Older breeds of pigs, some of them now officially rare, were bred when times were tougher and pigs could expect less attention and feeding. Many such breeds would be required to fatten on table waste alone. These pigs are easy for a home farmer to keep, and you will hardly know you have them. If you are producing hams and bacon for your own table (see p. 176), do not be afraid of a breed that is thought to carry too much fat by modern standards. The flavor of pig meat is in the fat, and pigs need plenty of it. It makes them hardier too.

HOUSING PIGS
Out in the open is the best place for pigs. They will need some kind of shelter, but it does not have to be fancy.

PIG BREEDS FOR THE SMALLHOLDER

	Large Black	Duroc	Saddleback	Hybrids	Landrace
Characteristics	A lop-eared, old, and rare breed, now out of fashion, but a hardy, mild-mannered pig with good mothering instincts.	Distinctive reddish-haired pig. Much favored breed in the United States.	Easily recognized by its lop ears and its black and white markings. Colored breeds of pig tend to be hardier than white animals.	Crosses between pig breeds, designed to produce pigs that suit market requirements.	A Scandinavian breed. White skinned, with lop ears. Good, prolific mothers. Found all over the world.
Management	An ideal pig to keep in outdoor housing. Very self-sufficient.	Can be kept happily as either an indoor or an outdoor pig.	A good pig for traditional rearing in field or sty.	Careful feeding and husbandry are needed to get the full potential from this sort of pig.	An easy pig to keep, farrows with little difficulty. Indoor or outdoor pig.
Meat	Excellent for pork or bacon production, but heavy pigs will carry plenty of fat.	Bacon breed, so grows quickly but matures late. The carcass has plenty of lean meat.	A dual-purpose breed for pork or bacon production.	Bred for either pork or bacon. Rather too specialized for the home farmer.	Offspring make long, lean carcasses, and are much prized as bacon-producing pigs.
Health and diseases	Older, hardier, multicolored breeds seem less susceptible to problems. Expect to have to attend to worms, skin lice, and mastitis in feeding mothers, and learn to recognize the symptoms of erysipelas (but you will need advice for this).				
Skills required	Little help needed at farrowing, but young piglets need informed watching. Feeding the right quantities, mucking out the sty (if used), and pig moving – an art in itself.				

Keeping a pig

THE PIG ASKS FOR only three things: shelter, space, and something to dig in. If you can provide all three, then your pig will be happy. A pig needs shelter from sun and rain, but this need not be elaborate. I have seen pig sties built like palaces, but I have known pigs that lived under a sheet of tin supported by bales of straw and were equally happy.

A pig also needs room to roam and exercise itself, but not as much as you might think – a small yard in front of a sty will do. And it needs something into which its snout can delve. I never like to see pigs kept on concrete alone. Pigs prefer earth, in which they can root for tasty bugs and worms, but deep straw will satisfy their natural instinct to get to the bottom of things. Do not be afraid to let pigs get filthy. In a wet winter, they will turn any green space into a sea of mud – and revel in it!

ACQUIRING PIGS
If new to pig keeping, buy a sow with a new litter. It will be a while before you need to worry about getting her "in pig," and, in the meantime, the piglets can be fattened.

WHERE TO KEEP A PIG

PIGS FIT NICELY into odd corners of a farm. They do not need the best grass to graze, so place them where they can work for you by ridding land of weeds or helping to plow the soil, and then move them on. Never let land become "pig sick" from too long a stay.

FREE-RANGE PIGS
These pigs have access to as much grass as they want, and plenty of space too. The movable arks are their sleeping quarters.

THE PIG STY
The sty is divided into two areas – a small, cozy sleeping area indoors, and an outdoor yard for exercise. This sty provides housing for two sows and their litters of piglets.

KEEPING A PIG IN AN ORCHARD
This pig is in heaven. In many parts of the world, pigs are traditionally kept in orchards, where they control weeds, make use of land that could not otherwise be utilized, and at the same time feed themselves on windfalls. But be warned – pigs will soon learn that by rubbing against the trees, the apples you wanted for a pie will fall to be their lunch.

ROUTINE PIG CARE

PIGS LIKE ROUTINE, so feed and water them by the clock. But don't be in too much of a hurry to finish each task. Pigs enjoy being talked to and tickled, and this is all part of the pleasure of keeping a pig. Bored pigs can be destructive, so provide your pig with enough mental stimulation, or expect to have to replace chewed wooden door frames occasionally.

If your pig lives in a sty, you must muck out regularly and provide fresh straw for bedding. If your pig lives outside, she will still need fresh straw for her shelter, and although she will constantly forage for herself, she will also require extra food. Apart from this, a free-range pig is very well able to run her own life, thank you very much.

HOW TO MOVE YOUR PIG
Pigs move best down corridors, so create one with boards held on either side of her. She will go forward only when she can see a clear way ahead.

WALLOWING IN THE MUD
This is not just idleness. The pig is getting a thick coating of mud to protect her skin from the heat of the sun. She digs her wallow, for you or the rain to fill.

HOSING DOWN YOUR PIG
Pigs can suffer severe sunburn in the height of summer and will appreciate anything you can do to help them stay cool. A hose-down is a real treat, and pigs will play as happily as children in the water. These black-haired pigs are less likely to suffer sunburn than a pink pig and might be better suited to hotter climates.

FOOD AND DRINK

PIGS WILL EAT MOST things, if you let them, and will quite happily eat household scraps. But they are vegetarians and should never be given meat. The best feed for pigs is soaked barley meal, and a fine wheat bran called "middlings." They will need no minerals if they can root in soil.

THE FOOD TROUGH
The trough needs to be heavy, or an excited pig will overturn it. It can be divided to stop greedy sows from stealing from others.

PIGS GRAZING ON ROOTS
Pigs are good at clearing land. Here they are foraging for roots left behind by sheep. Pigs will eat all root crops and kale.

THE WATER TROUGH
All pigs need clean, fresh water, but sows in milk need the most. The trough must be fixed to the ground, or the pigs will toss it over with their noses, for fun or to create a wallow. Do not make the trough too tall for piglets to get their heads over the rim.

Farrowing

YOU WILL ENJOY farrowing time. It seems to carry with it none of the anxieties that calving or lambing bring, possibly because of the greater intelligence of the sow. She seems to have a far better understanding of what is going on and orders her affairs accordingly. A pig that has been kept in as unstressed and natural an environment as you can provide is likely to present very few problems when she has her piglets.

MATING AND PREGNANCY

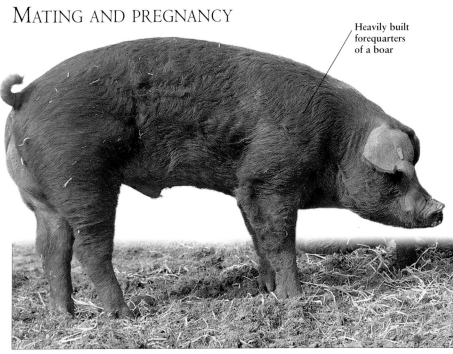

Heavily built forequarters of a boar

INTRODUCING THE BOAR
Mating can be a noisy, boisterous business, but it leaves you in no doubt as to when it happened and you can mark the calendar accordingly. A sow comes into heat every 21 days, and the boar should be kept with her for at least three cycles, to make sure.

FEEDING THE SOW

THREE DAYS BEFORE farrowing, feed your sow "sloppy food" (her usual meal made wet by adding bran that you have scalded in hot water) to clean out her system. If you have good grassland on which she can graze, she will do well on it. Or cut root or leaf crops (see p. 162) and bring them to her. After the birth, continue to give the sloppy feed for three days and then gradually return to the sow's usual feed. An old country way to calculate the amount is "as many pounds of meal [dry weight] as piglets, plus two pounds."

A BALANCED DIET
This pig is enjoying skimmed milk left over after the cream has been removed for butter making. Sows with piglets need a wide range of feed to ensure that all their mineral and vitamin requirements are met.

GETTING SOWS "IN PIG"
This is a job for the boar. There are test-tube methods, but using them requires some skill, and why should the pigs be deprived of their pleasure?

But be wary of boars. Some of them can be nasty fellows with wicked teeth, which are well concealed until the boar comes at you with an opened mouth. To ensure even-tempered boars, I have always reared my own, making sure they get plenty of attention and tummy-tickling from a very early age; then they are rarely any trouble.

Pigs interbreed well, and you do not necessarily need a boar of the same breed as the sow, unless you are rearing pedigree pigs. This is sometimes useful; for example, if you have a sow that tends to put on a lot of unfashionable fat, you can cross her with a leaner boar to slim down the offspring.

CARE OF THE PREGNANT SOWS
Pigs are pregnant for a total of three months, three weeks, and three days – easy to remember. Nothing out of the ordinary need be done until two weeks before farrowing. That is when the sow is moved to the farrowing quarters, unless you have planned for her to have her piglets in her existing sty.

It is also the time when you should pay special attention to the cleanliness of the sow's housing and to providing extra warmth if it is a cold time of year. An infrared lamp is a good source of heat, but it must be hung where the sow cannot use it as toy and swing it to and fro with her snout. Whatever the season, the bedding needs to be deep – short, chopped straw is best, if you have it, because the piglets will not get lost in it.

ONSET OF LABOR
Some sows will quietly get on with it; others will make a hell of a din. One of our sows used to announce that she was close to farrowing by getting her snout under her heavy feeding trough and throwing it in the air: when it crashed down, it sounded like the bells of hell.

The sow tends to make a nest for herself when she is close to giving birth. Milk may appear at the teats up to 12 hours before farrowing.

THE BIRTH

In the vast majority of cases, you have to do nothing. The piglets slither into the world, as many as 14 on occasion! The umbilical cord will break naturally, and each piglet will struggle out of the transparent sack that contains it. It is only moments before they are squealing and heading for the teat. Miraculous! Check that the afterbirth is completely expelled and remove it from the sty, and then leave the family alone.

CARE OF THE NEWBORN PIGLETS

It is a good idea to fit a sturdy rail across the sty roughly 2 ft (60 cm) from the wall and about 10 in (25 cm) above the ground. Place an infrared lamp over the space between the rail and the wall. This provides a warm, safe haven that the piglets can enter and leave as they please, but which the sow cannot enter. The piglets can sleep safely where their mother cannot roll on them. It is an annoying way to lose healthy piglets.

Some owners clip the teeth of piglets to avoid damage to the sow's udder, but I have never done this, or routinely injected or castrated young males. If they are not kept for breeding, boar piglets are long gone before their masculinity is likely to become a problem.

Make sure that each piglet is getting its fair share of the udder, and check that the inevitable runt is not being bullied out of its feed. After the first couple of weeks, the piglets will start to take an interest in solid food. Build a barrier to stop their mother from stealing it. Keep an eye on the piglets' tails: a curly tail is a sign of good health.

THE FIRST FEW WEEKS

Young piglets are prone to developing tummy upsets, which lead to scouring (loose droppings). Take a vet's advice if you think it is serious, but I have found these problems usually solve themselves after a day or two, and the piglets will be healthier for having found their own way to recovery. Mineral deficiencies, particularly iron deficiency, can be a problem and are best guarded against by making sure that the sow has a balanced diet – the minerals she eats will be passed on to the piglets in her milk.

FARROWING PEN

Infrared lamp must not be too low or piglets will overheat

Rail should be made of strong wood or iron

Bedding should be deep and fresh. Short straw is safer for piglets

DESIRABLE RESIDENCE

The farrowing pen needs to be warm and cozy, whatever the weather. The rail across the pen creates a safe area for the piglets where they cannot be accidentally crushed by their mother. At the same time, they can come out to feed whenever they wish.

SUCKLING AND WEANING

SOW SUCKLING

Piglets should suck in the first hour. Help them to the teat if they cannot find it. Each piglet has its own teat and returns to it every time it feeds.

OUT INTO THE FIELD

If the weather is fine, the sow and piglets can go outside after three days. The piglets will soon learn to nibble at the grass.

STUD BULL
Smallholders often do without their own bull if they can rent or borrow one locally.

HOME FARM COWS

ECAUSE THE COW is such a generous, placid creature she has been exploited by modern farming more than any other animal. I have just put down a manual on cows that opens with the words "Profit margins . . . " Have nothing to do with this sort of cow farming. Think of the cow's welfare before you start to think of your returns. Allow her to lead a life as she would wish it, and you will get your reward in the form of milk, cheese, butter, and beef – and even work in some parts of the world. There is no reason why you cannot keep a cow to supply all your needs, and give a surplus, without in any way having to inhibit her natural instincts. Such an animal is known as a house cow.

THE HEALTHY COW

Be aware of the existence of BSE! Make sure that any cow you buy comes from a herd that has always been grass-fed. Once you have put a wide distance between yourself and such dangers, you can safely judge a cow's health by how she looks.

Look first at her coat: unless it is winter and the coat is thick, shaggy, and soiled, there should be a gleam in the hairs, known as a bloom, which is a sign of health. Then look at her muzzle, which should be moist, and her nose, which should be clean and not runny. Her breath should be sweet and not foul.

Now look her in the eye. Don't intimidate her; just look, hard. What response do you get? If something passes between the two of you that says, "Yes, we could get on fine," then she is the cow for you. I am a strong believer in the "look of

IDEAL MILKER
The secret of having a good milking cow lies as much in the way she is looked after as in how she is built. Assuming she has four good teats and a healthy udder, then her milk supply will depend on how she is fed and kept. The cow shown here is a Friesian.

A healthy cow's coat has a gleam in the hairs (a bloom)

A clean rear is a good sign; a dirty one is not always bad

Udder should be soft, pliable, and free from lumps

Eyes should be clear, bright, and friendly

the eye" in choosing all livestock. We once had a young heifer whose eyes had trouble written right across them. We thought she might grow out of it, but she never did.

Now stand back and look at her; let her walk around and see how she moves, not so much to spot lameness, but more to see if she is generally happy with the world. A contented cow living on a small, friendly farm is a great marriage.

MILK OR BEEF?

I would not worry too much about this. It is true that some breeds give higher yields of milk, while butchers prefer other breeds for cutting; but the home farmer is into compromise, and there is no breed that is such a poor milker, and none whose beef is so poor, that it has to be avoided.

Choose a breed to suit the farm rather than the end product. There is no point in conducting farming as if it were a battle where nature and livestock are enemies. Some breeds enjoy life more in a rugged climate, while others will faint at the sight of a mountain. Above all, choose a cow that you simply like the look of and want to share your life with. You will form a working relationship with her more easily. This means that your cow is more likely to be in the right frame of mind to perform well for you, and you will be able to give her the respect she deserves.

OUTDOOR MILKING
If the milk is for your own use, there is no need for a milking shed and dairy. Milk out of doors with a bucket, and hope that it doesn't rain.

CATTLE BREEDS FOR THE SMALLHOLDER

	Friesian	Red Poll	Jersey	Charolais	Dexter
Characteristics	Large black and white breed. The premier provider of milk in much of the world.	Once prized as a dual-purpose animal, now a rare breed. Naturally polled (without horns).	As docile as any cow can be. Produces very rich milk. Adaptable animal suited to a wide range of climates.	Famed French breed of beef animal. Has a white or cream coat and a thickset head.	Can be black or red. Small animal, but not always easy to handle. Now a rare breed.
Management	Needs skilled management. Now a highly bred, high-tech cow best left to commercial farmers.	Good feeder that will fatten on traditional fodder such as oats, hay, and roots. Easy to handle; thrives outside.	Easily handled and milked, versatile in feeding habits, and hardy. Needs housing in cold winters.	Big, heavy animal needing strong housing and firm handling.	A traditional small farmer's cow, thriving in a variety of conditions and on a wide range of feed.
Milk/meat	Superb milk animal.	Dual-purpose. The fat is marbled through the meat, giving excellent eating characteristics.	Rich, creamy milk. Good meat, but with yellow fat that some will find unattractive.	Prime beef animal. Low proportion of fat.	Dual-purpose breed.
Health and diseases	All cattle are prone to lameness, attack by parasites, mastitis (cows only), worm infestation, bloat through overgrazing, foot-and-mouth disease, milk fever, and grass staggers.				
Skills required	Cattle handling, calving, feeding, care of newborn calves, recognizing symptoms of ill health, understanding dietary needs, calculating the correct amounts and combinations of feeds for milking cows.				

Keeping a cow

COWS DO NOT COMPLAIN MUCH, though that is no reason to neglect them. Your house cow is a hardy animal, adapts well to any circumstances in which she finds herself, and always has the ultimate weapon – she can stop giving milk if she is really unhappy or unwell. If you keep a single cow to provide milk for your own use, you will have little difficulty discerning her needs. The bond between farmer and cow is a strong one.

Apart from what might be called minor routine and maintenance, a cow's only requests are to be adequately fed and regularly milked. The latter is very important – a cow with a brimming, aching udder is not a pleasant sight. Once you have a cow to milk twice a day, you are well and truly shackled to the farm. But you also have a good friend to which all your troubles can be told.

COW HEALTH

YOU WILL SOON LEARN to spot a sick cow. When any animal is off its food, it is a bad sign, but this is even more true of cows. If your cow shows little interest in what is going on around her, hangs her head low, stares rather than looks, holds her ears back, or stands apart from the herd, then she is unwell and may need veterinary attention. Despite their natural strength, cows can die quickly – for example, from calcium or magnesium deficiencies. Get her examined immediately.

IN OR OUT OF DOORS?

THE ANSWER TO this question is "it all depends." Your cow needs shelter from cold winds and rain, but whether you have to bring her inside for the winter depends largely on the climate where you live.

The degree of shelter your cow requires also depends on her breed. For example, a Red Poll is a hardy cow and will be happy out of doors in weather that would make a Jersey cow miserable.

In hot weather, cows need to be in an outhouse, under trees, or in a field shelter.

WINTER QUARTERS
Food, water, deep bedding, room to roam, and no drafts make this an ideal winter shelter.

OPEN-AIR LIFE
Here is a happy cow, pleased to see you. She has good grazing and hedges to shelter her from the wind and rain. The farmyard is not too distant when she has to be brought home for milking.

GENERAL CARE

THERE ARE VETERINARY basics that you will need to master, but you are unlikely to need them very often. Learn how to administer drenches (liquid medicines given by mouth) and how to take your cow's temperature. Worms can be a problem with cows kept on the same pasture for a long time. Learn to administer wormers at the right dose.

Also watch for lameness, which can lead to general ill-health and a loss of milk.

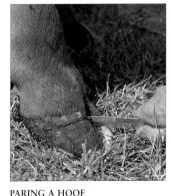

PARING A HOOF
You will not have to do this on a rocky or stony farm – the hooves will get worn down naturally. Be shown how to do this properly.

REMOVING A STONE
Stones can cause lameness and soreness. To ease a sore foot, apply a hot bran poultice after removing the stone.

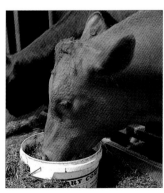

MINERAL LICK
Mineral deficiencies can be fatal. Provide a lick, either a block or this commercial type, and let the cow judge whether she needs it.

SILAGE
This is preserved grass, much loved by cows, but to make it you need expensive machinery.

HAY AND MANGELS
Some breeds of cow manage on no more than hay and mangels all winter, and still give sufficient milk. Add to these some rolled oats or barley, and you have a fine winter ration for any cow.

WINTER FEEDING

COWS NIBBLE GRASS in winter, but its nutritional level is so low that this is no more than a pastime. This is when all the hard work that you did in summer, sowing roots and making hay, finally pays off.

The trick in winter feeding is to give the cow just what she needs to produce the milk you require (see p. 77), while using no more of the precious stored fodder than necessary. Keep the fodder as close to where it is needed as you can.

THE COW AND KEEPER'S DAY

ONCE YOU START MILKING, you are signing a contract with the cow that runs for at least ten months. Of course, you can always dry her off, but what then is the point of having a cow, unless you intend to fatten her calves on the milk and no more? So do not embark on milking unless you have the time and are willing to take on the commitment, or it will become a torment for both you and the cow. Alongside milking go all the other tasks of the cow keeper's day, such as mucking out the cow's quarters, if she is living indoors, mixing feeds, and cleaning the dairy. Don't forget the growing calf too.

MILKING TIME
The more hasty you are about milking, the harder it gets. Clean all equipment (including the udder) first – warm milk is a perfect breeding ground for bacteria.

Cow fetched in from pasture

Morning milking

Keeper prepares shed for milking

Cow returns to pasture; keeper mucks out dairy

Keeper moves electric fence

MUCKING OUT
Deep bed litter, mucked out each week but with fresh straw added daily, is the best floor covering.

SUMMER PASTURE
You should spend a few moments every day checking electric fences and the water supply.

Evening milking

BACK TO THE MEADOW
Bring your cow into the milking shed for each milking, but return her to the pasture afterward.

WINTER HAY
Every day in the winter, your cow will go through a bale of hay, which you will have to carry. Remember this when building the haystack, and place it accordingly.

Milking

THERE IS NOTHING DIFFICULT about milking, nor does it need anything other than a stool on which to sit and a bucket to catch the milk. Once you start milking a cow, you are stuck with the job until her milk dries up, but that is a small price to pay for the pleasure of nestling close to your cow, speaking soothing words to her, and gently drawing the milk. There is another small price – you must feed her, in the right amounts.

IDEAL MILKING SHED

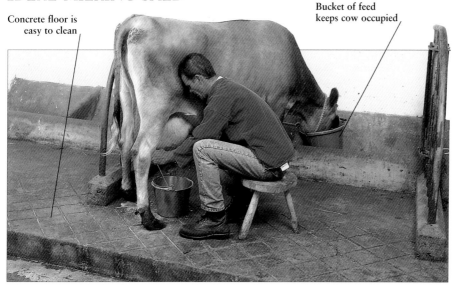

Concrete floor is easy to clean

Bucket of feed keeps cow occupied

CLEANLINESS AND SPACE
This traditional milking shed has all you need. There is plenty of room to move, and the raised concrete floor can be scrubbed down after milking. The cow can be tethered to a partition if necessary, but a bucket of feed is enough to keep most cows steady.

LIVING THE ROUTINE

Cows produce milk only to feed their offspring. You can squeeze all day at a cow that has never had a calf without ever seeing the tiniest drop of milk.

Once your cow has a calf, you are in business; you must get into a milking routine and stick to it. A cow's milk-making mechanisms are highly tuned, and if they detect that milk is being made needlessly, they will reduce the flow and you will end up with a dry cow. Regular milking will maintain the supply for at least ten months.

Assuming that milk production is going well, regular milking matters most. An unmilked cow has a distended udder and will be in some discomfort – take care never to inflict this on her.

Most people milk twice a day, but another option is to milk only once a day and leave the cow and calf together overnight. You can separate them in the morning, and then milk the cow for your own use in the evening. Under this system, the calf goes on suckling for longer than usual.

Whatever your routine, part of it must be aimed at getting both you and the cow in the right frame of mind. A cow has a reflex that prevents her from releasing milk if she is tense. It is up to you to soothe her into the right mental state to be milked.

HAND MILKING

DEVELOP PREDICTABLE habits, such as sitting on the same side of your cow every time, and she will feel easier.

Sit at a right angle to the cow, on a three-legged stool, and press your head into her flank. Now you will feel any muscular twitches that might herald a kick.

Using warm water and a clean cloth, wash the udder, not just for cleanliness but to relax the cow; this is the equivalent of a calf pressing its nose into the udder prior to sucking. Take hold of the teat firmly; don't grab. Now you are ready to start.

1 CLOSING OFF *If your cow has let milk down from the udder into the teat, you must stop it from going back as the teat is squeezed. Seal off the teat with thumb and index finger.*

2 SQUEEZE *Keeping the teat closed off, squeeze firmly downward, the upper fingers closing around the teat before the lower ones, so that the milk in the teat is forced down and out.*

3 RELEASE *Let the teat go, so that it can refill with milk. Then close it off and squeeze down again. You will develop hand muscles like iron and soon learn to milk two teats at once.*

MILKING PROBLEMS

Some cows hate being milked and will kick you. Even more irritating are the cows that will wait until the bucket is full, and then kick that. Patience is often enough to break a bad habit. If not, the cow may need to be hobbled by putting a rope around a hind leg and tying it up off the ground, but this is not a good working relationship.

Cows like to feel that the person who milks them is confident; they mistrust anyone who "tickles" around the udder. A lot of milking problems stem from hesitancy on the part of the milker.

FEEDING FOR MILKING

Grass is the very best food. In summer your cow will get all she needs from the meadow. But in winter she needs more: roughage in the form of hay or straw (oat straw is best), cereals for protein and carbohydrates, and "juicy" feeds, which cows relish, such as kale or mangels (see p. 162). Silage is expensive to buy, and difficult to make without specialist equipment.

Maintaining a year-round supply of food for your cow calls for very careful planning; once you have to go shopping for concentrates, your milk starts to get expensive.

A first-class milk cow can yield as much as 4 gallons (18 liters) a day

FORMULATING FEEDS

You can get deeply scientific when you formulate feeds, or you can simply think of the cow's diet as being divided into two parts – the part that keeps her alive, and the part that provides the additional nutrients she needs to produce milk.

A winter maintenance ration for a cow (enough to keep her alive and well) could be anything from 12 lb (5.5 kg) to 20 lb (9 kg) of good hay a day – it all depends on her size and the harshness of the climate. But you need not feed hay alone. It would deplete your stores of hay at an alarming rate, and would not provide much interest for the cow. Vary her diet by replacing some of the hay with other foodstuffs (see chart below), saving yourself money by using what is readily available and providing a more balanced diet for your cow. Make sure at least half of the ration is hay or straw to supply sufficient roughage.

For milk production, feed the equivalent of 5 lb of barley a day for every 1 gallon of milk you draw (or 1 kg barley for every 2 liters of milk). Once again, feeds consisting of nothing but barley every day would be monotonous for the cow, and you would need to have a mountain of barley in

BEWARE MASTITIS

THIS IS A HIGHLY infectious disease. There are two main symptoms: blood clots in the first few drops of milk, and a hot and swollen udder. It must be treated quickly, or the affected quarter can be permanently damaged and never give milk again. Veterinary treatment is best.

store. Replace some or all of the barley with one or more of the equivalent feeds listed in the chart below.

Even if you are feeding a balanced diet to your cow, it is worth adding some extra minerals, just to be on the safe side. Magnesium and calcium are particularly important. Provide a salt lick too. The cow is the best judge of whether she is short of salt or not.

Remember to have water readily available at all times – a cow in milk can drink 20 gallons (90 liters) a day!

FEED EQUIVALENTS FOR THE HOUSE COW

	Basic ingredients	Replacement formula	How the formula is used
Maintenance ration (for the cow's own needs)	A small cow, such as a Jersey, will need about 12 lb (5.5 kg) of hay, or its equivalent, each day in an average winter in a cool climate. A large cow, such as a Friesian, needs around 20 lb (9 kg) hay, or its equivalent, each day.	1 unit of weight (whether 1 lb or 1 kg) of average hay is equivalent to: 4 units of kale or 5 units of mangels or 5 units of cabbages or 1½ units of oat straw or 2 units of potatoes.	You could feed your cow on a diet of pure hay, but this would use up your reserves rapidly, and would end up giving an unbalanced diet lacking in some vital components. Instead, you can replace each weight unit (lb or kg) of hay with the correct quantity of kale, mangels, cabbages, oat straw, or potatoes. These quantities are given in the Replacement formula. Replacing hay in this way is cheap if you plan the year ahead and grow your own fodder crops for the winter.
Production ration (enables her to produce milk)	Feed 5 lb barley (rolled or cracked barley is good) a day for every 1 gallon of milk you draw (or 1 kg barley for every 2 liters of milk).	1 unit of weight (whether 1 lb or 1 kg) of barley is equivalent to: 1¼ units of dried sugar-beet pulp or 1¼ units of rolled oats or 7½ units of kale.	One way would be to give the cow pure barley and be done with it, but would you want to eat several pounds of barley every day? It is much better to give a varied diet by replacing different quantities of the barley ration with dried sugar-beet pulp, rolled oats, or winter kale in the proportions listed in the Replacement formula.

Calving

THE ARRIVAL OF A CALF is always a time of great excitement on a farm. It is miraculous to see the newborn, spindly creature work its way onto its wobbly legs and stagger to the cow's udder for the first suck of milk. There is also the question of whether it will be a bull calf or a heifer, which will have been much discussed in the preceding weeks. Because cows carry their calves for roughly nine months, there is also an extra sense of urgency about protecting the life of the new calf – it will be a whole year before the next one arrives.

GETTING COWS IN CALF

If you own a bull you have no problems, for he can manage perfectly well on his own. But as a home farmer, you may not have a bull and may have no wish to have one on your farm, even briefly. If this is the case, you will have to send the cow to visit a bull or else have her artificially inseminated. This is done by a technician who will offer a choice of bulls – it's rather like choosing curtain fabric. Don't go for the biggest bull in the book – match the size of the bull to the cow, or ask for advice. It is unfair to ask a small cow to carry a huge calf; she will struggle to give birth to it.

A cow can be inseminated only when she is in heat, that is, at a particular moment in her reproductive cycle, and spotting that time takes practice and luck. Some cows show a discharge of mucus; others don't. If she is part of a herd, a cow in heat will be mounted by other cows. Vets can jump-start the process, but it is undesirable. If it is the cow's first calf, it is worth finding a bull and sending her to him. If you know the date when she was successfully covered, you can work out the calving date by allowing nine months and seven days.

There is much debate as to which part of the year calves should be born in. The traditional wisdom is that "they grow best with the year"; this means that they should be born in the spring, when both they and their mothers get the nutritional benefit of the fresh grass.

A cow needs no special feeding until the last eight weeks of pregnancy, when she needs a modest increase in her diet.

BIRTH OF THE CALF

Give a calving cow additional rations of cereals, such as oats or barley, to get her in a fit condition to calve and to ensure a good flow of milk. Give an average cow an extra 2 lb (1 kg) of oats a day eight weeks before calving, and increase this gradually to 8 lb (3.5 kg) a day as calving gets closer. Fit, but not fat, is how you want her.

If the weather is warm and the cow's meadow is sheltered, let her calve in the open air. She will be happier in a field she knows than in a building that she has not seen before. Watch for the udder filling, which is a clue that the calf is on its way. The next sure sign is when the muscles at the rear end go slack, and the two bones just beneath the tail drop.

The calf should be born in a diving position, with its two front feet pointing forward and its head tucked between them. Any other birth presentation spells trouble, and you should get help. If the calf is positioned normally, avoid the temptation to jump in too quickly – just put your hands in your pockets and watch. Most healthy cows give birth without any trouble.

It is tempting to rush to the aid of a newborn calf, but if it is showing signs of life, coughing, breathing, or sneezing, then leave it alone. The mother's tongue

BULL IN THE HERD
A bull knows best how to get cows in calf. Some bulls are dangerous; others appear docile. But the best advice is never to trust a bull, for he will not hesitate to see off any threat to his cows. You may need the aid of a ring through his nose to control him.

CALVING KIT

WELL AHEAD OF THE EVENT, get these items together so you will have them ready: lubricating gel; a thermometer to check for hypothermia in the calf; iodine to treat the calf's navel; a calving rope (with wooden grips), in case the calf has to be pulled from the cow; and a bucket for hot water, which also serves as a holder for the kit.

THE FIRST 24 HOURS
If the calf shows good signs of life, its first 24 hours are best spent alone with its mother. Her strong tongue will stimulate its blood flow and heartbeat. The calf should suck in the first hour – keep an eye on it to make sure it does.

is far more effective at "licking it into shape" than you can ever be. The only time to intervene is if a thick layer of mucus envelops the head, preventing the calf from taking a breath.

CARE OF THE CALF

Watch to make sure that the calf takes those vital sucks of colostrum within the first hour. This thin, watery milk is produced by the mother for the first day or two after the birth of the calf and contains antibodies to help protect it from disease. If the calf fails to suck, it may be a matter for the vet, although such cases are rare.

Once the calf has drunk, you can leave it for 24 hours. The next day, catch the calf, which will already be a handful, and dip the dangling umbilical cord in iodine as a disinfectant. Insert an ear tag, too, if the law requires one.

With luck you will have no further problems, but should you lose the cow or if, for some reason, she has no flow of milk, you can make an emergency colostrum using this recipe. Add six egg whites and 1 teaspoon of cod liver oil to 1 pint (0.6 liter) of milk. Warm to body temperature and feed with a bottle.

HOW TO WEAN

You may not have to do it. Some calves will be self-weaning and give up the teat at six months old. But some hang on; this could mean a calf suckling from the mother when she is well into her next pregnancy. You do not want her to be dividing her resources at this time.

If you want all the milk for yourself, wean the calf (as most farmers do) when it is a week old, once it has drunk all the colostrum and the udder is full of

pure milk. Start gently, by separating the cow and calf for a few hours at a time and placing the calf where its mother can see it, but where it cannot feed. Milk the cow and feed the calf with a mixture of three parts milk to one of warm water.

You must make sure the calf knows how to drink from a bucket. You may have to teach it. When you are certain that the calf is feeding well, take it away from the cow for good. Expect pitiful bellowing, but this is not unduly cruel.

A HEALTHY CALF
Some calves have good health written all over them, like this one. Others do not, and you will soon learn how to spot the difference. A healthy calf has bright eyes, an interest in the world around it, and a curiosity about its mother. Some newborn calves get to their feet faster than others, but a calf that finds the teat and takes its first suck unaided is well on its way to good health.

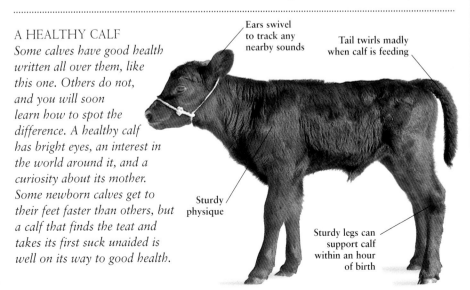

Ears swivel to track any nearby sounds

Tail twirls madly when calf is feeding

Sturdy physique

Sturdy legs can support calf within an hour of birth

WILD BOAR
The meat of these animals is highly regarded by those who have developed a taste for it. In the right location, wild boar can be a profitable enterprise.

OTHER LIVESTOCK

MOST PEOPLE TAKE livestock to mean horses, cattle, sheep, pigs, poultry, and goats. Outside this area of conventional farming, however, lies a separate realm of adventure, in which people keep all manner of animals for all sorts of reasons, including curiosity and enthusiasm. These animals range from rabbits, which you can keep on the smallest of holdings, to ostriches, which need lots of space and fencing. Even if you have no land at all, there is no reason why you should not become a beekeeper and place your hives (with permission) on other farmers' fields or in orchards, where the bees will not only help with pollination but also deliver the sweetest of honeys.

Keeping exotic livestock calls on your own inventive powers as you devise practical methods of care to suit your own situation. Such unusual charges require a high degree of dedication, and, in general, the more exotic an animal, the greater the effort that will be needed if it is to thrive.

LIVESTOCK FOR PROFIT
You may well be drawn to an animal simply for the fascination of keeping it and for no other reason. Nothing wrong with that – it is called a hobby. But if, for example, you are tempted to farm snails, then it is doubtful if it is out of affection for them. Nor would you keep a single deer as an ornament, for in your heart you would know that it would be better off as part of a herd, roaming wild. No, once you get into specialized areas, you have to start thinking about how you are going to make money. That is why farmers venture into these areas. And there is good money to be made. Food fashions come and go, and a good living can be made from venison, rabbit meat, game, or ostrich meat. But you will do well only if your enterprise is founded on research to establish exactly where you can sell, for what price, and how long the demand is likely to continue.

GOURMET FARMING

PHEASANT
Game birds are traditionally hunted in the wild, but, with careful management, they can be reared on a farm and sold as meat to specialty butchers and restaurants in the winter.

PIGEON
Young pigeons (squabs) are more suitable for eating than the tougher adults. Squabs are raised in small houses, a useful enterprise if you have little land on which to farm.

SNAIL
You can start snail farming on a very small scale, even in an old fish tank. Snails need fresh green plants to eat and access to chalk. They are well liked by some gourmet restaurants.

DEER
Deer are for only the larger farm. Farmed venison has become fashionable in recent years, but a large amount of capital expenditure is needed to fence the animals securely.

FITTING THE ANIMALS TO THE FARM

If you have a farm that is ideally suited to a particular livestock enterprise, then it would be foolish to try to bend it to accommodate another, unless money (making or losing it) is no object. A small farm set alongside a clover pasture is the ideal place to produce that most special of honeys made only by bees visiting clover and wildflowers that are associated with it. A resourceful beekeeper will always do well here.

On the other hand, if you have a small wood where wild boar can use their natural truffle-hunting abilities to seek out fallen acorns and other good things, then that might be the enterprise for you. Wild boar burgers could be the craze of the future, and I am sure they could be made to taste delicious.

As well as fitting the animals to the farm, there is a need to fit your choice of animal in with the law. There is a certain mystique about wild boars and ostriches. Some people keep them purely for profit, while others are enthusiasts for this kind of thing. No doubt it is exciting to own creatures that are officially classified, in most Western countries at any rate, as "dangerous wild animals." To keep them legally, you must get a license and display a notice warning the public. Emus do not require this, for they are smaller and more docile. They are also hardier birds, and this may be why the emu is gaining in popularity these days.

BEEKEEPING AS A SPECIALTY
You can keep bees even if you have no land at all. Some farmers and growers welcome bees onto their land to help with pollination. You can start at a low cost with only one hive, and grow from there. Honey will always be in demand.

OTHER LIVESTOCK

	Rabbit	*Bee*	*Boar*	*Ostrich*	*Llama*
Management	Easy to look after. Daily feeding and cleaning required.	Can take up a lot of time in summer if you have many hives. Not so much work needed in winter.	Feeding and ensuring they are confined.	Fencing needs checking regularly – you will have trouble catching escapees. Feeding and watering also required.	Hardy animals. Good fencing needed.
Cost of setting up	Very low. You can do it all yourself.	You can start small and build up from there.	Breeding stock can be expensive to buy.	High start-up costs.	High start-up costs.
Produce	Meat and pelts. Wool from Angora rabbits. Sale of young as pets.	Honey and beeswax. Maybe renting hives of bees out as pollinators.	Meat and sausages.	Meat and eggs.	Wool and possibly meat. Can also be used for work.
Type of farm suited to the enterprise	Smallest of garden farms will do.	No land at all needed if others will allow bees on theirs.	Wild boars need wild areas. Woodland is the most suitable for them.	A large farm is needed to give ostriches room to exercise.	Llama farming is an enterprise suitable for the larger farm.
Potential markets	Butchers, restaurants, or sell from a stand at the farm gate.	Grocers, health-food stores, or a stand at the farm gate.	Butchers and specialty restaurants.	Butchers and specialty restaurants.	Fleece sought by the manufacturers of fashion garments.

Keeping bees

DO NOT KEEP BEES unless you are fascinated by the mysterious ways in which they order their lives, go about their labors, and maintain the society within their hives. Here is an opportunity for a hard-pressed home farmer to steal a few moments a week away from regular farming tasks and get philosophical over the hive. There are greater rewards to be had from keeping bees than just the honey and the expert pollination services. A beekeeper must, however, keep a constant eye open for the mites that carry the Varroa virus. Systems for detecting this modern scourge are available, and, if the infection is found, treatment is possible. Do not hesitate to get professional advice on this.

The three castes – (from left) a worker, a drone, and the queen

WHERE TO KEEP BEES
Locate your hives in a spot that is quiet, sheltered from strong winds, and near sources of nectar and pollen.

THE HIVE
This is the bees' home, and if they are unhappy with it they will move out. Keep hives in a good state of repair. If any part of a hive is broken, you may handle it clumsily and upset the bees; broken hives also allow robbers (other bees and wasps) to steal your honey.

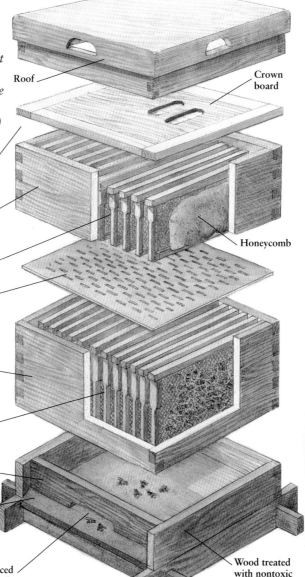

Roof

Crown board

More supers can be added on top

Super (upper chamber in which honey is stored)

Honey frame

Honeycomb

Queen excluder prevents queen from laying eggs in honey store

Brood chamber (in which queen lays eggs and young bees hatch)

Brood frame

Floor

Alighting board, on which bees land before crawling into the hive

Entrance can be reduced in winter to exclude moths and mice

Wood treated with nontoxic preservative

THE BEEKEEPER'S YEAR

EARLY SPRING
Queen bee starting to lay eggs. Food supply in hive at its lowest level after winter, and nectar and pollen in very short supply. Feed sugar syrup if necessary.

LATE SPRING
Rapid increase in the brood. Bees flying on fine warm days to gather nectar and pollen from early blossom. Prepare supers and put queen excluder in place.

EARLY SUMMER
Queen working flat out. Pollen and nectar at peak of supply. Add supers as required, and watch for signs of swarming, such as the formation of cells for new queens. Keep an eye on general health of hive.

MIDSUMMER
Careful watch needed for swarming. The queen's rate of lay drops. Fields of canola producing early pollen flows could cause your honey harvest to start early.

LATE SUMMER
Supers now full of honey. Watch for wasps trying to rob the hive. Colony starts to dwindle. This is the time of the main honey harvest: prepare equipment.

AUTUMN/WINTER
After the harvest, leave the bees to clear up. Now is the main time to check for and treat Varroa. Start feeding syrup or candy (confectioner's sugar and honey) in late autumn, for bees to form winter reserves.

EQUIPMENT YOU NEED

FOR CONFIDENCE, you need a bee-tight suit, helmet, boots, and gloves. Always use a smoker before opening a hive. The bees recoil from the smoke and fill their honey sacs with honey. The bloated bees find it difficult to use their stings and are easy to remove from the frames with the soft brush. Use a proper hive tool to open hives – screwdrivers do damage.

Feeder – a container for sugar syrup

Hammer for repairs – but not when bees are in residence

Soft brush removes bees from frames

Smoker – burns rags or dry grass

Hive tool for loosening frames or supers that are stuck together

BEEKEEPING TOOLS
Have everything ready when working with bees. They sense impatience and panic and will respond in a painful way!

MAKING A FRAME

YOU SHOULD NOT use second-hand frames – they can carry disease. You can save money by making your own frames from scratch or (as shown here) from kits. I have always found building hives, with its associated thoughts of spring and honey, to be a pleasant task for winter evenings.

Hives vary, and different countries and regions have their favorites. Check out the hives in your area – at some stage you are sure to want to borrow something.

1 TAPPING TOGETHER *Kits are a good way to start out. They are available for super frames and the larger brood frames. Precut ends should slot easily together to form the frame.*

2 FOUNDATION *Slot the sheet of foundation into the sides of the frame. This thin wax sheet is stamped with a hexagonal pattern that acts as a guide for the bees to construct their comb.*

3 FIXING PINS *Finish the frame off by hammering in the pins to fix the lower edge. The fixing needs to be firm, or the frame will come apart when laden with a heavy crop of honey.*

Capped honeycomb with honey inside

REMOVING THE HONEY
Cut off the wax cap the bees placed on the comb. A warmed knife will do the trick. After this, place the honey in a centrifuge to separate out the wax, then pass it through a honey strainer.

HONEYCOMB
You can estimate how much honey is in a comb as soon as you lift it. If there is no weight about it, it is better left for the bees. Lightly brush off any bees left after the clearing process (see right).

THE END PRODUCT
Remember that honey is food and put it in clean, sterilized jars. Finally, thank the bees that have worked so hard to achieve it.

HONEY HARVEST

THE HARVEST STARTS by parting the bees from their precious honey. A "clearer board" between the brood box and the supers provides a one-way door through which bees can enter the brood but not return. Allow at least 24 hours to clear a hive. Careful opening of the hive and quick removal of the supers to a place where the bees cannot follow are required. Here you will have set up your centrifugal separator, strainers, and jars to collect the golden crop.

Keeping rabbits

RABBITS ARE CHEAP TO BUY, breed easily (like rabbits!), and are naturally healthy. Their meat is not only delicious, but low in fat and therefore considered a healthy part of a modern diet. Rabbit skins can be sold, and one or two breeds, such as the Angora, are prized for their fleece. It all adds up to a formidable list of reasons for keeping rabbits; the proof is that there are 50 different breeds, all with qualities to match individual styles of rabbit farming.

Perhaps the biggest plus for the smallholder is that rabbits do not need a lot of room. I would not want to encourage anyone down the path of intensive rabbit rearing, where the creatures never leave wire cages. But with only a modest amount of space, you can offer a happy life to these easy-to-keep animals. And they don't make any noise.

CREAM OF THE CREAM
Clip the coats of your Angora rabbits and sell it to home-craft suppliers or direct to home spinners, who use it to produce a soft yarn that can be knitted or woven into fine fabrics.

RABBIT HOUSING

KEEP RABBITS IN HUTCHES (see below) or in arks (see right), which can be moved across the ground as new feeding areas are required. Rabbits do not like the heat. Their ideal temperature is 60°F (15.5°C). On hot summer days, hose the roof to cool things down. Arks ensure a good supply of fresh air, but hutches may need to be raised up on legs.

EXCELLENT ARK
These rabbits cannot escape, are safe from predators, and always have fresh grazing available. A healthy way to keep rabbits. Their droppings will also fertilize the grass.

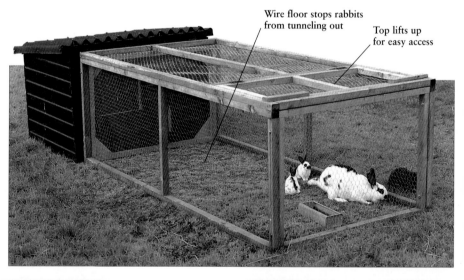

Wire floor stops rabbits from tunneling out

Top lifts up for easy access

GOOD HUTCH
A hutch is fine as long as it is large enough and you can keep it cool in the summer. Provide an area no smaller than 4 ft × 2 ft × 2 ft (120 cm × 60 cm × 60 cm) per rabbit.

Sleeping area will be dark, resembling a burrow, when door is closed

WIRE CAGE
These are widely used by commercial rabbit keepers because droppings fall through the mesh, leaving the cage splendidly clean, but I don't think they make for happy rabbits.

FOOD AND DRINK

RABBITS ARE BLESSED with those sharp front teeth, which grow continuously, so give something hard to gnaw, such as a block of wood, to keep their teeth down to size. If they get nothing else, they will happily chew their hutch! As for real food, all rabbits enjoy eating greenery, such as cabbage leaves or stalks, lettuce leaves, or other garden greens.

To fatten rabbits, give commercial concentrates (which are expensive) or a feed made up of whatever high-energy foodstuffs are around the farm, such as oats, barley, or cooked potatoes. Hay, for nibbling, should also be available.

DRINKER
Water must be available at all times. Rabbits will suck at a drinker like this, which has the advantage of keeping the water clean.

FEEDING RACK
Rabbits are skilled at eating off the ground, but a small trough like this will reduce the amount of food that gets wasted.

WHITE CLOVER
Clover is a high-protein feed: either in pasture or as cut greens, it helps to fatten rabbits quickly.

ACORNS
In the wild, rabbits would seek out acorns. This free food can be collected and fed when ripe.

DANDELIONS
Feeding rabbits is the best use for this weed – rabbits have a limitless appetite for it.

CHICKWEED
Rabbits will nibble a variety of weeds, such as chickweed, that other animals avoid.

RABBIT BREEDS FOR THE SMALLHOLDER

	Californian	Angora	New Zealand White	Tan	Dutch
Characteristics	White, with black or chocolate patches on nose, ears, tail, and feet. Large rabbit, weighing 7¾–11 lb (3.5–5 kg).	White form is most common. Other colors available. Medium-sized rabbit, weighing about 5½ lb (2.5 kg).	Albino rabbit, with dense white fur and pink eyes. Large rabbit, weighing 8¾–11 lb (4–5 kg).	Small, dark brown rabbit, weighing about 4½ lb (2 kg).	Distinctively marked rabbit. Fur is white with one other color. Small rabbit, weighing 4½–5½ lb (2–2.5 kg).
Reasons for keeping	Kept principally for meat. It may also be possible to sell pelts.	The fur is clipped and sold to home spinners and weavers, or their suppliers.	Kept principally for meat. It may also be possible to sell pelts.	Often kept as pets or for showing. Sales to the pet market. Quality meat for restaurants.	Often kept as pets or for showing. Sales to the pet market. Quality meat for restaurants.
Management	Careful feeding to get the benefit of this breed's fast growth.	Daily grooming, and seasonal clipping of the long coat.	Careful feeding to give maximum growth of this fast-growing rabbit.	Selective breeding for a productive strain.	Selective breeding for a productive strain.
Health and diseases	Rabbits may need their claws clipped if they have no opportunity to scratch. Protection from internal pests can be administered with feed if needed. Rabbits can catch colds; treat with a bran mash with onion and mint added. In high-risk areas, you may want to vaccinate against myxomatosis. Check ears regularly for presence of mites, indicated by orange-colored encrustations.				

Keeping exotics

KEEPING EXOTIC LIVESTOCK can call for exotic skills. Some of the animals shown here are highly sensitive to the conditions in which they live, and you should get good, clear advice before deciding if a particular species of animal will suit you and suit your farm. It is also likely that the basic breeding stock will cost you a considerable sum of money and, if only to protect your investment, you should acquire a working knowledge of your chosen livestock before starting out.

LLAMAS AND ALPACAS

USEFUL LLAMAS
Llamas are hardy, intelligent members of the camel family. They can be schooled to work, and they also produce meat and fleece. There are few farm animals that can match that.

ALPACA: A FINER FLEECE
The alpaca and the llama are closely related, both originating in South America. The fleece of the alpaca is particularly prized, as it can be spun into very high-quality wool.

RELATIVES OF THE CAMEL

Llamas are versatile creatures. Their fleeces can be used to produce rugs and ropes, but llamas can also perform light work as pack animals and can even be trained to work in teams. They can also be reared for meat, but the high cost of buying the stock often makes this option too expensive. Some cultures use llama dung as fuel. Alpacas, on the other hand, are kept principally for the fine wool that can be produced from their fleece.

Llamas and alpacas are camelids, members of the same family as camels. They have confusing digestive systems – although they are not ruminants, they do ruminate! When it comes to feeding, they should be fed more like cows than horses. Both llamas and alpacas were bred specifically as domestic animals, the llama as a beast of burden and the alpaca for its fleece.

KEEPING LLAMAS

Llamas are naturally hardy animals, but they will appreciate shelter from the hottest sun in warm climates. This need be no more than a three-sided shelter that will give the animal some shade throughout the day. The shade of closely spaced trees is even better. In colder climates, llamas need protection from wind chill, and a barn or stable may be needed, with doors that can be closed to exclude the worst of the weather.

Llamas do well on pastures, which need not be of the highest standard. In fact, a llama will thrive on a pasture so poor that it would not support a sheep. If you have doubts about pasture weeds, as a general rule, what is bad for horses, cattle, or sheep will usually be bad for llamas as well. They will relish hay in the winter, and a cereal supplement can be given if needed.

To confine llamas, the fencing will need to be at least 4 ft (1.2 m) high to keep them from jumping out. It should also finish low enough, within 1 ft (30 cm) of the ground, to prevent them from getting under it.

Do llamas spit at you? Yes, they do, particularly males. Alpacas do too, but less often. If you get spat at, it is more likely that you got in the way than that your llama meant you any offense.

KEEPING OSTRICHES

It is to be hoped that you get on well with your ostriches because they have a lifespan of up to 70 years, so you've got each other till death do you part!

The ostrich is becoming increasingly popular because of the exceptionally low fat content of its red meat, so prices of basic breeding stock can be quite high. But apart from the meat, ostrich leather is also much sought after, its strength and suppleness making it very popular in the fashion trade.

Are ostriches dangerous? Potentially, yes! A kick from one can be lethal. It is not for nothing that they are classed as "dangerous wild animals" (see p. 81). The male ostrich must be treated with special respect, as it is aggressive during the breeding season.

Ostriches are extremely agile birds – you will never be able to catch one by running after it. Those long, muscular legs will carry them at speeds of up to 40 mph (65 km/h).

PASTURE AND FEEDING

Ostriches feed largely by grazing and do not need specially lush pasture. They have evolved through the millennia to travel for many miles to find food and water so, unlike most domesticated farm animals, they do not need everything brought to them. As well as eating grass, ostriches browse on plants and bushes, taking some fruits as well as the leaves. They also eat small animals, including insects and lizards, which they hunt down on the ground.

With their athletic abilities, fencing high enough and strong enough to confine them is expensive.

QUAIL AND GUINEA FOWL

These are naturally free-ranging birds – Africa is their ancestral home, or winter home in the case of the quail since, in the wild, it is a migrant. This means that both must be securely confined, as once they escape they are not easy to catch. If you clip their wings to stop them from flying, rats or other vermin will be after them. Kept free-range, guinea fowl need less feeding in summer, as they catch insects. Even then, like all farm animals, they will need a basic ration of grain.

OSTRICH FARMING

OSTRICH HOUSING
This is a range shelter, which gives adequate protection from the wind and, for the female, a place to lay eggs. An ostrich farm is not complete, however, without a larger, more permanent building in which the birds can gather for protection in all kinds of weather.

OSTRICH FENCING
Long legs and the ability to travel at high speeds call for good fencing. This multi-stranded, high fencing is a good barrier.

OSTRICH EGG
An ostrich egg can weigh up to 3⅓ lb (1.5 kg) and hatches in 42 days. A breeding hen will lay 30–60 eggs in a nine-month laying season.

SMALLER EXOTIC BIRDS

CAPTIVE QUAIL
These small birds are prized for the table. Quail also produce small, tasty eggs, for which you may find a good market.

GUINEA FOWL FARMING
Free-range is best, if you think you can catch them again. If you have close neighbors, be aware that they can be the noisiest of birds.

FRUITS OF THE EARTH

IT IS NO ACCIDENT that "homegrown" has come to stand for quality, flavor, succulence, and, increasingly these days, safety. You can grow for your own table or to share produce with others by selling at the gate, but grow fruit and

vegetables you *must*. You may need to work hard digging the beds, especially in the first season or two.

But at the end of a long day, when you come exhausted to the supper table, as soon as you taste the first forkful of what you have grown, you will remember why you do it.

THE KITCHEN GARDEN

THE KITCHEN GARDEN may take up a large or small part of your land, or it may be the entire farm. The larger your holding, the greater the amount of thought you will need to put in to ensure that the vegetable area runs with a minimum of effort. I have always considered my kitchen garden to be a retreat where I can put the pressures of the rest of the farm behind me and indulge in the simpler pleasures of growing my own vegetables. Plan for abundant crops, but do not expect them in the first couple of years. Instead, build the garden up gradually. Start from firm, organic foundations and let it develop from there.

HEAVY CROP
Years go into creating a kitchen garden that has plentiful beds and established fruit bushes.

CHOOSING A SITE

If you have a choice, go for the best soil. It will need the least work to make it into a garden. Bear in mind that clearing land of thistles, grasses, and brambles can take a full year. Overhanging trees can be a problem, and any vegetable garden that is in shade for much of the day is never going to do well. A garden

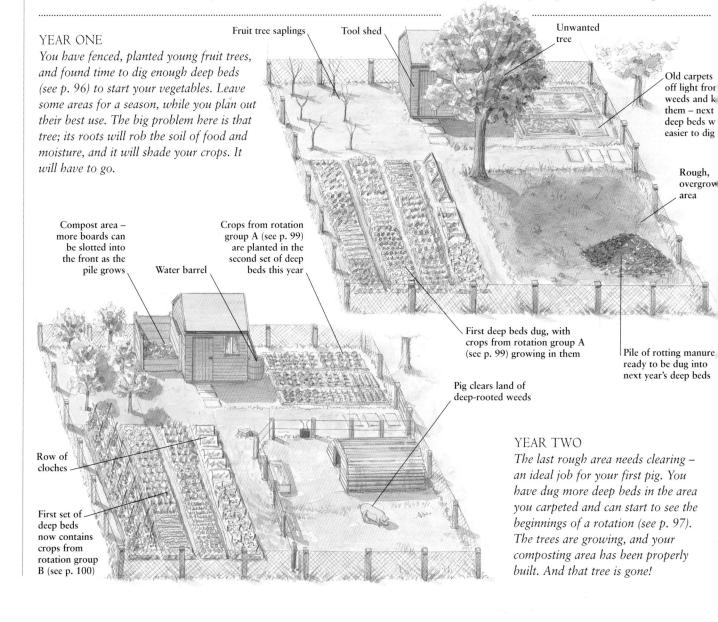

YEAR ONE
You have fenced, planted young fruit trees, and found time to dig enough deep beds (see p. 96) to start your vegetables. Leave some areas for a season, while you plan out their best use. The big problem here is that tree; its roots will rob the soil of food and moisture, and it will shade your crops. It will have to go.

Fruit tree saplings

Tool shed

Unwanted tree

Old carpets off light from weeds and k them – next deep beds w easier to dig

Rough, overgrow area

Compost area – more boards can be slotted into the front as the pile grows

Crops from rotation group A (see p. 99) are planted in the second set of deep beds this year

Water barrel

First deep beds dug, with crops from rotation group A (see p. 99) growing in them

Pile of rotting manure ready to be dug into next year's deep beds

Pig clears land of deep-rooted weeds

Row of cloches

First set of deep beds now contains crops from rotation group B (see p. 100)

YEAR TWO
The last rough area needs clearing – an ideal job for your first pig. You have dug more deep beds in the area you carpeted and can start to see the beginnings of a rotation (see p. 97). The trees are growing, and your composting area has been properly built. And that tree is gone!

facing the noon sun is ideal. A moderate slope to the land is also a good feature. Cold air, which can cause damaging ground frosts, will roll over it without lingering. But too steep a slope may lead to topsoil being washed away in heavy rains, and it certainly makes walking from one end of your plot to the other with a loaded wheelbarrow much harder.

GARDEN STRUCTURES

Before you do anything else, erect fencing to keep rabbits out – they will consume a year's work in a single night and enjoy doing so. In warm climates, where winters are not harsh, you may find that the only building you need is a shed to store your tools. But elsewhere you will need a greenhouse or a polytunnel too, and possibly a shed in which to store your harvest. If you don't have room for a greenhouse, you could opt for a smaller cold frame or even a few cloches. All kitchen gardens need a properly constructed compost area that is built to last a lifetime, and a water barrel or other provision for collecting rainwater for garden use. You need not have them all from day one, but if you have a clear idea of where your garden is heading, it will save much retracing of steps in later years.

> *❝ I have always considered my kitchen garden to be a retreat where I can put the pressures of the rest of the farm behind me . . . ❞*

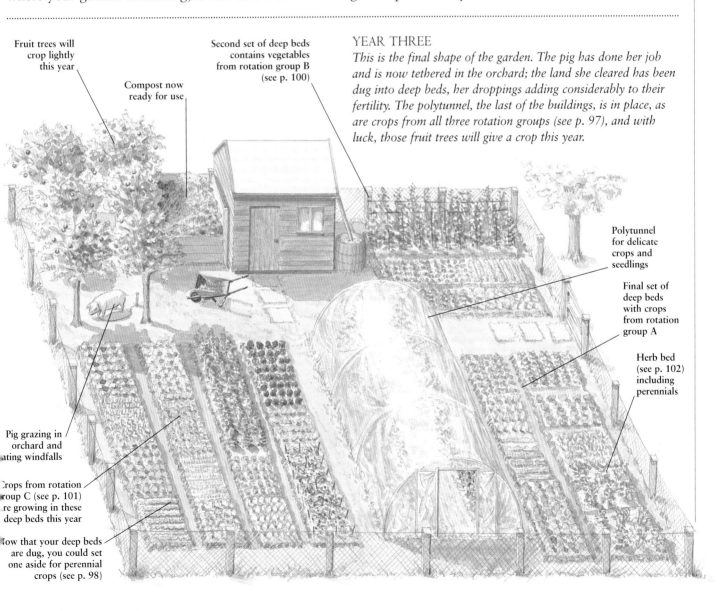

Fruit trees will crop lightly this year

Compost now ready for use

Second set of deep beds contains vegetables from rotation group B (see p. 100)

YEAR THREE
This is the final shape of the garden. The pig has done her job and is now tethered in the orchard; the land she cleared has been dug into deep beds, her droppings adding considerably to their fertility. The polytunnel, the last of the buildings, is in place, as are crops from all three rotation groups (see p. 97), and with luck, those fruit trees will give a crop this year.

Polytunnel for delicate crops and seedlings

Final set of deep beds with crops from rotation group A

Herb bed (see p. 102) including perennials

Pig grazing in orchard and eating windfalls

Crops from rotation group C (see p. 101) are growing in these deep beds this year

Now that your deep beds are dug, you could set one aside for perennial crops (see p. 98)

Working with nature

YOUR AMBITION AS A HOME FARMER is to ensure that, as you grow your crops, you are on the side of nature, not fighting against it. In the war on weeds, pests, and diseases, you can avail yourself of natural means alone. Here are four ways of working with nature: companion planting, encouraging predators of pests, chemical-free weed control, and the use of compost (see p. 94) to boost the health and strength of your crops.

COMPANION PLANTING

PLANTS IN THE POLYTUNNEL
Marigolds and morning glories have been planted alongside tomatoes as a form of natural pest control. Hoverflies will visit them and lay their eggs on the tomato plants. When the larvae hatch, they will feed on the aphids on the tomato plants.

COMPANION PLANTING
The principle behind this stratagem is that growing plants in certain useful combinations brings better results than growing them singly.

First, there is the physical effect of two plants being next to each other: green-bean plants are bushy enough to protect delicate lettuce seedlings from the wind.

Second, it is believed that some plants (we don't know enough about how this works) drive away or inhibit the growth of certain pests. Nasturtiums, spearmint, garlic, and stinging nettles are said to help control aphids. In part, ideas of this kind are rooted in tradition: you may find they work well for you, or you may not. Why not try them?

MARIGOLDS AND HOVERFLIES
One plant that most would agree does possess special properties is the highly aromatic French marigold, also known as *Tagetes*. When this flower is planted with cabbages, its scent masks their presence. This hides them from the cabbage white butterfly, the insect that produces those marauding caterpillars. Marigolds are also believed to suppress nematodes, which can do great damage to a potato crop.

The female hoverfly, a true friend of the organic grower, feeds on marigolds (both kinds, *Tagetes* and *Calendula*). To ensure plenty of food for her larvae, she lays her eggs where tasty aphids are abundant. So put the marigolds next to crops with an aphid problem, and let the hoverfly sort it out for you.

ANIMAL ALLIES

GROUNDHOG SURPRISE
Although infamous for their ability to destroy a vegetable garden overnight, groundhogs do help out by eating slugs.

INSECT POWER
Bees carry pollen from one plant to the next, helping many orchard trees, on which any unpollinated blossom will not produce fruit.

SONG THRUSH
Birds often cause more problems than they solve, but some, like the song thrush (above) and the robin, feed on slugs.

OTHER PEST-HUNTERS

Other predators are less easy to attract because they do not feed on flowers. This applies to ladybugs and lacewings, both great enemies of the aphid. The way to encourage them is to do nothing that will deter them! Avoid all sprays, and hope they move in. If you are lucky, ground beetles, too, will arrive, to feast on slugs and cabbage root fly eggs.

Find out from local experts about the predators you can best aim to cultivate in your area. Birds, beetles and other insects, and even frogs and toads can be encouraged to visit. There are useful mammals too: the hedgehog in Europe and the skunk in North America (and, in some states, the porcupine) eat invertebrate garden pests. These animals occupy individual or family territories in which they forage for food. If you see them in your garden, encourage them to visit more often by providing drinking water near their hiding places.

NATURAL WEED CONTROL

All green plants need light, so you can kill weeds by covering them with old carpets or black plastic. Or you can use a mulch (see right). A good solution that is available from garden centers, and does no harm to the soil despite its industrial origins, is landscape fabric of polypropylene or a similar plastic. This lets moisture in but keeps weeds down.

There will come a time, though, when the only way to get rid of weeds is to remove them physically: pull them up or dig them out. Hoeing is a possibility, but deep-rooted perennial weeds see this as a challenge and spread their roots even farther. Then you have to dig deep and remove every trace.

TRADITIONAL REMEDIES

Talk to people who have faced these problems over a lifetime, and a few words of conversation can yield tried and tested local remedies.

Soapy water from washing dishes has been used to control aphids for generations, and people still control aphids by blowing tobacco smoke on them. A remedy for mildew on grapes is to boil lime and sulfur in water, cool the solution, and pour it on the plants.

NATURAL WEED CONTROL

Deep bed planted with four rows of seedlings

ELIMINATE THE COMPETITION
If you can kill the weeds before they have a chance to grow, you are well on your way to controlling them. These young cabbages need protection from competing weeds if they are to grow into healthy plants. Accurate hoeing, although time-consuming, does this best.

MULCHES FOR WEED CONTROL

GARDEN COMPOST
The mulch must be deep – say 5 in (12.5 cm) – to keep weeds down effectively.

HORSE MANURE
A thick layer will stop weeds, but if it is not well rotted it will "burn" your plants.

GRASS CUTTINGS
Make the mulch as deep as you can: start with 6 in (15 cm), as it will rot down.

BARK AND TWIGS
This is expensive to buy, but you can make your own by using a garden shredder.

SAWDUST
A sawdust mulch stops weeds but rots slowly and uses up nitrogen in the process.

BROWN PAPER
This is ideal for deep beds. Just roll it out to cover the beds, and plant through it.

Composts and fertilizers

THERE ARE TWO WAYS to fertilize a garden. The first is to buy a box of manufactured chemicals, for which great claims are made. You won't be improving the soil, but you will get big cabbages. Home farmers use the second way, the organic way, for the good of their health as well as that of soil and crops, and for the wider world's sake. There are five kinds of organic garden inputs: manures (see p. 136), green manures (p. 137), garden compost, worm-worked compost, and general organic fertilizers.

GARDEN COMPOST

COMPOST PILE
Don't hide it away! A well-made compost pile is something to be proud of. It shows your deep commitment to natural ways of growing food. Too often they are built in shady corners where they never see the warming sun, and become damp and dead.

COMPOST BOX
This is made from slats of treated wood, which admit air. Adjust the height of the front by adding or removing slats, to match the amount of compost. The box has no floor: fork the soil under it to encourage earthworms to invade. At the same time, the frame is held a little above ground level by its feet (or by bricks) for ventilation.

Nail slats to the frame (in other types, slats slide up and down in grooves)

Grass cuttings need to be mixed in with other material

Mixture of garden and kitchen waste

Base of twigs for ventilation

SOIL-MANAGEMENT PLAN

Your aim is to grow healthy crops and create healthy soil as you do so. Your best way to achieve this is to work to a four-stage plan: (1) assess the soil (see p. 132) and correct chemical deficiencies with soil conditioners such as lime or potash; (2) dig in bulky organic matter (see p. 96), either manure or garden compost; (3) if you cannot get enough bulk organic matter, provide nutrients by means of general organic fertilizers; (4) apply any organic fertilizers needed individually by your crops.

The first stage is dealt with on pages 132–133, while information on manure is found on pages 136–137. Here I shall describe ways of making compost and the general organic fertilizers you will need as substitutes if you cannot get enough compost or manure.

MAKING COMPOST

Making compost is rather like cooking. If you get the right ingredients, in the correct quantities, and cook them at the proper temperature, it cannot fail.

Make compost boxes out of wooden slats, as shown on the left. Even on a tiny farm, you need a series of two or three boxes, side by side. With a series, you can fork material from one heap to the next, reducing decomposition time.

Fill each box with a variety of things, such as waste from the vegetable garden or kitchen, tree and shrub leaves, a little soil, shredded bark and twigs, and grass clippings, but do not make thick layers of any one of them. You can put weeds in, but only if you are sure your pile will get hot enough to kill the seeds.

As the composting process takes place, the temperature will rise – a good pile can achieve 150°F (65°C). Allow the pile to heat up for a few weeks and then fork it inside out. Worms will gradually make their way into the compost and finish off the process. Compost can be made in as little as eight weeks this way.

A slower, less labor-intensive method is to build a compost pile (above left) and leave it. You will get compost in a year. Of course, you can always start off with the quick method, and if it doesn't work you can tell yourself you planned to use the slower method all along.

WHEN COMPOST GOES WRONG

There are a number of reasons why things might not go according to plan. If the ingredients are too wet or too dry, the heating process will not start. They should be damp to the touch, but not sodden. Exclude rain. A square of old carpet across the pile will do this, and help conserve the heat.

Other reasons for failure are using leaves that are too large and not mixing the pile enough at the start. Finally, the composting process needs air, and if the holes in the sides of the pile are blocked, the process will come to a halt.

GENERAL ORGANIC FERTILIZERS

These are plant and soil nutrients that occur naturally, are not manufactured by chemical companies, and contain nothing that is derived from petroleum. Examples are seaweed, dried animal manures, wood ash, dried blood, bone meal, fish meal, and rock potash. Where organic fertilizers score over all artificial fertilizers is that they help preserve the natural life-forms in the soil, rather than destroying them. Most of these microorganisms are on your side and should be encouraged.

Fertilizers need be used only when compost will not do the trick or is unavailable. If you live in a town, animal manure might be hard to come by, and there is a limit to how much compost you can produce in a kitchen garden.

WORM-WORKED COMPOST

WORM-WORKED COMPOST is made from the same ingredients as garden compost, but instead of the usual rotting process, you harness the digestive power of worms to convert the raw materials into a rich compost.

Compost worms are sold in the angling shops as bait, but it is best to buy from a specialist supplier (these are not rare). Build a worm compost box, place paper over the mesh, add a layer of manure, then put in the worms. Add a thin layer of kitchen or garden waste; cover it with a piece of old carpet. Add new layers as the colony grows, creating the compost in the process.

ADDING COMPOST WORMS
Put the worms on the layer of manure, and they will climb up into the layer of compost materials, where they will not be injured by the scrapers (see right).

THE WORMERY

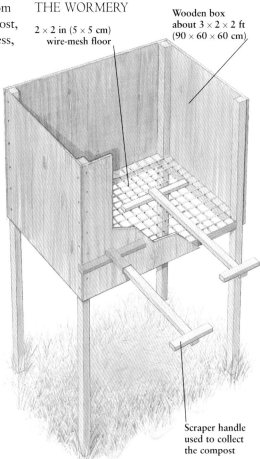

2 × 2 in (5 × 5 cm) wire-mesh floor

Wooden box about 3 × 2 × 2 ft (90 × 60 × 60 cm)

Scraper handle used to collect the compost

HOMEMADE WORM COMPOST BOX
Rake the finished compost through the mesh with the scrapers and place a wheelbarrow underneath to catch it. If you do not want a homemade box, commercially made wormeries are very efficient.

WHICH COMPOST OR FERTILIZER?

	Manure	Garden compost	Blood, fish, and bone meal	Seaweed	Green manure	Worm compost
Good points	Readily available in large quantities if you have livestock. A good way to make use of this natural waste.	A uniform, fine compost that will add fertility in all gardens.	A manufactured organic fertilizer that contains all the nutrients that growing plants require.	A good, all-around organic fertilizer containing trace elements. Useful for adding to compost pile to encourage the process.	Cheap to grow, encourages soil life and structure, and adds fertility and organic matter when it is dug in.	Rich in nutrients and minerals, in forms available to plants. Worm population doubles in 90–120 days, increasing capacity.
Bad points	Until it has been rotted for a year, it can be rich and may burn tender plants. Chemical properties vary, depending on the source of the manure.	It takes plenty of care and attention to produce good compost, and it can be difficult to achieve sufficient quantities.	The nitrogen is contained in the dried blood, which is easily washed away. Makes use of animal residues to which some people may object.	Expensive, unless you live by the coast. Fresh seaweed should be composted for a year before use.	Takes up valuable space in the garden for the best part of a season, therefore preventing other crops from being planted.	Requires careful moisture and temperature control. Simple wormeries are slow producers: you can add only about 3 in (7 cm) to the top each week.

Deep beds

IF TIME IS AT A PREMIUM – and on all home farms it is the most precious commodity – then a system of growing vegetables that gives the greatest reward for the least effort becomes a necessity. Once dug, deep beds concentrate the growing area into defined plots where, due to the deep cultivation of the soil, plants can be grown closer together than in a conventional vegetable bed. This not only produces more crop for the same area, but also means that the plants grow up quickly to cover the ground, cutting light off from the surface of the bed and effectively stifling the growth of weeds. I promise you, the work in digging deep beds is hard, but it has to be done only every five or six years, and it will be more than repaid.

THE BENEFITS

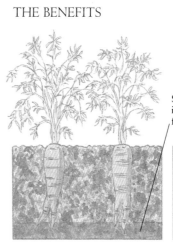 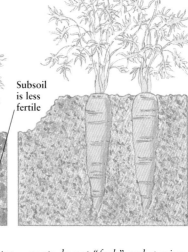

Subsoil is less fertile

SHALLOW VERSUS DEEP BED
In a shallow bed (left), plants try to send roots sideways to find nutrients. In a deep bed (right), roots do not "fork" and spacing can be closer, as the roots reach deeper into more fertile soil.

DOUBLE DIGGING

THIS METHOD consists of digging to one spade's depth, called a spit, and then using a fork to break up the soil to the depth of a second spit. This means digging twice as deep as in a conventional plot, which allows you to put in compost or manure at a far greater depth than in a single-dug bed.

The depth and friability of double-dug soil is the deep bed's secret of success, and the extra time spent will be well rewarded in the future.

1 **MARKING OUT** *Mark out the bed before you start digging. It can be any length, but make it narrow enough for you to reach the middle without walking on it.*

2 **FIRST SPIT** *Dig a trench at one end of the bed to the depth of the spade – one spit – and move the dug soil along to the far end of the bed.*

3 **SECOND SPIT** *Break up the soil at the bottom of the hole with a fork, to a further spade's depth. Don't turn it, or you will expose the less fertile subsoil.*

4 **FIRST MANURING** *Place a good load of well-rotted manure or compost in the base of the trench and fork it lightly into the second spit.*

5 **SECOND TRENCH** *Now dig the second trench, filling the first hole with what you dig out. When the first hole is half-full, add a second dose of manure.*

Raking the finished bed gives it an even shape and creates a fine tilth

6 **COMPLETED BED** *You will arrive at the far end and find you still have a hole left. Fill it with the soil you dug out of the first trench. Rake the bed to a raised, level surface. Keep your feet off!*

Planning a rotation

PLANTS, LIKE PEOPLE, have different appetites and food needs. Some will gobble up everything you put before them, while others seem content with very little. If you grow hungry vegetables in the same plot every year, you will soon starve the soil. So it makes sense to divide your crops into groups on the basis of their nutrient requirements, and grow the hungry ones in the most fertile soil and the lighter feeders to follow.

Legume crops, such as peas and beans, are generous and actually feed the soil while growing, by "fixing" nitrogen – these plants have a special relationship with certain bacteria that have the marvelous ability to enrich the soil with plentiful, nutritious nitrates. So follow your legumes with a crop that will make full use of that "free" fertility.

Crop rotation also helps to keep down pests and diseases, and there is no better way of encouraging disasters than by trying to grow the same crop in the same place year after year.

PRODUCTIVE BEDS
These healthy vegetables are the result of a carefully planned rotation that matches the fertility of the soil to the needs of the plants.

THREE-YEAR ROTATION PLAN

DO NOT THINK OF A ROTATION as a straitjacket into which your plot is tied. Keep it in the back of your mind, and stick to it if you can, but do not despair if you are forced to deviate from it for a while. Just return to it at the earliest opportunity. First, decide which of your vegetables refuse to be rotated. These might be perennial crops such as asparagus or rhubarb, which take time to establish, but then crop for several years. Three years is a good period over which to plan a rotation for the rest of your crops. Divide them into groups, as suggested below. Start by placing the greediest crops (group C) in the most fertile bed and the legumes (group B) in the poorest bed. You then move the groups around from bed to bed each year.

THE CROPPING GROUPS

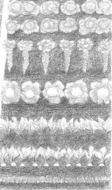

PERENNIALS
This group contains the perennial crops, which need to stay in the same place for several years. After that, the perennial bed might be brought into the rotation and a new area set aside for this group. In addition to crops on page 98, perennial herbs could be grown with this group.

ROTATION GROUP A
This group contains the green, leafy brassicas, such as cabbages and cauliflowers, and some of the root crops (see p. 99). These do best in a slightly alkaline soil (pH 6.5–7, see p. 132), and you may have to adjust the pH of the plot by applying lime well before planting.

ROTATION GROUP B
This group includes the legumes, which help fix nitrogen in the soil. Suitable crops for this group are shown on page 100 and include corn, lettuce, spinach, and okra, as well as the legumes. The plot may need a general fertilizer (see p. 95) early in the growing season.

ROTATION GROUP C
Crops in this group are shown on page 101. Of all the groups, this one has the highest feeding requirements. Nourish the soil with fertilizers, compost, or manure (see pp. 94, 136), but if you choose manure, it must be well rotted; otherwise, carrots and parsnips will tend to "fork."

ROTATION PLAN

YEAR 1			
PER	A	B	C

YEAR 2			
PER	C	A	B

YEAR 3			
PER	B	C	A

MANAGEMENT OF THE BEDS
Deep beds will last five or six years before they need redigging. In the intervening winters, check the pH (see p. 132) and adjust the fertility of the soil to suit the incoming crop by forking in an organic fertilizer or compost.

Vegetables

I CANNOT IMAGINE a home farm without a vegetable garden. Growing vegetables is one of the easiest of all farming activities, requiring only common sense and a willingness to have a go. The worst that can happen is that some of your cabbages become so caterpillar-riddled that they are fit only for the goat. She will be delighted and, in return, will provide the manure to fertilize your deep beds for the next attempt.

I have given planting distances that are appropriate for normal, single-dug beds, as I cannot assume every reader has prepared deep beds: if you have, you are free to experiment with considerably closer spacing.

PLANTING CABBAGES
These cabbages are being planted out in a deep bed dug on a field scale. The farmer knows he can sell this sort of quantity locally. Make sure you have a market before you plant on this scale.

PERENNIALS

Asparagus

A relatively pest-proof crop, asparagus is eagerly sought after in spring, when customers will pay good prices. It can be sown from seed, or named cultivars can be planted from divisions. Once plants are established, they will continue to crop for up to 20 years. Good drainage, however, is essential.
PLANTING DISTANCES Sow in drills 2 in (5 cm) deep in early spring. Lift plants the following spring and plant 12 in (30 cm) apart in their permanent positions.
YIELD Up to ten spears from each crown. Do not cut later than early summer.

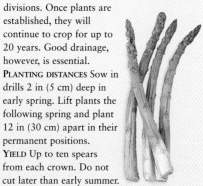

Rhubarb

Rhubarb crops early in the year when other produce might not be available. It likes a neutral soil (pH 7, see p.132), so add lime to achieve this if you have an acidic soil. To multiply rhubarb, simply lift a crown, chop it in half, and replant both parts.
PLANTING DISTANCES Plant crowns in early spring. The leaves can grow to a very large size, so allow roughly 3 ft (90 cm) between plants. Pull the stalks from the crown; don't cut them.
YIELD Expect about 4½ lb (2 kg) of rhubarb stalks from each crown.

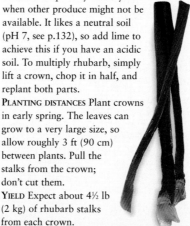

Globe artichoke

Easily grown, the globe artichoke is more popular in continental Europe than elsewhere. It was once thought to be an aphrodisiac and a cure for baldness. It needs well-drained soil and shelter from wind, and the roots must be kept moist in summer.
PLANTING DISTANCES Sow seeds outdoors in early spring and transplant to 3 ft (90 cm) apart. Expect just one head in the first year. This vegetable can also be grown as an annual in rotation group A (see p. 97).
YIELD About ten heads from a fully grown plant.

Jerusalem artichoke

Few things are easier to grow than this root crop, described as "potatoes with knobs on." The plants grow tall and leafy, and need hilling up (like potatoes) to prevent wind damage; they also need a stretched-wire support. The crop can be left in the ground and harvested throughout winter as required.
PLANTING DISTANCES Plant individual tubers in early spring 12 in (30 cm) apart and 6 in (15 cm) deep with 3 ft (1 m) between rows.
YIELD 7 lb (3 kg) of tubers will yield about 55 lb (25 kg) of crop.

Perennial herbs, such as this rosemary, will last for many years; plant them with other perennial crops.

Salsify and scorzonera

These two vegetables are similar, but salsify has white roots; scorzonera, black. As overwintered crops they produce edible flower buds, shoots, and leaves in their second spring.
PLANTING DISTANCES Sow seeds in spring and thin to 4 in (10 cm) apart in rows 6 in (15 cm) apart. Both vegetables can be grown as annuals in rotation group C, in which case the roots are eaten.
YIELD About 8 lb (3.5 kg) of roots from a 20-ft (6-m) row of either vegetable. Yield of leaves and flowers is highly variable.

ROTATION GROUP A

Cabbage

There is a cabbage for every season of the year. In general, cabbages are hungry beasts, needing rich, fertile, well-manured soils. Sow seeds in packs or seedbeds and transplant about five weeks later. They need to be firmly planted, as they do not like to wobble in the wind. The winter varieties grow slowly, and plants might need extra feeding if they falter. This is a crop that will never be wasted, whatever the time of year. You can cook cabbages, eat them raw in salads, or pickle them; and animals will always relish them, even when you don't.
PLANTING DISTANCES Depend on the variety. Plant the large, leafy types 2 ft (60 cm) apart; space the smaller, more pointed varieties more closely.
YIELD A good, dense cabbage can weigh up to 3¼ lb (1.5 kg).

Winter cabbage

Red cabbage

Spring cabbage

Savoy cabbage

Brussels sprouts

Sprouts often crop from autumn through to spring, if scavenging birds don't get to them first. If the ground is too rich in nitrogen, the sprouts will open like cabbages. They don't like to be swayed about by the wind, so hill them up as they grow to keep them stable. Sprouts are slow growing, so they can be interplanted with faster-growing vegetables. Tradition has it that they taste best after the first frost.
PLANTING DISTANCES Sow in spring, when the ground is warm enough to encourage germination, and plant out 2 ft (60 cm) apart each way.
YIELD About 2 lb (1 kg) of sprouts per plant. Cattle will happily chew stalks and leaves.

Kale

Both curly and smooth-leaved varieties of kale are grown in gardens, whereas the field crop tends to be smooth. Kale belongs to the cabbage family and will survive rather harsh winters. Because of the spread of its leaves and their height, it can be used as a windbreak for more tender crops. Taller varieties grow to a height of 3 ft (90 cm).
PLANTING DISTANCES Sow in seed trays in the spring and transplant in midsummer, spacing plants about 2½ ft (75 cm) apart.
YIELD About 2 lb (1 kg) of leaves per plant.

Cauliflower

Temperamental things are cauliflowers. If not treated with due respect, they cease to play the game and will throw shoots in all directions, rather than into the neat ball expected of a cauliflower. The secret is to keep them growing steadily throughout the season without interruption. This means regular watering to prevent checks in growth.
PLANTING DISTANCES About 2½ ft (75 cm) apart for plants grown from seed.
YIELD Heads vary in size. An average head might weigh 1½ lb (0.7 kg).

Broccoli

Sprouting broccoli is an easy vegetable to grow and will give a crop at a time of year when other vegetables are scarce. These plants need space, as they can grow up to 3 ft (90 cm) tall. Headed broccoli (calabrese) is much more compact and produces a single main head rather than lots of shoots.
PLANTING DISTANCES Sow in spring. Sprouting broccoli can be sown in seedbeds and planted out at least 2 ft (60 cm) apart. Sow calabrese seeds in their final location; don't transplant.
YIELD 9 lb (4 kg) from a 10-ft (3-m) row.

Rutabaga

The rutabaga is of Swedish origin. Rutabaga is similar to turnips, but is able to withstand cold winters better because of its lower water content. It also has a milder and sweeter flavor than turnips. Rutabaga takes about half a year to grow and can be stored in a clamp (see p. 153). It is excellent for feeding to sheep if you have a surplus that you are unable to store or sell.
PLANTING DISTANCES Sow thinly in rows ¾ in (2 cm) deep, and thin in stages to keep plants 12 in (30 cm) apart.
YIELD 31 lb (14 kg) from a 10-ft (3-m) row.

Turnips

You will grow smaller and sweeter turnips in a garden than if you were growing them on a field scale. The young green leaves of turnips are delicious and can provide a meal in themselves while the turnips continue to grow. Turnips grow much faster than rutabaga; some of the small, white varieties grow particularly fast.
PLANTING DISTANCES Turnips will grow to a pleasant size if thinned to 4 in (10 cm) apart.
YIELD 13 lb (6 kg) from a 10-ft (3-m) row.

Radishes

There are many varieties of radish, from the long, white daikon radish and the large, round, black winter radish to the small, round, red summer radish. Summer radishes have the advantage of being swift growers that can be harvested only a few weeks after planting. Plant them between slower-growing crops to make full use of land.
PLANTING DISTANCES Thin summer radish seedlings to 1 in (2.5 cm) apart and winter radish or daikon to 6 in (15 cm).
YIELD 30 summer radishes or 3¼ lb (1.5 kg) winter radishes from a 3-ft (1-m) row.

ROTATION GROUP B

Peas

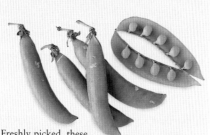

Freshly picked, these are the sweetest of all vegetables. Eat the peas yourself and give the animals the pods (or make wine with them). There are many varieties, but most will need support from netting or stakes while growing.
PLANTING DISTANCES Sow the seeds 2 in (5 cm) deep, about 2 in (5 cm) apart.
YIELD 10 lb (4.5 kg) from a 10-ft (3-m) row.

Runner beans

A joy to the eye as well as the palate, these beans are vigorous, ornamental, and prolific. They were originally intended for decoration. They need well-fertilized soil, rich in compost, and supports up which to grow. The supports should be strong, for by autumn, when storms can strike, the beans will have put on considerable foliage.
PLANTING DISTANCES Put up supports before planting. Sow seed into warm, well-manured soil, about 2 in (5 cm) deep. Water well during dry spells.
YIELD About 2 lb (1 kg) of beans from each plant.

Broad beans

These are rather hardy beans and in some areas can be sown in the autumn for cropping the following season. They need no support and can be usefully grown where space is limited. Some varieties are short enough to be grown under cloches for very early crops. The big enemies are mice and slugs, which view them as a handy winter treat.
PLANTING DISTANCES For maximum yields, plant about 8 in (20 cm) apart.
YIELD 20 lb (9 kg) of beans from a 10-ft (3-m) row.

Peanuts

This is a crop for the warmer parts of the world, as it needs temperatures of 68–86°F (20–30°C). For those who have never seen peanuts grow, it may come as a surprise to learn they grow underground on tendrils produced by the fertilized flowers. Sandy soil is best for growing peanuts because it warms quickly.
PLANTING DISTANCES Grow from proper seed rather than shelled peanuts, and plant 12 in (30 cm) apart in rows 2 ft (60 cm) apart.
YIELD Varies with climate and variety, but roughly 1 lb (0.5 kg) of nuts to each plant.

Corn

The hotter the weather, the better corn will do. It will not grow successfully in areas with cool summers. It is an amazingly fast grower once summer arrives, when ears can swell up overnight.
PLANTING DISTANCES Corn is pollinated by the wind, so to ensure full ears, it is better planted in blocks of at least four plants each way than to plant in regular rows. Sow seed in late spring and thin plants to 30 cm (12 in) apart.
YIELD Corn grows to a height of about 6 ft (1.8 m). Expect two or three ears per plant.

Okra

Okra is grown for its immature seed pods (also known as ladies' fingers), which are cooked whole. Okra will not grow in cool, wet weather or in places where there are surprise late frosts. It is a vegetable best picked and used fresh from the garden, as it does not store well. Plants are 4 ft (120 cm) high with leaves 1 ft (30 cm) wide.
PLANTING DISTANCES Soak seeds for 24 hours before sowing. Sow outside if soil temperature reaches 61–64°F (16–18°C); otherwise, sow inside and transplant when they are 4–6 in (10–15 cm) tall. Plant seedlings about 12 in (30 cm) apart.
YIELD Each plant can produce anything from 4 to 20 pods.

Lettuce

There are many varieties of lettuce for all tastes and most seasons. The soil needs to be light, with added compost to ensure it retains moisture. In a hot climate, growing lettuce is not advisable, as it bolts (goes to flower) in hot conditions. Lettuce will grow reasonably well in a moderate climate, although it should be watered often on hot summer days and harvested only in the cool of the morning. In cooler climates, it grows all year round, but needs cloches or cold frames some of the time.
PLANTING DISTANCES Sow in rows, and thin to keep plants 12 in (30 cm) apart. Transplanting is not always as reliable as growing from seed. If you sow your lettuces all at once, you will have to eat them all at once. Spread the sowings over several weeks to produce a continuous supply. Looseleaf varieties can be cut just above ground level and left to come again with a new crop.
YIELD 15–20 lettuces from a 10-ft (3-m) row.

Looseleaf lettuce

Romaine lettuce

Boston lettuce

Spinach

The principal requirement of spinach is that there is plenty of nitrogen for it to gobble up. For this reason, it needs richly fertilized soil to give the best crops. Damp soil suits it, and so do cool conditions: this makes spinach a useful crop that can find a place in most gardens. It also likes some shade.
PLANTING DISTANCES Sow during spring in rows 12 in (30 cm) apart. Thin to leave about 6 in (15 cm) between plants.
YIELD Up to 10 lb (4.5 kg) from a 10-ft (3-m) row.

ROTATION GROUP C

Potatoes

Choose between a multitude of varieties to suit the season and your taste. Potatoes prefer an acidic soil, which should be rich and moist, and they like it to be well manured.
PLANTING DISTANCES Set the seed potatoes 4 in (10 cm) deep, 12 in (30 cm) apart, with 24 in (60 cm) between the rows.
YIELD Up to 22 lb (10 kg) of potatoes from a 10-ft (3-m) row.

Tomatoes

In warm climates, tomatoes will grow out of doors. Otherwise, you will have to grow them in a frame, greenhouse, or polytunnel. Soil should be enriched with rotted manure.
PLANTING DISTANCES Sow indoors and transplant when 6 in (15 cm) high. Plant about 20 in (50 cm) apart.
YIELD About 4½–9 lb (2–4 kg) of fruit per plant, depending on the variety.

Peppers

These can be grown out of doors in milder climates as long as you can be sure of plenty of summer sun. Otherwise, grow them in a polytunnel. The soil should be well manured and must be adequately watered.

Green peppers are the unripe version of the red or yellow pepper. Some varieties are best for producing green peppers; others are better for red or yellow.
PLANTING DISTANCES Sow in warmth in the spring. Plant 18 in (45 cm) apart when you can be sure there will be no more frosts.
YIELD Expect at least six peppers per plant.

The onion family

This group embraces onions, leeks, shallots, garlic, and scallions. The whole family likes to grow in a rich, well-manured soil. When you are growing onions, you have a choice whether to grow from seed or from "sets," which are dormant onions that are waiting to be planted out.
PLANTING DISTANCES Sow onion seed thinly and thin to 1½ in (4 cm) apart for medium-size onions, or double this for large ones. Leave scallions ¾ in (2 cm) apart. Grow leeks from seed; transplant them into holes 6–8 in (15–20 cm) deep when they are 8 in (20 cm) tall. Shallots are best grown from sets planted 6 in (15 cm) apart; garlic is grown from cloves.
YIELD About 7 lb (3 kg) of onions or shallots, 11 lb (5 kg) of leeks, or 20 bulbs of garlic from a 10-ft (3-m) row.

Scallions

Leeks

Shallots

Onion

Zucchini and squashes

This group of vegetables includes zucchini, squashes, marrows, and pumpkins. Most varieties form leafy, trailing plants, but some are compact and bushy. They flourish only in warm weather. All need generous compost or manure, and plenty of water.
PLANTING DISTANCES Trailing types should be sown 6½ ft (2 m) apart, bush types 3 ft (90 cm).
YIELD One healthy plant may produce up to 20 zucchini.

Butternut squash   *Zucchini*

Carrots

Carrots do best on light soils with plenty of well-rotted organic matter. They are a delicate crop that needs care. Wait until the soil is warm enough for speedy germination, and rake the seedbed to a fine tilth. The seedlings will not compete well with weeds, so expect to spend some time on your knees.
PLANTING DISTANCES Sow seed ½ in (1 cm) deep and sparsely. If you thin out seedlings, the dreaded carrot fly will smell them and move in.
YIELD About 9 lb (4 kg) of carrots from a 10-ft (3-m) row.

Parsnips

You need a light, stone-free soil, which will encourage the parsnip to send its root straight into the soil. Parsnips will tolerate poor soils, but do best with well-rotted manure. They can be slow to germinate and to grow, especially in a cool spring. Do not give them too much water at once, or the roots will split. The flavor of parsnips is improved by frost, so leave them in the soil for the winter and lift them as required.
PLANTING DISTANCES Sow ¾ in (2 cm) deep. Thin to 4 in (10 cm) apart in rows 8 in (20 cm) apart.
YIELD Up to 8 lb (3.5 kg) of parsnips from a 10-ft (3-m) row.

Beets

Beets can be either long (as examples shown) or round, and as well as the traditional deep red varieties, yellow and white beets are available. Choose monogerm varieties, or you will find that each seed produces two or three plants and you will have to thin them by hand. Provide plenty of compost or rotted manure.
PLANTING DISTANCES Sow seed in spring, 6 in (15 cm) apart and ¾ in (2 cm) deep, in rows 8 in (20 cm) apart.
YIELD About 15 lb (7 kg) from a 10-ft (3-m) row.

Homegrown herbs

HERBS DESERVE A PLACE in any kitchen garden. They are easy to grow and are attractive, with the pink flowers of thyme, the yellow ones of fennel, and the purple or white ones of comfrey. They have many uses, from flavoring food to making cosmetics. As an organic grower, you will be glad to see herbs attracting insects, some of which hunt garden pests, while others pollinate your fruit. Even more satisfying, to my mind, is the knowledge that herbs are part of an ancient, and possibly wiser, approach to solving medical problems in ourselves and our livestock.

WHAT ARE HERBS?

My dictionary has two definitions of an herb. One is "a flowering plant which, unlike a shrub or tree, has no woody stem above the ground." This is close to the meaning of the original Latin word *herba*, which simply means a grass or a green plant, but it is not what I mean when I talk about herbs.

The second definition is "any of the aromatic plants such as rosemary, mint, and parsley, used in cooking or in herbal medicine." This describes the range of plants you find in a traditional kitchen garden, but to me, herbs mean more than this: there are hundreds of plants with health-giving properties, both for humans and for animals.

If you can take the time, a close study of traditional uses of herbs is fascinating. Quite apart from the remedies for livestock and humans, herbs can play a part in so many aspects of daily life: dyes, cosmetics, herbal teas, and even in making potpourris.

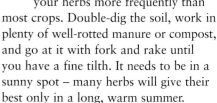

Ladybug feeding on aphids

GROWING HERBS

Naturally you will want to grow herbs for your own use, but don't forget your livestock. There are some herbs that can be included as part of a meadow (see p. 154) that will greatly enhance the health of grazing animals. They provide essential minerals, many of which have been brought to the surface by the very deep root systems of the herbs.

For yourself, reserve a warm corner of the farm in which you can cultivate a wide range of herbs, and never miss an opportunity to snip and taste, grind, dry, or freeze, and gradually work them into every aspect of your diet. The herb patch must be close to the kitchen – you will certainly not bother to walk a hundred yards for a couple of leaves of parsley or mint, and you will be harvesting your herbs more frequently than most crops. Double-dig the soil, work in plenty of well-rotted manure or compost, and go at it with fork and rake until you have a fine tilth. It needs to be in a sunny spot – many herbs will give their best only in a long, warm summer.

HERBS AS REMEDIES

Herbal medicine, to those who have not looked into it, seems an obscure field of knowledge made up of oral traditions inherited from our ancient ancestors. This is far from true – today there are many good books on the subject. There are homeopathic herbal books too, both medical and veterinary.

An increasing number of people are taking an interest in herbal remedies, and home farmers are among them, as herbalism is an aspect of "working with nature." Some cures prove their worth frequently. Feverfew has relieved many a migraine, and garlic alleviates colds.

Herbs can also be beneficial for animals. I have often found that a sickly sow will feel better after a good feed of nettle soup, made by soaking fresh nettles in water for 24 hours.

Of course, seriously sick humans or animals should always be treated by a doctor or vet. But do not dismiss the power of herbs to bring good health to all the occupants of the farm.

COMFREY
The leaves of this perennial herb are rich in potassium, and you can make an excellent plant food by cutting comfrey and steeping it in rainwater. Comfrey has traditionally been used as a food and a medicine, but doubts have recently arisen about its safety.

ANNUALS AND BIENNIALS

Angelica

An upright, tall, thick-stemmed herb, angelica grows well in shade and moist conditions. The stalk is candied for kitchen use. The hollow stem is said to be an aid to fertility, and the seeds good for the digestive system. Angelica has been described as the "ginseng" of Europe.

Cilantro/coriander

This grows best in a dry, light soil. The leaves (cilantro) are an herb, used especially in Middle Eastern and Southeast Asian cooking, and the seeds (coriander) are used as a spice. Oil is extracted from the fruit and mixed with less tasty ingredients for treating wind.

Dill

This fast-growing herb can be found growing wild. It has fine leaves and pale yellow flowers, and although it is the leaves that are chopped and used in the kitchen, it is the seeds that are prized in animal medicine. Mixed with bran and fed to stock, they are used to treat digestive disorders.

Chervil

This is a parsley relative that will grow in semishade, but not in dry conditions. It is used in the kitchen in a wide range of dishes, such as fish, soups, and stews. On the farm, chervil seeds help to increase the appetites of animals that are off their feed.

Borage

Borage grows to 2 ft (60 cm) tall and has rough, spiky hairs along its stems and under its leaves. It spreads its seeds widely, and will need regular trimming. It is an excellent bee attractor. Added to animal feed, it is said to increase milk flow and cure eye problems.

Basil

A fragrant Mediterranean herb, basil must be planted out late in the season where frosts are a problem. There is little evidence to suggest that it has any medicinal value, but basil is a cheering ingredient to find in any salad. It is also the key ingredient of pesto.

Nasturtium

This trailing plant has bright orange and red flowers. It grows easily if the soil is not too rich. The leaves are often eaten in salads. The fresh seeds are a good substitute for capers, while an infusion of dried, crushed seeds makes an antiseptic.

Parsley

A very important herb that goats and sheep (as well as farmers) adore, parsley is said to increase milk yields and should be planted in meadows as well as gardens. It provides an herbal remedy for colic and for kidney disorders. Note that parsley will not grow in acidic soils.

PERENNIALS

Mint

This is a quick-spreading plant and is often *too* easy to grow. Mint tea is particularly refreshing, and there is evidence that mint is effective in reducing the milk supply in livestock. This might be needed once young have been weaned and the udder needs to be dried off.

Chives

The upright, cylindrical leaves of chives can be chopped into salads and taste like onions. This is not surprising because they are closely related. If left, the plants flower, giving vivid, purple heads. Chives sometimes grow wild, and grazing livestock seek out these plants enthusiastically.

Tarragon

The aromatic leaves are used in seasonings for fish and meat dishes, and as an ingredient in soups and salads. Tarragon needs warmth and sunshine to flourish, and dry conditions will not worry it. It grows new stems, which must be divided and replanted every two or three years.

Marjoram

In cooler climates, marjoram will not survive winter and may have to be resown every year. Sandy soil is best. If fed to livestock along with bran, it will help with problems of digestion. Its botanical name, *Origanum*, means "joy of the mountain," a clue to its natural home.

Bay

Bay is usually grown as a bush or small tree (sometimes not so small) from which leaves are plucked, dried, and then crumbled to give flavor to soups and stews. It will survive in moderate climates, but cold winter winds can do great damage.

Rosemary

This evergreen herb grows best on a light, dry soil. On a chalky soil, plants are smaller, but more fragrant. Besides a culinary herb, the plant (as an infusion) is a good fly repellant. It is also effective as an astringent and as a remedy to stimulate circulation of the blood.

Sage

An evergreen herb native to southern Europe, sage can stand the winter well in colder countries. It is used for flavoring, and the many varieties each have subtly different flavors. Sage tea is said to be good for the throat, lungs, and ears.

Thyme

Thyme grows easily in light, dry, stony soils. It is a fragrant herb of Mediterranean Europe. Its many varieties all share a distinctive flavor, despite interesting differences. Thyme is a good tonic for the digestive system, whether of humans or animals.

Cool-climate fruit

SINCE MANY OF US now have access to global markets, many types of fruit are available throughout the year, and the joy of eating the first fruit of the season, picked fresh from our own garden, is disappearing. So recapture it! The deep intensity of eating the first ripe strawberry of the year was always heightened by the waiting. First the plants flowered, then they set fruit, then after that worrying cold spell, the fruit was finally ready for picking. Now we can buy strawberries any time. But no fruit can compare with what has just come from the garden.

WHERE TO GROW STRAWBERRIES
Strawberry plants need to be replaced every three years, so they may fit in better as part of your vegetable rotation (see p. 97).

PLANNING FOR FRUIT

Unlike most of the vegetables, fruit (with the exception of the strawberry) does not form part of a rotation system, moving around the garden from year to year, so it is important to undertake some careful planning before planting your fruit garden.

Whatever fruits you choose must suit your local conditions. Be realistic about how the weather *really* is in your area. If frosts come early and stay late, there is no point in going to endless bother trying to grow the most heartbreaking peaches in the world. Grow hardier fruits, and investigate varieties that have become rare because they do not suit intensive growers. There will be plenty of customers for such "interesting" fruit, especially with an organic label.

The soil must be right for fruit to succeed, and because you can't replant every year, as you do with vegetables, you have to get it right to start with.

Water is your first consideration. Fruit will not grow in waterlogged soil or in drought; and when the fruit is ripening, you must have plentiful water.

If the land is heavy, you will have to double-dig it, add compost, and provide drainage. If the land is light, you will need to enrich it by adding compost, straw, and farmyard manure.

PLANTING TREES

The right place for tree fruit is at the end of the garden. If you plant trees too close to the house, they will cause problems of shading, and their roots may undermine the foundations.

Autumn is a good time to plant fruit trees. It gives their roots time to become established over the winter, before the drier summer months.

Don't forget that the orchard is part of the whole farm and can provide good pecking for a flock of chickens or fine foraging for a tethered pig.

A mature plum tree can produce 50 lb (23 kg) of fruit

PLANTING PLAN
Place the trees that will grow tallest on the side farthest from the sun, and rank the smaller plants toward the sun, in order to minimize shading.

Apple crops improve if the trees are cross-pollinated with another variety of apple

GOOD DRAINAGE
If growing fruit on sticky, heavy land, you will have to ensure that drains are laid to remove surplus water before planting. Fruit trees do not like their feet too wet.

Once dug, the drains should last a lifetime

FRUIT PROTECTION

WHEN THE BIRDS steal your entire crop of blueberries overnight, try to remember that birds *are* useful as predators of harmful insects and snails at various times of year.

Even so, bird damage is hard to tolerate. The only way to be sure of excluding them is to cage the fruit. This can be an expensive business, but with a high-value crop it might be worth it, and a good cage will last for years. This is a commercially made cage, but you can make one yourself that will be just as effective.

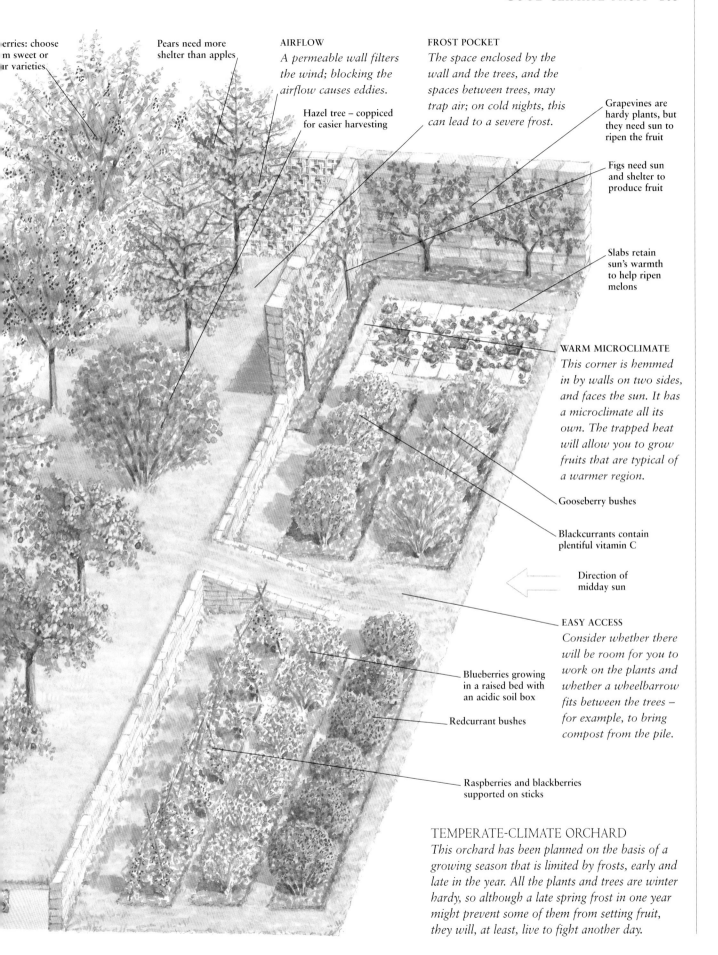

...erries: choose
...m sweet or
...r varieties

Pears need more
shelter than apples

Hazel tree – coppiced
for easier harvesting

AIRFLOW
*A permeable wall filters
the wind; blocking the
airflow causes eddies.*

FROST POCKET
*The space enclosed by the
wall and the trees, and the
spaces between trees, may
trap air; on cold nights, this
can lead to a severe frost.*

Grapevines are
hardy plants, but
they need sun to
ripen the fruit

Figs need sun
and shelter to
produce fruit

Slabs retain
sun's warmth
to help ripen
melons

WARM MICROCLIMATE
*This corner is hemmed
in by walls on two sides,
and faces the sun. It has
a microclimate all its
own. The trapped heat
will allow you to grow
fruits that are typical of
a warmer region.*

Gooseberry bushes

Blackcurrants contain
plentiful vitamin C

Direction of
midday sun

EASY ACCESS
*Consider whether there
will be room for you to
work on the plants and
whether a wheelbarrow
fits between the trees –
for example, to bring
compost from the pile.*

Blueberries growing
in a raised bed with
an acidic soil box

Redcurrant bushes

Raspberries and blackberries
supported on sticks

TEMPERATE-CLIMATE ORCHARD
*This orchard has been planned on the basis of a
growing season that is limited by frosts, early and
late in the year. All the plants and trees are winter
hardy, so although a late spring frost in one year
might prevent some of them from setting fruit,
they will, at least, live to fight another day.*

Warm-climate fruit

THE MEDITERRANEAN CLIMATIC ZONE is a worldwide belt (see p. 22) in which summers are long and dry, and rainfall is concentrated in winter. Here, fruit growers are in their element. If you are lucky enough to have a fertile lowland site in any part of this zone, where frosts are unknown, the choice of fruits to grow is enormous. You can enjoy the sweet scent of orange blossoms in the spring and savor the pleasure of eating a ripe fig, freshly picked and still warm from the sun. A well-planned garden not only will provide a wide range of interesting fruits but also will give welcome shade during the long, hot months of summer.

ALMONDS IN BLOSSOM
Most almond trees are self-sterile, but if there are other ones nearby, bees will pollinate them efficiently.

WHAT TO GROW

Do not hesitate to take long walks around the area in which you live, noting the contents of other people's fruit gardens. Local practice is a reliable guide to what will suit the soil type in your region. On the other hand, don't be afraid to experiment: imagine the pleasure of harvesting your first home-grown banana or mango! Some fruits can be grown from seed – it's fun, but it takes time and you have to be prepared for disappointment.

PLANNING THE ORCHARD

Take advice from a reputable nursery and choose named varieties of proven performance. Go for flavor rather than high yield, and for compact varieties on dwarfing rootstocks, as these take up less room and are easier to manage. A little extra money spent at the beginning on young trees of high quality will pay dividends over many years.

Many fruits, including most varieties of peach, are self-fertile, and you need only one tree for a crop. However, others, including many varieties of apple and plum, are self-sterile. This means that a tree cannot pollinate itself and needs additional trees nearby to act as pollinators if it is to produce any fruit. The other tree needs to be of a different variety, and it is up to you to choose trees that work well together.

Fruit growth depends on pollination. Insects do this well, but don't think you can't help. You can achieve a great deal by transferring pollen between flowers, using a small, soft paintbrush.

ROOF GARDEN
A roof garden or patio area is ideal for growing trees in pots. Pomegranates, kumquats, and limes are attractive, but remember to feed and water them regularly in this confined situation.

Apricots flower very early, so may need pollinating by hand if no insects are around

ORCHARD WALL
The wall serves as a sun trap; it is ideal for training apricots, figs, peaches, and nectarines. The soil at the base of a wall may get very dry in summer.

Quinces have a wonderful scent

WARM-CLIMATE ORCHARD
The site must be well drained. At the same time, it needs all the water it can get: water is vital for growth and fruiting throughout the hot summers. Setting up an irrigation system is one of the first tasks to be tackled. Any soil deficiencies (see p. 132) are easier to correct than shortage of water.

HOW TO STORE FRUIT

STORE LATE VARIETIES of apples in a cool, frost-free, well-ventilated shed or cellar. Choose medium-size, healthy fruits and wrap them individually in waxed paper or newspaper. Check the store, and remove any rotting fruit regularly. Watch out for mice – they like apples too!

LEMONS AND OTHER citrus fruits can be stored much like apples, or you can keep them in boxes of sand. Put layers of unblemished fruits into wooden crates or paper-lined boxes, and cover each layer with dry sand. The fruit will keep for up to two months in this way.

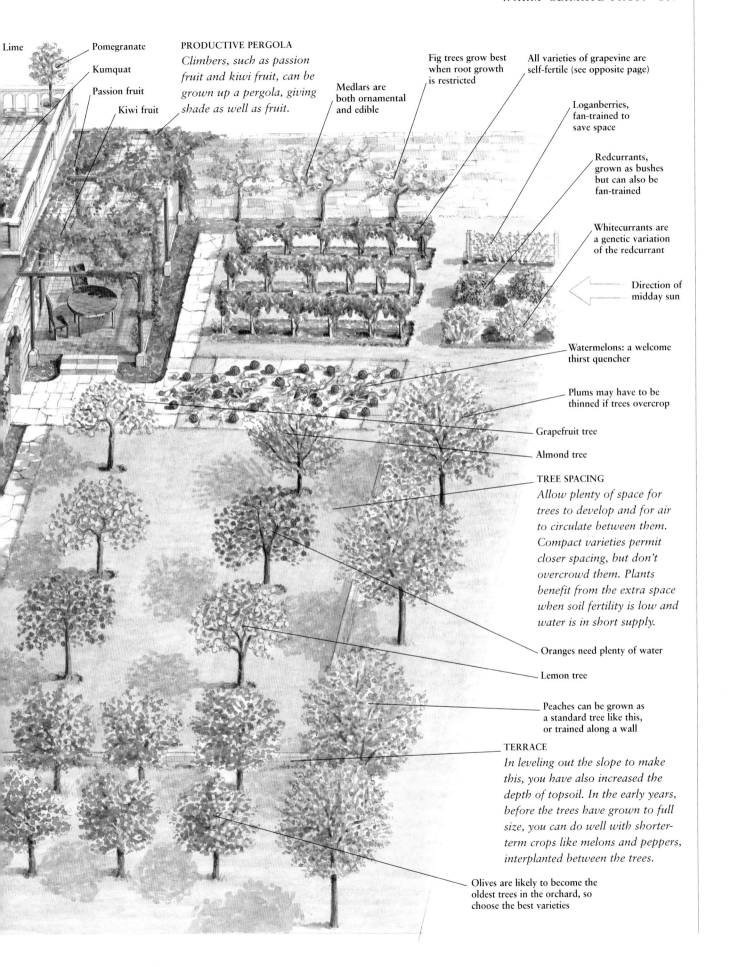

Lime

Pomegranate

Kumquat

Passion fruit

Kiwi fruit

PRODUCTIVE PERGOLA
Climbers, such as passion fruit and kiwi fruit, can be grown up a pergola, giving shade as well as fruit.

Medlars are both ornamental and edible

Fig trees grow best when root growth is restricted

All varieties of grapevine are self-fertile (see opposite page)

Loganberries, fan-trained to save space

Redcurrants, grown as bushes but can also be fan-trained

Whitecurrants are a genetic variation of the redcurrant

Direction of midday sun

Watermelons: a welcome thirst quencher

Plums may have to be thinned if trees overcrop

Grapefruit tree

Almond tree

TREE SPACING
Allow plenty of space for trees to develop and for air to circulate between them. Compact varieties permit closer spacing, but don't overcrowd them. Plants benefit from the extra space when soil fertility is low and water is in short supply.

Oranges need plenty of water

Lemon tree

Peaches can be grown as a standard tree like this, or trained along a wall

TERRACE
In leveling out the slope to make this, you have also increased the depth of topsoil. In the early years, before the trees have grown to full size, you can do well with shorter-term crops like melons and peppers, interplanted between the trees.

Olives are likely to become the oldest trees in the orchard, so choose the best varieties

Homegrown fruits

NOTHING ADDS MORE to the beauty of a garden or farm than the sight of fruit blossoming and ripening. Fruit gives pleasure from the start of the growing season to its very end; it fills the garden with scents as the first warm days of spring arrive, and then, later in the year, the ripe fruits are ready to be picked and eaten or stored for the winter. One of the greatest pleasures of autumn is to return from a long day in the fields and pluck a reviving apple from the tree.

Many fruits can be trained to grow up the sides of buildings, against walls, or over arches, making good use of odd corners where nothing else will grow.

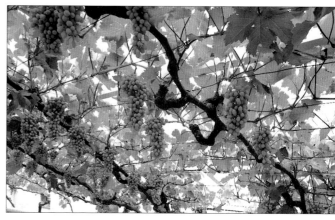

GRAPES IN A COOL CLIMATE
Grow grapes in a conservatory, if your summer cannot be relied on. Why not grow two varieties of grape, say a red and a white? You can also grow passion fruit or kiwi fruit in a conservatory.

NUTS AND VINES

Hazelnuts

There are two species of hazelnut: the rounder cobnut (left), which is only partly covered by its husk, and the longer filbert (right), which is fully enclosed by the husk. Both occur in woodlands, growing in light shade, sheltered by larger trees. When planting hazel trees, avoid heavy shade. They tolerate most soils, if drainage is adequate. The crop may be erratic from year to year.
PLANTING DISTANCES 11½ ft (3.5 m).
YIELD About 24 lb (11 kg) from mature trees.

Almonds

Almonds are grown widely around the Mediterranean, in California, and in East Asia. The trees, dormant in winter, have a tendency to start flowering at the first hint of spring. In the cooler parts of their range, there is a danger that, if a frost follows, you will lose the blossom and hence the almonds. If frosts are a risk, plant the trees against a warm wall.
PLANTING DISTANCES 15 ft (4.5 m).
YIELD About 20 lb (9 kg) from mature trees.

Walnuts

The roots of a walnut tree go deep, drawing nutrients from deep in the soil, rather than from the surface. This means that if you are planting walnut trees, it will make sense to plant them around the edge of the soft fruit garden where they will provide a useful windbreak without robbing other crops of nutrients. Remember, though, that they can live for up to 200 years.
PLANTING DISTANCES 20 ft (6 m).
YIELD About 50 lb (23 kg) from mature trees.

Grapes

Expect no fruit until three years after planting, but after that a properly tended vine may fruit for 20 years. If you are trying to grow grapes outdoors in cooler conditions, grow them next to a warm wall. The best grapes are produced in arid parts of the world, and roots that become too wet spell disaster. A sandy soil, with plenty of grit to keep it open, is ideal.
PLANTING DISTANCES Plant vines 4–5 ft (1.2–1.5 m) apart.
YIELD About 15 lb (7 kg) from a mature vine.

Passion fruit

Also known as the granadilla, the passion fruit grows on vines with dark green leaves and large, white flowers. The vines flourish in the sunniest sites and will not survive frosts. Provide manure until the start of flowering, and water regularly. Fruits take a long time to ripen. You can grow passion fruit from seed or buy high-quality "clonal" plants from specialist suppliers.
PLANTING DISTANCES One vine may be enough, but if you have more, plant them about 13 ft (4 m) apart.
YIELD 20 lb (9 kg) from an established vine.

Kiwi fruit

Kiwi fruit, also called Chinese gooseberries, grow on vines that are extremely vigorous climbers. The original form of the plant needs an eight-month growing season, but now shorter-season varieties, suitable for temperate regions, are available. Kiwi fruit need plenty of water during the growing season. They need feeding, too, in all but the most fertile soils. The male and female flowers are on separate plants – you will need both to get any fruit.
PLANTING DISTANCES Plant a male plant and a female plant together, 13 ft (4 m) apart.
YIELD 20 lb (9 kg) from an established vine.

SOFT FRUIT

Raspberries

You can get a lot of fruit from each raspberry cane, so this is a good soft fruit if you have limited space. The main problems are birds (you may have to net your crop) and virus infection (discard any infected canes).
TRAINING/PRUNING Train along wires, and prune old canes to the ground after fruiting.
PLANTING DISTANCES Plant canes 16–24 in (40–60 cm) apart.
YIELD 12 lb (5.5 kg) from a 10-ft (3-m) row.

Blackberries

You can gather blackberries for free from wild brambles, but cultivated varieties will give fatter, sweeter fruit.
TRAINING/PRUNING Train along wires, and prune old canes to the ground after fruiting. Alternatively, you can plant blackberries as part of a hedge.
PLANTING DISTANCES Set plants at 8–11½ ft (2.5–3.5 m) apart.
YIELD About 11–20 lb (5–9 kg) per plant.

Loganberries

Loganberries were first discovered by Judge James H. Logan of California in 1881 and were thought then to be a cross between a raspberry and a blackberry. Botanists now think probably not. Loganberries are larger fruits than either raspberries or blackberries and can be grown from thornless stock, which makes life easier when you are picking and pruning. Make sure that you buy virus-free stock and plant in a slightly acidic soil.
TRAINING/PRUNING As for raspberries or blackberries.
PLANTING DISTANCES Set the plants at 10–11½ ft (3–3.5 m) apart.
YIELD 13 lb (6 kg) per plant.

Currants

Whitecurrants and redcurrants are the same species, the white being a variant of the red. Blackcurrants are a separate species; they require richer soil, so dig in manure or compost before planting them. All kinds of currants need a soil with plenty of potash and prefer a well-drained site. They will grow in semishade.
TRAINING/PRUNING Redcurrants and whitecurrants fruit on old wood, so there is no need for severe pruning. Blackcurrants fruit on one-year-old stems, so you cut out the older wood after the harvest. Year-old stems are pale, while those that are two years old or more are darker and thicker.
PLANTING DISTANCES Allow about 5–6 ft (1.5–1.8 m) between bushes for all currants.
YIELD About 11 lb (5 kg) of fruit per bush, once it is mature. Bushes may take three years to establish themselves fully.

Whitecurrants fruit on the older wood

Blackcurrants fruit on year-old stems

Redcurrants fruit on the older wood

Gooseberries

This is not a difficult fruit to grow, and once it is properly established, you can expect crops from a gooseberry bush for up to 20 years. The soil needs to be well drained, but retaining enough moisture for growth.
TRAINING/PRUNING No need to train; prune only to make a handy shape for harvesting.
PLANTING DISTANCES About 5 ft (1.5 m) apart.
YIELD About 6½–11 lb (3–5 kg) per bush.

Blueberries

Unless you have highly acidic soil, you will have to create a special area for planting blueberries or grow them in containers in acidic soil mix. Feed with potash while fruit is forming.
TRAINING/PRUNING No need to train. Prune only to make a handy shape for harvesting.
PLANTING DISTANCES Plant 5 ft (1.5 m) apart.
YIELD 6½ lb (3 kg) per mature bush.

Strawberries

Plant in soil that has been well dug, but given time to settle. Add well-rotted manure. When the fruits develop, keep them off the ground with a carpet of straw. Birds are the great enemy, and you must provide protection.
TRAINING/PRUNING No special need.
PLANTING DISTANCES Set plants 18 in (45 cm) apart in rows 3 ft (1 m) apart.
YIELD About 9 oz (250 g) fruit per plant.

Melons

If the climate is cool, start seeds under glass. In some areas, the melons will be happier spending the rest of their lives there.
TRAINING/PRUNING No training needed. Pinch out the growing tips of the side stems when they have five leaves: the fruit grows on the resulting shoots.
PLANTING DISTANCES Set the plants at least 3 ft (1 m) apart, as they need generous space.
YIELD Approximately four fruit per plant.

TREE FRUIT

Cherries

There are two types of cherry – sweet and sour. Grow sweet cherries for eating, sour ones for preserving.

GROWTH FORMS Trees can be quite large, although today, as with other fruit trees, small size is achieved by grafting onto dwarfing rootstocks. Standard trees are hard to defend against birds. Fan-trained ones can be netted.

POLLINATION Not normally a problem with cherries.

PLANTING DISTANCES Allow 20–30 ft (6–9 m) between standard trees, or 18 ft (5.5 m) if fan-trained.

YIELD 70 lb (32 kg) from a standard tree.

Black cherry

'Montmorency' cherry

Plums

There is a vast range of varieties of plum, and these include the damson and the greengage. All need deep soil and need to be safe from frost at blossoming time. If you want to grow these fruits on a commercial scale, you will need to take action to prevent pests and diseases (see p. 92). Otherwise, all the plums are easy to grow. They are best left to get on with it!

GROWTH FORMS All plum varieties are grafted onto rootstocks. The rootstock that is used will control the size of the resulting tree. Choose a dwarfing rootstock if you want to fan-train along a wall.

POLLINATION Not normally a problem.

PLANTING DISTANCES Plant standard trees 20 ft (6 m) apart, and fan-trained trees 11½ ft (3.5 m) apart.

YIELD About 50 lb (23 kg) from a freestanding tree, or 31 lb (14 kg) from a ten-year-old fan-trained tree.

'Marjorie's Seedling' plum

'Victoria' plum

Damson

Greengage

Apricots

Sunshine is the secret of a well-flavored apricot, and only the warmest sites will do unless you can provide shelter, such as a wall. Apricots flower early in the year and are prone to frost damage.

GROWTH FORMS If the climate is cold, fan-train against a warm wall or in a greenhouse.

POLLINATION Apricots are self-fertile (see p. 106), so one tree can be grown alone. If the flowers appear early in spring, before insects are flying, hand-pollinate with a soft brush.

PLANTING DISTANCES Space fan-trained trees along a wall about 15 ft (4.5 m) apart.

YIELD About 20 lb (9 kg) from a good fan.

Nectarines

Nectarines are grown in the same way as apricots, but they need more protection from frost.

GROWTH FORMS If the climate is cold, fan-train against a warm wall.

POLLINATION As for apricots.

PLANTING DISTANCES Space fan-trained trees along a wall about 11½ ft (3.5 m) apart.

YIELD About 20 lb (9 kg) from a good fan.

Peaches

Peaches need a well-drained soil with as neutral a pH (see p. 133) as can be achieved.

GROWTH FORMS In colder areas, peach trees are best fan-trained against a warm wall.

POLLINATION If flowers appear very early in the year, before sufficient numbers of insects are on the wing, you will need to pollinate them yourself by hand, using a small, soft paintbrush.

PLANTING DISTANCES Space fan-trained trees along a wall about 11½ ft (3.5 m) apart.

YIELD About 20 lb (9 kg) from a good fan.

Apples

Apples should give you few problems, and there are sufficient varieties worldwide for you to find apples that will flourish wherever you are.

GROWTH FORMS Apples can be grown on trees of all sizes thanks to modern grafting techniques. Varieties are available that are suited to fan-training and pleaching.

POLLINATION If planting a small orchard, remember that an apple tree will produce a full crop only if it is pollinated by apples of another variety, so make sure you plant at least two compatible varieties that will be in flower at the same time. The pollen is carried from tree to tree by insects, so you could help by keeping bees in the orchard.

PLANTING DISTANCES Plant standard trees 20 ft (6 m) apart, bush trees 12–20 ft (3.6–6 m) apart, and fan-trained trees 15 ft (4.5 m) apart.

YIELD Much depends on weather, variety, and age of tree, but over 110 lb (50 kg) from a mature tree.

'Jonared'

'Suntan'

'Bramley'

'Star King'

Pears

Plant in a fertile site, and weed around saplings while young. You may have to water pears, for they suffer more in drought conditions than apples do.

GROWTH FORMS Can be grown as standard or bush trees, pruned to grow as fans, or trained along wires or frames.

POLLINATION Self-fertile varieties exist (see p. 106), but most need cross-pollinating.

PLANTING DISTANCES Plant standard trees 30 ft (9 m) apart, and bush trees 20 ft (6 m) apart.

YIELD Very variable depending on weather, variety, and age of tree, but you can get over 165 lb (75 kg) from a large, mature tree.

TREE FRUIT

Oranges

Some growers have done well with oranges in the unpredictable weather of the cool temperate zone, but only under glass, with expensive heating. In warmer climes, they are much easier. Orange trees will grow up from seed and produce a good crop within three years of planting. If you are growing your fruit in a greenhouse, consider mandarins or tangerines, which generally find buyers more quickly than oranges do.
PLANTING DISTANCES Leave 25 ft (7.5 m) between bush trees, more for larger forms.
YIELD 100 to 300 fruit from a mature tree.

Lemons and limes

In all but the warmest climates, you will have to grow limes and lemons indoors. Although they are quite hardy, they will not make any reasonable growth except in the warmest conditions. If you are thinking of starting one by growing a seed taken from a lime or lemon, expect a wait of ten years before the first flowers. As with all citrus fruits, lemons and limes like the soil to be slightly acidic.
PLANTING DISTANCES 15 ft (4.5 m) between bush trees.
YIELD 100 to 300 fruit from a mature tree.

Grapefruit

The grapefruit originated in the West Indies, and that gives a clue to its needs: warmth for the fruit to ripen, and good drainage. Despite its love of the sun, the grapefruit is a hardy tree, and if you take cuttings they will root with little difficulty. You may want to grow one solely for the scent of the flowers. It is said that the perfume of one flower will fill an entire greenhouse.
PLANTING DISTANCES Even the bush form is large. Allow 30 ft (9 m) for all forms.
YIELD About 100 fruit from a mature tree.

Kumquats

The small, sweet, orange fruits of this member of the citrus family are eaten whole. They are borne on small, heavily branched trees that, like all citrus trees, have evergreen foliage. The trees benefit from protection from wind damage, but prefer an open, sunny position. Kumquats should be grown much like oranges, but have the advantage of being slightly more cold tolerant.
PLANTING DISTANCES Leave 15 ft (4.5 m) between trees (practically all are bush forms).
YIELD Varies a great deal with conditions.

Mulberries

Mulberry trees need plenty of space and do not grow well if trained along a wall. In cold sites, or dull seasons, they are unproductive, but with enough sun and shelter they produce good crops. However, they are slow-growing trees: expect at least eight years from planting to first fruiting, and then expect to lose some of the crop to the birds, which will produce copious droppings over a wide area around the tree. To gather the fruit, spread a large sheet under the tree, and shake the branches.
PLANTING DISTANCES Space 30 ft (9 m) apart.
YIELD 165 lb (75 kg) from a mature tree.

Olives

This native of the Mediterranean region should be protected from frosts and grown in the sunniest of situations in well-drained soil. The olive is a small tree whose trunk becomes gnarled and twisted with time. Under the right conditions, it can grow to a great age, perhaps as much as 2,000 years! Varieties of olive grown for eating have a higher proportion of flesh than those used in oil production. All are drought tolerant and thrive on the poorest soils.
PLANTING DISTANCES Leave about 25–39 ft (7.5–12 m) between standard trees.
YIELD 110 lb (50 kg) from a mature tree.

Quinces

These grow on a beautiful tree with stunning pink and white flowers. It is said that a quince tree grew in the Garden of Eden and that it was in this tree that the snake resided. Quinces are relatives of pears and are not difficult trees to grow, fruiting in four or five years. They are self-fertile and need no special pollination. The strongly scented fruits are not for eating raw, but are used in baking – particularly with apples – or in making wine or preserves.
PLANTING DISTANCES Up to 20 ft (6 m) between bush trees, farther between larger forms.
YIELD 50 lb (23 kg) from a mature tree.

Figs

Fig trees can grow very large, but they need special attention if they are to set fruit and not simply put on leaf. In a cool climate, grow them against a warm wall. If you do not restrict root growth, the trees will not fruit. You may have to dig a hole and line it with bricks or concrete to contain the roots. Another method is to grow the fig in a container, but sink the container beneath the ground and restrict the roots that way. Do not overwater while the figs are ripening, or they may split.
PLANTING DISTANCES Leave 10 ft (3 m) between bush trees.
YIELD 66 lb (30 kg) from a mature tree.

Pomegranates

The pomegranate is an apple-size fruit that grows on a small tree with beautiful red flowers. It needs sunny conditions to ripen. Protect the tree from frost. In warm countries, it retains its leaves all year, but in cooler climes they are shed each winter. It should be grown in a well-drained situation and watered regularly, but not excessively, during the growing season.
PLANTING DISTANCES 16 ft (5 m)
YIELD 100–150 fruits from a mature tree.

WIDER HORIZONS

WORKING ON A LARGER SCALE does not mean you give any less attention to the crops you grow or show less concern for the land. Instead of a garden you have a

series of fields, and it is only the techniques and machinery that change, not the frame of mind in which you carry out the tasks. You will still use a rotation system for cropping and keep animals in as natural a way as possible. In short, you can farm bigger, without thinking bigger. This is the beauty of home farming.

HEART OF THE FARM

L ARGER FARMS, IN THE CONTEXT of home farming, mean anything above, say, 10 acres (4 ha). Such a farm might have half a dozen large fields and a real herd of sheep or cattle. It will have buildings in which to keep implements, produce, and fodder crops; outhouses for milking, dairying, or wine making; and an area in which to hold livestock brought in for milking, for shearing, or for housing in the winter. On larger farms, life revolves around the farmyard, which is one of the great institutions of farm life, at one and the same time a working center of operations and a place charged with atmosphere and associations. If you are looking at farms to buy, you have to develop a shrewd judgment of the yard and buildings – they are the very heart of the farm.

LIVING OVER THE SHOP
The house should be close to the farmyard – it is a farmer's lot to be needed at short notice for one thing or another in the yard.

AN IDEAL LAYOUT
The main purpose of the yard is to enclose cattle and sheep whenever you need to do so; if you have horses, they should have their own separate yard. Close to both yards there should be space for a manure pile (see p. 136). For small livestock, multipurpose holding pens are most useful for home farmers, who may change from poultry to pigs or from sheep to goats while experimenting to see which suit them best. You will always be glad of a Dutch barn – a cheap and extremely versatile farm building.

Practical considerations demand that the milking shed be close to the dairy. Pigs, too, like to be close to the dairy, for they will be the recipients of some of the by-products, such as the buttermilk. Cowsheds, stables, and multipurpose stock pens should be laid out in such a way that their outer walls together form the enclosure for your main livestock yard. Your house, and the kitchen garden, should be conveniently close at hand.

Wind-driven generator as an auxiliary power supply

Manure pile must be some way from house

Barn is used as a general livestock shelter

Stable yard: horses need to have their own separate exercise area

INFRASTRUCTURE AND MAINTENANCE

GATES AND DRIVEWAYS
Reinforce gates with wire mesh to keep foxes out and poultry in. Be prepared to spend time repairing your driveway, too.

FIELD DRAINAGE
In wet winters, your field crops could rot if the land becomes waterlogged. Ditches must be kept clear with regular digging.

FARM WORKSHOP
Something will break almost every day, and you need a workshop large enough for you to be able to carry out repairs.

Milking shed
close to house for
home dairying

Kitchen garden helps to
increase self-sufficiency
on the farm

A pond is always
a focal point for
wildlife

Telephone lines and
main electricity
supply

Locate the Dutch
barn so that you
have easy access to
it from all sides

This stable
has enough
room for
three horses

Allow plenty of time
to dig and maintain
ditches for drainage

Multipurpose
housing and pens
for pigs, goats,
sheep, or poultry

THE FARMYARD

Here you will shear sheep, load pigs, milk cows, cart manure, and store hay and straw. A farmyard evolves to suit the needs of your farm, and you will find your farmyard changes over the years as you refine your farming ideas.

BARNS, STABLES, AND SHEDS

GENERAL-PURPOSE BARN
On many farms in the United States, barns like this store produce and shelter livestock.

DUTCH BARN
These barns have high, curved roofs and are used to store hay, straw, and equipment.

STABLE
Horses need a comfortable stable in which to feed and rest when they are not working.

COWSHED
This will shelter cows in winter, and enable you to confine them whenever you need to.

DONKEY PADDOCK
Contrary to popular belief, donkeys are no cheaper than ponies or light horses.

CHOICE OF POWER
This chart sets out the main factors to be considered when choosing a power source. While it is important to be realistic in assessing the needs of your plot or farm and the tasks you have to accomplish on it, you must feel happy with your final choice – you will be spending a lot of time together.

HUMAN POWER
If you are fit enough and your plot is small, you may manage without machines altogether.

POWER TO YOUR ELBOW

WHEN RUNNING A large home farm, you will not be able to take spade, fork, hoe, and shovel and do everything yourself. You have important decisions to make about how you will work the land and gather the harvest. It is tempting to think that you can go back to the days, often glimpsed in old photographs, when entire families and villages would take up pitchforks and head for the meadows to make the hay or dig the potatoes. But those days of cheap and abundant labor are gone, and more often than not you will find the greater part of the work will fall on your shoulders. If you do not choose wisely

	Simple cultivator	Mini-tractor
Purchase price	Buy secondhand: this type of machine is of only limited use, for only part of the year. But if you do buy a modern one, attachments exist for a variety of tasks.	Up there with a brand-new car. There is a secondhand market, which may be worth exploring. Beware of "imitation tractors" (small machines that are no more than glorified garden implements).
Maintenance	Routine requirements for a gas-engined implement.	Top up oil, grease, and water; but anything more than that would have to be done by or through an approved dealer.
Expert services needed	Try to fix it yourself.	Sophisticated and often expensive.
Feed/fuel	Gasoline, using about the same amount as a big lawn mower.	Diesel (some models run on gas).
Most appropriate tasks	Preparing land on small-scale farms.	Pulling a light plow or harrow; moving loads; pulling a cart. Can be fitted with a lifting bucket.
Most appropriate location	Small, flat plots of land.	Excellent on small farms due to compact size. Good on steep slopes.
Level of operator skill needed	Low skill level, but some stamina required.	Easily learned skills.
Level of maintenance skill needed	Think of it as a motorcycle.	Anything more than routine needs a mechanic – do not try it yourself.

A mini-tractor fits easily inside a polytunnel

Sit-on cultivator adapted for harvesting

in planning to relieve that load, you could end up adding to your burdens instead of lightening them. You may, for example, be tempted to think that, because you are farming on only a small scale, it would be appropriate to use animal traction. You may like the idea of working with horses. Animals were, after all, a primary power source before mechanization. But the work involved in keeping a working horse alive and well fed is considerable, and the best part of the day can be gone by the time the horse is ready for work. Tractors are less demanding.

But one word of caution: you have become a home farmer because of your love of the land. It is easy to be tempted into buying ever grander machinery. The implements are impressive, but if you use them you will find yourself divorced from your main source of satisfaction – the fact that you are working on the land.

TRACTOR-DRAWN BINDER
If you love the old ways, why not borrow or purchase a binder (see p. 146) to cut your cereals?

Basic tractor	Light horse/pony/donkey	Heavy horse	Ox
Buy cheap at auction or beg off a farmer who has upgraded. Pay more if it comes complete with matching implements.	Beware of cheap horses. Remember, used-car salesmen learned all their tricks from horse dealers!	Do not pay a high price for a pedigree horse. You want it for what it can do, not how it looks.	Breed your own: oxen are basically cattle adapted for work. They need to be schooled from quite a young age. Good beef when the working life is over. Can live for a long time.
Oil and grease regularly. Tires will wear. *Routine servicing for a tractor*	Daily feeding in winter, daily visits in summer. Grooming. Mucking out. Harness also needs cleaning.	As with light horse. Collar and harness need cleaning.	Less prone to foot and leg problems than horses. Good self-feeders, on decent pasture.
Mechanic needed for major breakdowns, but routine maintenance quite simple. One wrench fits most nuts and bolts.	Vet and farrier. Neither of these is a job for an amateur, and in both cases the money is well spent.	As with light horse. Also, you may want to employ a horseman who specializes in draft horses to do the fieldwork – at least at first.	Hard to find experienced people who can teach oxen to work. Usual stockmanship skills needed.
Diesel. Some basic tractors will run on as little as ½ gallon (2.25 liters) an hour, working at usual rates of output (for example, tasks like chain harrowing or transporting light loads around the farm).	Bulk feeds: grass in summer, hay in winter. Concentrated feeds: cereals and commercial mixes. How much you feed of each type, and in what proportion, varies with workload.	As with light horse. Grow plenty of fodder crops; otherwise, you will have an expensive time catering to a cart horse.	Oats, barley, grass, hay, silage.
All tillage and haulage tasks. It will refuse few jobs. *Tractor pulling a spring-tine cultivator*	You need weight to pull weight, so the pulling power of any light horse or pony is limited. However, some breeds can carry loads well out of proportion to their size.	Excellent for cultivation on a field scale. Ideal for hoeing between row crops, and working with a cart in confined spaces. Very good, too, for haymaking and cereal harvest.	*American home farmer using oxen to pull a plow* Slow but steady workers, best used on decent-size patches, as oxen need a large area to turn.
Excellent on small farms due to compact size.	Good, hardy animals, well proven in all terrains. Some ponies work particularly well in upland areas.	Almost any. Can work more safely on steep land than a tractor, and in tighter corners too.	Flat, regular fields larger than 5 acres (2 ha).
Everyone's tractor.	Considerable, plus animal instinct.	As with light horse.	High skill level, as well as a deep sense of the romantic.
Try it, in the safe knowledge that there is not much scope to do any serious damage.	Horseman's eye.	As with light horse.	High.

Collar and harness

Body brush, used for grooming

Tractors

TRACTORS HAVE HARD LIVES. They are the most abused thing on a farm, expected to perform to order, often used to carry out tasks heavier than those for which they were designed, kicked if they fail, and cursed when they break down. You may start off with the best of intentions toward your tractor, but very soon you will find yourself on the slippery slope to tractor abuse. Try not to be too harsh on it.

THE "MAID-OF-ALL-WORK"

Hydraulic hose

Hydraulic lift arm

Height of each arm can be adjusted separately

Bottom link is attached to the lower end of a farm implement

Top link is attached to the top of a farm implement

Safety guard

Power takeoff shaft

Drawbar used in pulling mode

POWER CONNECTIONS
A great deal happens at the back, behind the driver's seat. The power takeoff shaft is located here, and the output of the hydraulic pump, which can power the lifting arms or a fork attached to the front of the tractor. It is essential that proper safety guards be fitted.

NEW OR OLD?
A small farm does not need a brand-new tractor. Most modern tractors are too big and powerful for your needs, and "mini-tractors" are overpriced and are often more pretty than useful.

The world is littered with tractors that have become outdated by modern developments, and I would seek out one of those. Find someone who knows and loves tractors, and take him or her with you when you go to buy.

In many ways, the faithful Ferguson (shown on the right) is an ideal tractor for the home farmer. But there are many other good models, and your older neighbors will know which they are.

DO I NEED ONE?
On very small farms, you can use only a mini-tractor or rotary cultivator. Mini-tractors are popular, but slow, and in my opinion, most are more useful for mowing lawns than cultivating land or hauling manure. A rotary cultivator is a better bet for tilling the soil, if you can manage the other tasks by hand.

On a larger farm, there are tasks that are too heavy to be done manually. You need either horses or a tractor. Bearing in mind a huge range of variables, the comparison is like this: for some tasks, like plowing, a basic tractor can do the work of two or three heavy horses. A basic tractor, purchased secondhand, might cost as much as a horse, but its maintenance and fuel cost only about a tenth of what it costs to keep a horse.

THREE WAYS OF WORKING

PULLING POWER
This tractor is in the pulling mode, hauling an old plow. Two things determine the pulling power of a tractor: the engine size and the depth of tread on the tires.

HYDRAULIC POWER
Many tractors are fitted with hydraulics and can be used for lifting things. On this tractor, a fork has been fitted at the front. It could be used for shifting manure or straw.

POWER TAKEOFF
This tractor is stationary, and the power from its engine has been diverted to the power takeoff (PTO) shaft. PTO shafts are used to drive machinery, such as this shredder.

THREE WAYS OF WORKING

Well-schooled horses are capable of a wide range of tasks, but in some ways tractors are more versatile. Tractors are often thought of simply as machines for pulling, but almost all are also fitted with hydraulics and are therefore useful for lifting. Most tractors can also drive machinery via a power takeoff (PTO) shaft, connected through a gearbox to the engine (see left). With hydraulics and PTO, you have a truly versatile machine. You can plow, fork manure, lift sacks, drive saws for logging, and chop straw and hay into chaff.

MAINTENANCE

A small diesel-powered tractor can run for many years with only a minimum of maintenance, but that does not mean you can get away with doing nothing to it at all. I was told, by a man who understood tractors better than I did, that washing them down was one of the best favors you could do yourself. You will never spot a fuel or oil leak if it is buried beneath a thick layer of mud.

The process of combustion at the heart of a diesel engine needs two things – fuel and air – brought together, at the right time, in the cylinder. If you can get this right, you will have no problems. Most breakdowns result from fuel and air mixing too early (in the pipeline, for instance, which happens if the tank runs dry). Study the fuel line from tank to cylinder, and learn how to "bleed" it, as this may get the engine running again.

TRACTOR SAFETY

TRACTORS CAN TURN OVER and crush you. In some countries, new tractors are fitted with rollbars by law, but older ones may not be. If you have a hilly farm, be extra careful. The power takeoff can also be a lethal piece of equipment, causing nasty accidents if not used with care. Hydraulics, if not properly fitted and serviced, are dangerous. Never let children ride on tractors. Even though I never intended to do much tractor work, attending a safety course at a college was time well spent.

DAY-TO-DAY MAINTENANCE

FUELING UP
It may be too obvious to state, but tractors need diesel fuel in order to work. It can be a long walk back to the farm if you run out of fuel on the far side of a field.

BATTERY CHECK
Checking the electrolyte levels in the battery is the only way to ensure that your tractor will start on cold, frosty mornings. You could get away with doing this once a week.

OIL CHECK
An engine that runs out of oil will seize up and be ruined almost before you can shut it off. Check the oil level often, and suspect a problem if you notice a sudden drop.

TOPPING UP OIL
The maximum and minimum levels of oil will be marked on the dipstick. Fill to just below the maximum mark. Some tractors have dipsticks for both engine and gearbox.

GREASING
Grease points may be in places where they are hard to spot, and there may be more than you think. Wipe off any dirt from the grease nipples before applying the grease gun.

TOPPING UP COOLING WATER
Soft water is better for the radiator than hard, and rainwater is better than tap water. Check the water early in the day – the cap is easier to unscrew before it has heated up.

Horses

UNTIL YOU HAVE EXPERIENCED the deep satisfaction of working land with horses, I doubt if your farming career will be complete. That is how I started mine, behind a pair of Suffolk Punches, a native British breed of chestnut cart horse. They practically taught me to plow. A very special kind of dialogue takes place between farmer and horse, and it will not be many years before you hardly have to give your horse a command – if he or she is anything of a horse, the two of you will be of one mind.

One person on the field needs to be aware of the needs of the horse

POWER ON THE FARM

Working with horses can make for pleasant days in the field. For repetitive tasks, such as pulling this wagon along slowly, stopping every few minutes to allow the people to load sheaves of corn, a horse is easier to use than a tractor – and a good deal quieter.

HOW TO CHOOSE A HORSE

Nearly every country has a native breed of horse that has been bred over many years for working the land. I am a firm believer in the principle that an animal plays best on its home ground. In other words, choose the working horse that is traditional to wherever you farm.

Do not bother too much about the horse's pedigree – manners and health matter more than looks. Temperament is the single most important quality you have to consider in a working horse: for much of the day, a farm horse will be expected to obey important commands precisely, and horses with minds of their own have no place on a farm.

Avoid a young, inexperienced horse, and instead buy one that has worked the land. Then you can learn from the horse. That's good value.

HOW TO WORK WITH HORSES

Find yourself a good teacher. In most parts of the world, farmers of the last generation that worked with horses are dying out and taking their secrets to the grave. Get a little of their wisdom if you can. You yourself will need to have an even temper to work horses and an understanding of when the horse needs to rest, when he or she is to be urged on, and when the animal is confused because your orders were not clear.

GOOD PHYSIQUE

YOU MAY HAVE to choose from a range of possible horses if you are going to buy the cart horses you plan to work with. If you want a thorough assessment of an animal, ask a veterinarian, who will examine in particular the limbs, heart, and eyes. But generally speaking, a successful working horse is one that has some weight about him or her; this is based on the principle that you need weight to pull weight. In order to be an effective pulling machine, the horse also needs strong, muscled legs and good-size feet with which to get a grip.

Despite appearances, the collar does not rest on the horse's neck, but on the chest and shoulders, and it is from here that the animal pulls. Look for a broad, strong chest on a working horse.

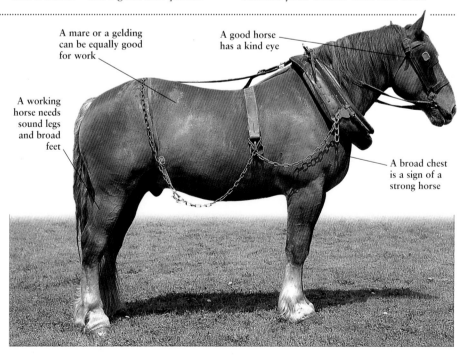

A mare or a gelding can be equally good for work

A good horse has a kind eye

A working horse needs sound legs and broad feet

A broad chest is a sign of a strong horse

CLEAR COMMANDS

In my early days with horses, I cursed and shouted at them for not doing as I said, but now I realize that the fault was mine: I should have sounded clearer and more commanding in telling them what I wanted. Talk to horses as they work, and they will work better for you.

Working with horses is a knack that you develop in time, but if you have a natural fear of horses, you will not get very far because they will sense it.

WHAT HORSES CAN DO

Pulling is the only type of work a horse can do, but agricultural engineers have devised ingenious ways of turning their forward plod into various sorts of useful work. The hay mower and side-delivery rake (see p. 158) and the potato spinner (p. 152) are good examples of this.

The main drawback with horses is their relatively slow working speed. This matters only to the larger farmer. Why would a home farmer want anything more than to follow a pair of horses as they plow a handful of acres?

I have successfully used horses for plowing, harrowing meadows and plowed land, carting manure, sowing seed, planting potatoes, mowing grass, turning hay, and cutting and carting corn, which covers just about all the heavy work in the entire farming year.

HORSE SAFETY

EVEN THE MOST experienced and benign horse sees things differently from you and may surprise you. A horse will have fears you know nothing about, and may be startled into a dangerous panic by things you do not even notice. Always carry a pocket knife (see p. 37), in case you ever need to cut the harness to free a fallen horse or one that is panicking. In your early days of handling horses, be sure to have an experienced person with you, and watch the way he or she handles and harnesses the horse and leads it out to work. And watch where you step, for the horse's feet will always be bigger, and less fragile, than yours.

FARM PONIES
In some countries, smaller and lighter horses, even ponies such as these, are used on farms. They are effective, providing they are not asked to perform tasks that are too much for them. On a light soil that is not being turned too deeply, these ponies are perfectly happy.

LEARNING ABILITY

The horse's talent for learning a job is impressive. For the vegetable grower, a horse-drawn hoe is a highly efficient and nontoxic way to control weeds in row crops. When harnessed to a hoe, horses will walk with precision, in a straight line, between rows of plants. It is amazing just how few plants even the large feet of a heavy horse will trample. You will need to have as much skill as the horse does.

Farm horses are schooled for their work by professional trainers. The obedience

Horses enjoy the companionship of being part of a herd

natural to farm horses shows when they are plowing. This task requires one horse to walk on the unplowed side of the furrow, while the other has to walk in the furrow. Treading in bare soil is exactly the opposite of what the horses were taught to do in their first stage of training, yet, once they know that this is really what is required of them, they will not let this confuse them.

HORSE-DRAWN MACHINERY

Without machines to pull, the horse is of no use, and so before you embark on horse-drawn farming, make sure that harness and machinery can be found that will fit the breed of horse you favor. You will have more luck in some places than others; a wide selection of implements, along with an impressive array of harness, is available in some American states and eastern Europe. Elsewhere – in Britain and much of western Europe, for instance – harness and gear were thrown onto the bonfire when the tractors took over. Finding horse-drawn equipment can be a matter of looking in the back of other people's barns, and making offers for things they don't know the purpose of and never knew they had. I have also rescued old, forgotten plows from ditches where they were dumped decades ago. Old machinery is prone to break down, and your repair skills will be called on almost as much as your horsemanship.

Keeping horses

HORSES NEED RATHER MORE care and attention than other farm animals, mainly because they work. Their feet and their coats need regular care, and they must be kept active. Let "keep them fit, and keep them fed" be your motto. Horses like routine, and providing you can keep to one, there is no reason why your horse should not thrive. Your routine in winter will be different from the one you follow in summer. In winter, when the ground is wet, the broad feet of a heavy horse can damage the turf of the meadows, so bring the horses in and let them live in stables or strawed yards. In summer, they need never see the inside of a stable, unless you bring them in for feeding, grooming, or harnessing.

STABLING

FRESH AIR, BUT no drafts is the first rule for a good stable. A horse feeds from a manger, which should not be too small, because the first thing horses do when presented with their feed is to give it a good blast of air from their nostrils to spread it around. If your horse is in regular work, you should make good hay available for him to nibble at during the day, either from an overhead rack, as seen in the picture below, or from a rack mounted head high on the wall.

Overhead hay rack   Large manger   Plenty of straw on floor stops horse from slipping

A WORKING HORSE STABLE
In winter, this horse is tied to the manger during the day when not at work. There is hay in the rack overhead, and other feed is put in the wooden manger. A well-strawed floor is safest and prevents slipping.

HARNESS FOR THREE CART HORSES
Harness should be hung on the wall, out of reach of rats and mice and close at hand for harnessing. The box contains a grooming kit and items for dealing with cuts and grazes.

HORSE CARE

ONE OF THE WISEST sayings is "no foot, no horse." What it means is that lack of attention to vital working parts, such as feet, can lead to problems. Grooming and cleaning out the hooves are tasks done for the sake of the horse's health, not just for an eye-catching appearance.

GROOMING
Working horses can get filthy. Groom them particularly in areas where the harness is likely to rub, and remove all mud and sweat.

REMOVING A SHOE
Shoeing should be done only by a qualified farrier. But a loose shoe can be dangerous – remove it, and every nail, with pincers.

CLEANING THE HOOVES
Stones and mud collect in the horse's hooves, where they can cause lameness. Scrape well with a hoof pick, getting into every cranny.

FEED

OVERFEEDING HORSES IS as dangerous as underfeeding them, and the skill is to match the feed to the work. Horses that are not being worked will be fine on meadow grass in summer and hay in winter. Working horses need concentrates. These consist of cereals and commercial feeds of various types.

Feed your horses at the same time every day and look for any leftovers, which might indicate illness. Always give water before feeding, and do not work a horse within an hour of the most recent meal. Allow plenty of time for digestion.

WATER TROUGH
Rainwater makes an enjoyable drink. Do not give a sweating horse too much cold water.

WINTER FEED
In or out of work, horses need plenty of roughage; in winter, it is best supplied by good hay.

HORSE FEEDS MADE SIMPLE

	Bulk feeds	Concentrated feeds	Supplements
Homegrown feeds	These provide roughage – a vital part of any horse's diet. Grass may be fed either fresh, as grazing, or conserved, as hay. Silage is best avoided. Alfalfa and clover are highly nutritious feeds: make them into hay, but do not use them fresh. You can also feed horses with chopped oat straw or dried corn stalks.	These are principally cereals, which give horses the energy they need to work. If you grow oats, roll them in a mill before feeding. Barley can be fed whole, but boiled. Wheat grains are not suitable for horses, but the bran is, and you can recover it when milling your grain, or you can ask the miller to do it for you.	Horses will be happy to munch on surplus carrots and apples. Apples are safest chopped in quarters; cut the carrots lengthwise to prevent choking. Fresh-cut corn can be fed to larger horses in the late summer, and some horses will enjoy the sweetness of chopped mangels in the winter.
Bought feeds	You can always buy hay, but making your own is cheaper. Other possibilities are chaff (chopped hay or straw), which is often sold sprayed with molasses, and dried alfalfa. But these are expensive ways of feeding bulk, and should be considered only in an emergency, when there is no alternative.	Most of the feeds that you buy are commercial ones, coming in the form of cubes or nuts designed to give a balanced diet if fed with grass or hay. Corn, dried and rolled to make flakes, is a valuable concentrated feed. Sugar-beet pulp *must* be soaked for 24 hours before feeding.	To maintain health, add cod liver oil to regular feeds. Some oils, such as corn oil, also give energy to horses in heavy work. Molasses is a useful, sweet additive, disguising any foods a horse might shun. Provide a salt lick in the stable for horses to use whenever they need. Various forms are sold.

GRAZING
A rich, well-seeded meadow (see p. 154) can supply all a horse's needs when not working.

STABLE FEED
Feed by the clock; a horse likes to know when the next meal will be.

HARNESSING

THE MOST COMMON cause of accidents with working horses is a harness breaking, causing the horse to panic. A good habit is to check the harness each time you put it on: look for frayed stitches or cracked leather. If you are a beginner, have the horse held by an experienced handler while you learn the correct order in which to harness a horse. You must also learn how to tell if the horse is comfortable in the harness.

PUTTING ON THE COLLAR
Put this on upside down (as seen here), then twist it right side up while it is resting on the neck. Keep hold of the leading rein.

THE HARNESS
A horse wears chains to pull a cart or a saddle (shown) to pull a plow. Place the harness on the horse's back, and tighten it.

THE BRIDLE
Finally, add the bridle. To get the horse to open his or her mouth, insert your finger in the corner of the mouth, and it will open.

Farming and wildlife

OWNING A FARM carries with it responsibilities, not only for the crops you plant and the animals you rear, but also for everything that was there before you started to mold the holding to your own needs. The trees, meadows, and ponds, and all their inhabitants, from the smallest insect to the largest mammal, were all there before you, and conserving them should be as much a part of your farming as crops and livestock.

GRASSLANDS

HEADLAND HABITAT
Headlands are strips of land bordering fields. They lie so close to hedges or ditches that they are often neither plowed nor sown. Leave them that way! This is where animals scurry for safety and shelter, and birds and insects find the plants on which they feed.

TRADITIONAL HAY MEADOW
This meadow is rich in grasses and herbs, and better for wildlife than a field of just one type of grass. It is all right to let your cattle graze it, but keep them off in spring, to allow the plants to flower and set seed.

WHOSE LANDSCAPE?

The countryside we see around us has been changed by farmers: it looks the way it does because of centuries of forest clearance, drainage, enclosure, and now modern agricultural methods. It might be argued that, since farmers made the landscape, they have a right to destroy it, if that is what suits their purposes. But we must not accept this argument, and it is easy to refute it.

Yes, a farmer *did* plant your hedges centuries ago, but since then animals and plants have come to rely on them for their survival. Farmers *did* plow the prairie to create those fields of wheat. But they left stubble there all winter, and this has now become a food source for some of North America's ground-nesting songbirds, such as the eastern meadowlark. Yes, that pond *was* once dug as a wagon-wash, but it is now a breeding site for frogs and toads.

To destroy these and any other wildlife habitats is irrational, particularly if done for profit, for the creatures in them will help to increase profits by keeping down farm pests. Birds pick the caterpillars off your kale, and frogs feed on the insects that plague your cows. Rotten trees provide nest sites for owls, which will rid you of the mice that are after your grain store.

Eastern meadowlark

NOT TOO TIDY

There is a fashion among farmers to tidy every corner of the farm ruthlessly, cutting the grass short and removing every weed, dead tree, or fallen branch. This might be a great temptation for some, but nature has never cared for the human idea of tidiness and cannot cope with it if applied too rigorously.

This is not an excuse for doing nothing. You need to aim for a balance: a farm that is workable, but still meets the needs of its wild inhabitants.

Hedges are a good example. When they are old and untended, they become straggly. Don't just continue neglecting them: rehabilitate them by stages.

RESTORING A POND

A POND BECOMES DERELICT if it is not managed. The streams or ditches that bring water to the pond also bring silt, and over time this will accumulate and fill in the pond – unless you dredge it.

If you let too many trees grow up around the edge of the pond, they will block out the light, and aquatic life will die. Leaves and twigs will fall from the tree and choke the water. Organisms in the pond will feed on fallen material, multiply, and use up all the oxygen in the water. The water in the pond will become acidic and dead.

If this is a description of a pond on your farm, do not despair – restoring it to a rich wildlife habitat is not difficult.

DERELICT POND
This pond has gradually filled up with silt over the years. The trees have grown tall, blocking out light and filling what is left of the pond with decaying leaves.

RESTORATION WORK
Dig the silt out with machinery (or an army of volunteers in waders). There will probably be a layer of clay under the silt – don't break through it, or your pond will leak.

IN GOOD SHAPE
Once the pond has filled, the combination of clean water and light will soon bring it back to life. An annual cut of overhanging growth will keep the pond well lit and alive.

CLEARING ALGAE
Too many algae can be a problem. Barley straw is slightly acidic: throw a bale into the pond and it will clear!

HEDGE MANAGEMENT

Straggly hedges are useless as barriers, and they are not much use for wildlife. They need trimming and tidying. But if you did this all at once, it would be an ecological crime. Tidy up a third of the hedges on your land each year until all are in good order: nature can cope with this, and you will cause no problems.

Some hedges are so badly neglected that they will have to be cut right back to the ground and allowed to regrow. If all your hedges are in this category, plan to do this work over a ten-year cycle to get the maximum benefit for you, while causing the minimum disruption to those who live among them.

Never spray or burn the bottoms of hedges to reduce weeds. It may look tidier, but it is not nature's way. It is a common mistake to think that weeds lurk at the base of your hedges, ready to invade your crops the next chance they get. Most of the weeds affecting arable crops are "pioneering annuals"; that is, they belong to a category of plants that specialize in colonizing newly disturbed ground, such as a plowed field. Most plants in the hedge bases, and a good deal of those that grow on headlands, are perennials: they cannot invade fields that are cultivated annually.

ESTABLISHING WILD AREAS

If the land you farm, or are about to start farming, has lost a lot of wildlife in the course of intensive farming, why not create habitats anew and undo some of the damage? Wherever your farm is, there will be some animal and plant species that have suffered as a result of modern farming methods. As a home farmer, working to a different agenda, you are well placed to devote a corner of land to conservation of these species.

Only in recent years has it been fully realized how rapidly certain songbirds that live in open farmland

Dormouse numbers are decreasing fast

are disappearing as their habitats are being destroyed and their food sources reduced by insecticides. These birds include the skylark in Europe and the eastern meadowlark and grasshopper sparrow in North America.

If you can create a refuge for birds like this, no matter how small, it will help. The majority of cereals are now planted in the autumn rather than the spring, so the bare winter stubble birds need has become rare. Early-season

harvesting, mechanized into the bargain, has driven the harvest mouse from the wheat fields. The meadows, full of herbs and flowers, that were home to so many tiny creatures have nearly all been plowed under to make room for more profitable crops. Woodlands have gone, and with them most of the dormice. But you will be returning to the old ways, and your whole farm can be a refuge.

If you are creating wildlife areas, start now. Don't leave it until next season. Trees take time to grow, and it will be several years before you see any rewards for your efforts. Even then, don't expect that just because you have planted a hedge or two, the rarest birds and butterflies in the world will be so grateful that they will flock to your farm. They are not pets that can be enticed; the best you can do is make a clear sign that they are welcome, and leave the rest to them.

MAKING A CONSERVATION PLAN

Having an overall conservation plan is a great way to start, and there is no doubt that a little experienced help in making it is a valuable thing. There may be a representative of your local government or wildlife group who will be delighted to help you draw up a plan and who will also know if you are eligible for any grants to carry out the work. You might even discover delights you never knew you had. My attention was drawn to a pond on our farm that I never knew existed. It appeared to be no more than an overgrown, boggy patch until we dug it out, and watched it fill naturally and burst into new life.

A good starting point is to aim to conserve species you already have, and then let any others join in if they wish. In some conservation activities, you will have to be brave: coppicing, for instance, can seem brutal, because so much of it consists of sawing and chopping. But it is in the long-term interest of a vitally important habitat, and in the end most woodland will benefit a great deal from this kind of sympathetic management.

Farming with wildlife is a great balancing act, but a hugely rewarding one that should be high on the agenda of every home farmer.

HEDGES – LINEAR WOODLANDS

HEDGES ARE WORLDS of their own, where plants and animals lead hidden lives. But they also confine farm animals and provide them with shelter. The trick is in getting the full benefit for both wild and domestic animals. No livestock will get through the one shown here, and at the same time it is a luxury home for wild creatures. The hedge's multicolored appearance is a good sign: the stretch seen here contains five species of woody plant: hawthorn, elder, ash, oak, and holly. They support a varied population of insects that – together with the leaves, fruits, and dense structure – meet the needs of a healthy range of birds.

MANAGING WOODLAND

WOODS GET FORGOTTEN, or perhaps left to get on with their life unaided. There may be some good in this, but the right management will make a wood into a better, more lasting source of forest products and a better wildlife habitat.

Coppicing keeps a wood young. It consists of felling sections of the wood, year by year. The first section will have regrown by the time you get back to it. Pollarding consists of cutting branches back to the trunk, to let them regrow. Both systems allow light into the wood and create new wildlife habitats.

WELL-MAINTAINED WOODLAND
The varied structure of this wood gives a range of different habitats: mature trees support a leafy canopy, cleared areas let in sunlight, and smaller trees and flowers on the ground support a variety of butterflies and other insects.

COPPICING
In coppice management, the harvest is a crop of poles. A craftsman cuts a swath across the wood, leaving the stumps to grow again.

PRODUCE OF THE FOREST
Poles of different thicknesses are useful for different things – for instance, hurdle making (see p. 29), hedging (p. 31), or thatching.

COPPICE STOOLS
From these freshly cut stools, new shoots will quickly emerge, and in five years another crop will be ready to harvest.

POLLARDING
This looks brutal, but it will be in the tree's best long-term interests. Infected wood is cut away, extending the life of the tree. The tree in the foreground is making new shoots: these will grow into poles just like those from a coppice stool. Meanwhile, the aging trunk is a great habitat for insects and other wildlife.

Old trees are nesting and roosting sites for many different birds, from owls to wrens

FOOD FROM THE FIELDS

THERE IS UNDENIABLE PLEASURE in the sight of a field of flourishing crops ripening under the summer sun. But there is even greater joy to be had from knowing that it is only through your efforts that the soil has been fertilized and duly tilled, the seeds sown, the weeds hoed and kept down, the pests deterred, and the plants tended

until the food is ready for harvest. When farming fields, you are laboring on a larger canvas, but it can still be as much an art as working the smallest of gardens.

WHICH FIELD CROP?

WARM-CLIMATE CROP
Rice needs high temperatures, long hours of sunshine, and an enormous amount of water.

THREE THINGS DETERMINE which crops are grown on any given farm. Even though you are a home farmer, you will make your choice in the light of these three factors. Two of them you can do relatively little about, but, because you are working the land for the love of it, the third is entirely in your hands. You have no control over the climate, and there are limits to what you can do to improve the soil. They sing their own tunes, and their music might be sweet to some plants, but not so for others. You cannot expect to grow corn halfway up a north Canadian mountainside; the soil may be rich and well drained, but the growing season is too short. Nor is there any point in trying to grow potatoes on

YOUR CHOICE OF FIELD CROPS

	Wheat	Barley	Oats	Rye
General	Most demanding of all field crops in terms of nutrients.	High nutrient needs in early spring. Requires moderate temperatures and well-distributed rainfall.	A versatile cereal, growing well in most situations with temperate conditions. Ideal in cool, moist districts.	A hardy cereal, easily grown. It shades out weeds with its long stems. A good "pioneer" crop for land on which no cereals have grown before.
Variety	Choose between winter wheat (sown in autumn) and spring wheat. Winter wheat gives greater yields. Older varieties often do better in organic systems.	Choose between winter or spring barley. *Threshed barley*	"Naked" oats, which have no husk, are now available. This makes milling considerably easier.	Few available to choose from. Consult a local farm supplier.
Soil/conditions	Will grow on most fertile soils, but a rich clay is best.	Does not tolerate poor drainage or acid conditions.	Will grow on heavy clay soils, on acidic soils, and in wetter environments.	Will do well on poorer, lighter land. Drought resistant.
Diseases	Prone to diseases, pests, and fungal infections, including eyespot, take-all, cereal cyst nematode, and mildew. New ones discovered every year.	Eyespot, take-all, cereal cyst nematode, and mildew.	Not susceptible to take-all. Fruit flies can be destructive, and slugs can be a problem.	Few disease problems.
Work involved	Plowing and harrowing. Sowing in autumn or spring. Harvesting in middle or late summer. Weed control.	As for wheat, but seedbeds need to be "as light as a feather." More care and attention needed than with any other cereal crop.	Cultivation as for wheat. Winter oats must be sown well before winter starts.	Prepare seedbed as for other cereals. Sow two or three weeks before winter wheat. Rye is the first of the cereals to ripen.
Yield	1.6 tons per acre (4 tonnes per ha). *Cracked wheat*	1.4 tons per acre (3.5 tonnes per ha).	1.7 tons per acre (4.2 tonnes per ha).	1.8 tons per acre (4.4 tonnes per ha). *Thatching straw*
Uses	Milling for bread- or pasta-making, or for animal feed. Long-strawed varieties also good for thatching.	The best barley is sold for malting to make beer, while other grades are used as an animal feed.	Useful as a livestock feed. Organically grown oats are always in healthy demand among millers.	Can be grown as a green crop for grazing. Also in demand for crispbread. Straw can be used as thatch.

a thick, sticky clay, for although the weather may be perfect for planting, there is a risk that wet autumn soil will prevent you from ever taking a harvest. Over the generations, farmers have worked out what grows best in the area in which they live, and that is why it is good to look carefully at your neighbors' fields.

If your neighbors are commercial farmers, they will be tied by the third factor, profitability. For them, the most important question is whether a crop can be sold for good financial rewards. This is not a game the home farmer has to play. In fact, selling cereals on a small scale is often more trouble than it is worth, and you are better off growing the crops you *need* in order to run your farm, rather than those that you think will bring in the most money. So grow oats or barley because they are staple foods of horses, cattle, and sheep, and ignore the fact that wheat is more profitable. For you, profitability is an option, no more.

> " *For commercial farmers, the question is whether a crop can be sold for good financial rewards. This is not a game the home farmer has to play.* "

Triticale	Potato	Rice	Corn	Sunflowers
Cross betwen wheat and rye. Yields nearly as high as for wheat, but crop is as tolerant as rye. Deserves consideration.	Good as a cash crop or for home consumption. On suitable soils, an easy crop to grow.	A staple food, but suitable only for parts of the world where there is plenty of rain or adequate irrigation water from rivers or other sources.	Requires high levels of soil fertility. Controlling weeds can be the main difficulty in organic-farming systems.	Grown for its seeds, which can be crushed for oil or eaten whole.
Few as yet. Consult a local farm supplier.	Early and maincrop (autumn) varieties. Choose from hundreds for the best disease protection in your area.	Long-, medium-, or round-grain varieties. Some are suitable for lowland areas, others for highlands.	Varieties include sweet corn (see p. 100), popping corn, and those grown to produce other foodstuffs. There are also many varieties for livestock feed.	Consult a seed merchant for varieties suitable for your district.
Will tolerate poorer soils than those required by wheat.	Likes rich, moist, acidic soils. Needs plenty of well-rotted manure.	Needs a five-month stretch with temperatures at 68°F (20°C) or above.	Needs deep, rich, easily worked loams.	Thrives on almost any soil provided it has plenty of sun and warmth.
Few disease problems. Less susceptible than wheat.	Discourage potato cyst nematode by leaving four or five years between crops. Potatoes are also prone to potato blight.		Prone to stalk rot, a fungal infection. Not susceptible to the same diseases as straw crops and can provide a useful break between them.	Extremely resistant plant. The greatest threat comes from birds, immediately after sowing and before harvesting.
As for other cereal crops.	Needs deeply worked, well-manured soils. Plant when soil has warmed in spring. Harvest in autumn.	Cultivation, transplanting, keeping water at right levels.	Applications of manure may have to be made to growing crop. Sow in late spring when soil has warmed. Weed control needed between rows.	Sow as soon as frosts are finished. To prevent bird damage, you may have to net your crop in the weeks before harvesting.
Almost as high as wheat.	12 tons per acre (30 tonnes per ha).	8 tons per acre (20 tonnes per ha) fresh weight.	1.6 tons per acre (4 tonnes per ha) of ears, but about 20 tons per acre (50 tonnes per ha) of greenstuff.	A generous plant. Lots of it in return for little work.
High in crude protein, so makes a good replacement for concentrates in animal feed. Can be grazed.	Food for humans or for pigs and cattle. If you feed potatoes to pigs or cattle, chop them first.	For human consumption.	Livestock varieties may be fed green or as silage. Dried ears store for long periods.	The seeds can be crushed for oil, and the residue fed to pigs. They are also in demand as a health food.

Shock of triticale

Harvesting rice

Assessing the soil

SOIL IS ALIVE, bursting with vigor and vitality, all of which you must harness. Sometimes soil gets sick and needs treatment, but you cannot prescribe the medicine until you understand the patient. The first step in understanding your soil, and what it will be good for, is to walk over it. In some places, it will stick to your boots like grim death; in others, it will be as loose as sand on the beach. After judging it with your feet, try a chemical analysis. You may be able to make use of your findings and correct any harmful imbalances, for the good of your land and crops.

VARIATIONS IN THE SOIL
In this field on a big American farm, you can see dark streaks from left to right. These indicate small variations in the composition of the soil from one spot to the next. When the crop grows and ripens, these variations may be reflected in the quality of the plants.

HOW DEEP IS THE TOPSOIL?

Topsoil is the raw material with which you have to work. If you are lucky, your topsoil will be good and deep, but you might find rock just below the surface. Either way, the fertility is in the topsoil, and has been put there over centuries by the rotting of plant and animal remains.

The topsoil is the powerhouse of the farm: miraculous chemical interactions occur here, making nutrients available to the growing plants. It is worthy of the highest respect, and it has ways of dealing with farmers who ill-treat it. Never turn the soil to such a depth that subsoil is brought to the surface, or you are burying your greatest asset.

CLAY SOILS

It is one of the cruelest things about farming that the most fertile soils can also be the most difficult to work.

Soils containing clay are heavy and sticky when wet, and hard as iron when dry. They are dreadful to work with: it is hard enough to walk across the field in the rain without leaving a boot behind, and it is impossible to plant potatoes in clay soils. But they are packed full of plant nutrients, and if you are working on a garden scale, you can tame them over a period of time by mixing in well-rotted manure and other organic matter, a little more each year.

SOIL TYPES

Clay

The particles in clay are very small, and so water does not easily drain from soils like these. It makes for a heavy soil, damp to the touch and "cold," in that it takes longer to warm up in spring. But clay soils are highly fertile and with the right choice of crops, such as cereals, can be rewarding.

Medium loam

This type of soil gives you the best of all worlds. It has the fertility of a clay without the "heaviness." It has none of the chilly feeling of a handful of clay, nor is it rough to the touch like a sandy soil. You will be able to work a soil like this in almost any weather, within reason, throughout the year.

Peat

Providing that peat soils do not become waterlogged, they can be highly fertile, and thus are a vegetable grower's dream. Peat soils are usually black because of the large proportions of organic matter that they contain. They also tend to be acidic, and for some crops you will have to add lime to correct this.

Sandy

Sandy soils always feel dry, and if you rub the soil between your fingers, it feels, as you might expect, like sandpaper. The chief problem with this type of soil is that because water drains from it so easily, so do nutrients, and to get good crops you will have to add large quantities of organic matter.

Calcareous

A bedrock consisting of limestone or chalk gives a calcareous topsoil, which in layman's terms is a soil rich in calcium carbonate. It is usually thin and tends to lose water easily, which in turn leads to a loss of nutrients. Soils of this type are alkaline, a condition that is difficult to correct. They are often stony too.

SANDY SOILS

Unlike clay soils, these are a joy to dig and work, and easily maintain a fine tilth. Alas, their fertility washes away with every shower of rain, and you will put much effort into keeping it high. On most farms, the soils will prove to lie somewhere between the two extremes of clay and sand (see facing page, below).

ACIDIC OR ALKALINE?

Test every plot or field at least once a year. Just after harvest is a good time, so that any corrections can be made ahead of the next season. You need to know the pH of your soil – a precise measure of how acidic or alkaline the soil is. There are simple tests, as described on the right, or you can send a sample to a laboratory to clear up any doubts.

If the soil is too acidic or alkaline, this hinders the release of minerals and other nutrients from organic matter, stunting crop growth. If you can assess the soil correctly and understand how to correct extremes, this maximizes the range of crops that you can grow.

One substance that makes soil acidic is peat; another is fresh animal manure. There are some situations in which land grows increasingly acidic – for example, when a meadow is overgrazed. The animals eat the turf down to the roots, at the same time putting down a layer of

TESTING SOIL pH

TEST A REPRESENTATIVE sample of soil. This may mean gathering several samples from various points across a field or garden and mixing them. Simple pH testing kits are available and are generally accurate enough for a home farmer's purposes. With most kits, you add chemicals to a soil sample, and compare the resulting color against a chart. Be careful not to unearth any dog bones in the process.

manure, which contains acid. The acid upsets the chemistry of the soil and the health of the community of organisms it contains. In normal health, the turf and soil organisms together are able to break down this amount of acidity, but under the pressure of overgrazing they can't.

SOIL MAINTENANCE

Making acidic land more alkaline is a straightforward matter. Buy lime from a farm supplier and spread it on the land in the way specified by the supplier. For some other chemical imbalances, such as potassium deficiency, there is a chemical remedy, in this case rock potash. There

are other organic fertilizers (see p. 101) and they are effective, although they are too expensive to apply on a field scale.

Making alkaline land more acidic is a much more difficult proposition. Fresh manure and compost are acidic, but a properly cultivated soil has no difficulty breaking down acidity, so you have to add more manure on a regular basis.

On a garden scale, you can build a "soil box" (see p. 105) to isolate a bed from a strongly alkaline environment. Even this works well only if you import an acidic soil. In the box, the soil is to some extent protected from alkaline water running off the surrounding soil.

TESTING BY HAND

TRY TO MAKE A BALL
Scoop up a handful of soil, and right away you will notice how heavy or light it feels and whether it is cold to the touch. Roll it between your hands and try to make a ball.

LIGHT, SANDY SOIL
This soil will not play the game, no matter how hard you work at it. The ball will always crumble and fall apart because the grains of soil are so large. The soil will feel quite warm to the touch.

GOOD SOIL
This intermediate soil is the best for most purposes. You might not get a perfect ball with it because organic matter gives it quite a coarse, open texture, but it will hold some shape.

HEAVY CLAY SOIL
A heavy clay soil will form a ball as soon as you roll it and will hold together whatever you do to it. An hour in the sun and this cold, damp soil would be baked as hard as a cannonball.

Crop rotation

GROW THE SAME CROP on the same piece of land year after year, and soon there will be no crop at all. The land will be exhausted and drained of nutrients, and the soil will be riddled with pests and diseases, which will flourish on the constant supply of their favorite food. Admittedly, all these problems can be solved by applying synthetic fertilizers and pesticides, but this is no remedy for the home farmer, who does not seek to crack every farming nut with a sledgehammer. Use a properly planned crop rotation, and most of these problems will never arise in the first place.

PLOWING AFTER ALFALFA
Plow the alfalfa stubble under after the last hay of the season has been cut. Leaving the roots of legumes such as this in the ground allows the nitrates they contain to be slowly released.

LEGUME FODDER CROP
Some legumes are cut for hay, as is the alfalfa crop shown here; others, such as white clover, are grazed. Peas and beans, too, are legumes, and they are harvested as food for humans or animals.

TYPICAL PLAN
This is a typical rotation, but you will have to devise one to suit your farm. The principle of all rotations is the same: hungry crops are followed by ones that replenish the land.

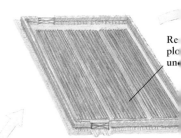

Re
plo
un

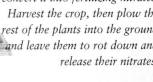

Legume crop

STAGE ONE – LEGUMES
Bacteria in the roots of legumes take nitrogen from the air and convert it into fertilizing nitrates. Harvest the crop, then plow the rest of the plants into the ground and leave them to rot down and release their nitrates.

STAGE FOUR – POTATOES
Potatoes and other root crops are hungry feeders and will relish the highly fertile soil left after the plowing of the ley. Potatoes should not be grown in the same field within five years. Follow roots with legumes to replenish the soil again.

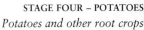

Residue plowed under in autumn

GROWING POTATOES
Potatoes need rich soil, but the elaborate method of plowing and sowing, and the hilling up of the crop, ensure that weeds have little chance of taking advantage of the good feeding.

Potatoes planted in spring

VIRTUES OF ROTATION

CROP ROTATION is about keeping the soil alive and allowing the farmer to utilize to the full the natural methods that are at his or her disposal for maintaining the fertility of the farm. The principle is similar to that of livestock rotation (see p. 156): pests and diseases have a hard time surviving because the hosts they depend on (your crops or livestock) keep moving on. Also, each phase of crop rotation alters and improves the chemistry and condition of the soil.

HARVESTING A CEREAL CROP
Cereals will lap up the nitrogen left by the legumes. You can sow cereals in autumn or leave the plowed land bare until spring, so that winter frosts can break the soil down to a finer tilth.

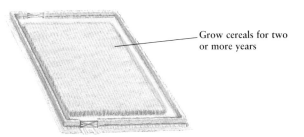

Grow cereals for two or more years

STAGE TWO – CEREALS
Cereals need nitrogen to produce high yields, and the nitrogen left by the preceding legumes will feed them well. You might plan a series of different cereal crops: for example, greedy wheat first, followed by rye or oats.

Harrow and undersow with pasture grasses in final year of phase

STAGE THREE – PASTURE
This is known as the ley phase. Animals can graze the pasture, and their droppings will enrich the resting land. Plow in the grass at the end of the phase, adding to the organic matter in the soil. You may also be able to take the occasional cut of hay.

Once the cereal is cut, the field soon becomes a meadow

UNDERSOWN PASTURE GRASSES
In the last year of stage two, sow grasses when the cereal is 12 in (30 cm) high. Initially, they will grow slowly, but once the cereal has been harvested, they will form a meadow in six weeks.

Grass plowed under in autumn has time to rot and release its nutrients

PRODUCTIVE PASTURE
You can leave land under pasture for several years if this suits the needs of the farm. The livestock are acting as manure spreaders, and are increasing the fertility of the land just by being there.

Nourishing the soil

ALL FARMING IS ROBBERY. You are stealing precious fertility from the soil every time you harvest a crop, and if you take no trouble to replace that fertility, the soil will soon stop playing the game and you will have no crops at all. There is much public condemnation of those who are cruel to animals, but cruelty to soil is nothing to be proud of either.

Modern farming nourishes soil with manufactured fertilizers. While these add nutrients, they do nothing to improve the structure of the soil or to help valuable organisms to multiply. Soil is a living thing and has to be kept alive to be healthy. How can we hope to grow healthy plants if the soil we plant them in is basically sick or dead?

The basic ingredient of the best fertilizer is animal manure, and even if you have only one goat or a few chickens, their litter should never be regarded as waste. Indeed, it is among the most valuable products on the farm. If you don't have animals, other good fertilizers you can use are vegetable compost (see p. 94) or a green manure.

GOOD SOIL
Worms know good soil when they find it. Counting earthworms is a good way to monitor the changing health of the soil.

BUILDING A MANURE PILE

"BUILDING" IS THE important word here. A manure pile is not just a dump. It has to be constructed so that it will not dry out too much and so that rain will not wash away the nutrients. Air is needed too, or the composting process will not take place.

YARD STRAW
Horses have overwintered in this yard. The mixture of straw and dung will be dug out in spring to form the basis of a rich compost.

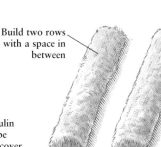

THE CURING PROCESS
Heat is generated when organic material rots. Steam is an indication that your manure pile is healthy and that the composting process is well under way.

TWO METHODS OF CONSTRUCTION

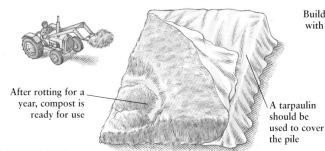

After rotting for a year, compost is ready for use

A tarpaulin should be used to cover the pile

Build two rows with a space in between

Merge the rows and mix inner and outer layers

METHOD ONE
This is the "make it into a big pile and hope it works" way. Often it will, but the composting will be variable and so will the resulting compost. Cover the pile with a tarpaulin. If it is left uncovered, there is a danger of nutrients being washed away, and the resulting concentrated runoff can be toxic.

METHOD TWO
Make two long rows of manure and leave them to rot down. After they have cured for a few months, break each row open and turn the contents together, forming a new row in a central position. By breaking up and mixing outer and inner layers, you create a more uniformly rotted, better-quality compost.

APPLYING COMPOSTED MANURE

THIS IS HARD WORK, and if you have a large area to cover you will need a mechanical spreader. You should be able to find a dealer who rents them. Time your manure spreading carefully. If you spread it in the autumn and leave it lying, the rain will wash away nutrients. If you spread compost on grassland, the ideal time is spring, when the growing grass can feed on it. For plowing in, spread the manure just before you plow.

COMPOSTED MANURE READY TO DIG IN
A conical heap of rich, dark composted manure has been placed in this garden, ready to be spread between plants. It has been in the manure pile for a year. The curing, or composting, process has broken down the manure and given it a fine, crumbly texture.

USING A MANURE SPREADER
A mechanical spreader (above) gives an even, controllable spread of manure. A farmer with a shovel (right) can do the job just as well, but with much more sweat. The spread will not be as even, but the task will have been accomplished at far less cost.

YOUNG MUSTARD
This green manure grows very quickly and will make plenty of organic matter. It is an excellent weed supressant too.

READY TO PLOW
Once this field of mustard has set seed, you may have problems getting rid of it. Plow it under now. This is a good green manure to plant before a potato crop, because it will rid the soil of wireworms.

GREEN MANURE

THE IDEA OF A GREEN manure is to plant a fast-growing, green, leafy crop, then plow it under and leave it to rot. This puts the nutrients stored in the plants back into the soil. The stems and leaves add bulk, which improves soil drainage and aeration, both of which are good for biological activity in the soil. If you use a legume as a green manure, it puts more nitrogen into the soil (see p. 134).

Leaving land bare is asking for weeds to flourish and nutrients to be lost. A green manure can be used to cover the ground, binding the soil together and competing with weeds. Crops used include buckwheat, vetches, mustard, field beans, clovers, alfalfa, and grasses.

Plowing

The coulter, share, and moldboard

GOOD PLOWING, it has been wisely said, is the basis of good farming. It is the job of the plow to turn the soil, allowing the freshly turned earth to be exposed to wind, rain, sun, and air; burying the weeds and any remains of the previous crop; and also placing any fertilizer or manure where the roots of the crop can best get at it. It is the job of the plowman to ensure that the plow turns the field evenly, leaving no great dips or lumps, and to the correct depth for the subsequent crop.

Plowing, whether by horse or tractor, is one of the most difficult farming skills to learn, but one of the most satisfying. You are turning an old field into a new one, and time spent developing your skill will be well rewarded. Styles of plowing, and the method of cutting the first furrows, vary according to local custom. I have described the process in the way I learned to do it – and it works. There is no better way to learn the ways of the land, and the feel of the soil, than to follow a plow.

HORSE OR TRACTOR?

THE PRINCIPLES of plowing are the same, whether you use a basic tractor (see p. 118) or horses. Both are suited to plowing in "lands," as shown on the facing page. An advantage of the tractor is that it can draw a two-furrow plow, as on the facing page, or even a three-furrow. Horses are valued for their quietness, companionship, and reliability.

ACTION OF THE PLOW

THE CUTTING ACTION OF THE PLOW is achieved by three components. The coulter cuts vertically into the ground. The share cuts horizontally along the bottom of this cut. These two cuts loosen a slice of earth, which is lifted and turned by the moldboard, or bottom, as the plow moves forward.

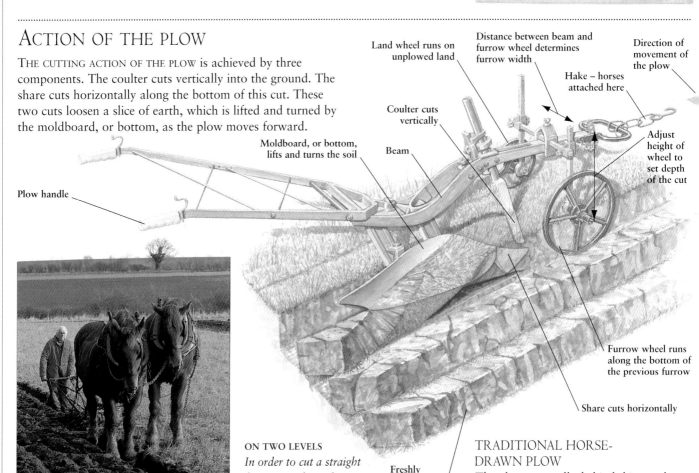

Plow handle

Moldboard, or bottom, lifts and turns the soil

Coulter cuts vertically

Beam

Land wheel runs on unplowed land

Distance between beam and furrow wheel determines furrow width

Hake – horses attached here

Direction of movement of the plow

Adjust height of wheel to set depth of the cut

Furrow wheel runs along the bottom of the previous furrow

Share cuts horizontally

Freshly turned earth

ON TWO LEVELS
In order to cut a straight furrow, one horse has to walk in the previous furrow while the other walks on unplowed land.

TRADITIONAL HORSE-DRAWN PLOW
The plowman walks behind this two-horse plow to keep it straight. Several parts of the plow, such as the wheels and coulter, can be adjusted for the perfect cut.

PLOWING IN LANDS

UNLESS YOU USE A REVERSIBLE PLOW (see p. 141), your plow will "throw" the soil in only one direction. Therefore, the plow must go around its work, tracing a series of widening rectangles around a central ridge. Eventually, the increasing width of the plowed area will mean that more time is spent turning than plowing, so the field is divided into a series of manageable areas called "lands," each with a central ridge.

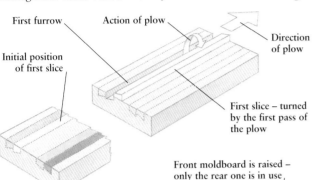

First furrow
Action of plow
Direction of plow
Initial position of first slice
First slice – turned by the first pass of the plow

Direction of plow
Action of plow
Third slice
Third furrow

3 **THE THIRD FURROW** *Turn to the right, set the furrow wheel against the wall of the first furrow, and cut the third furrow alongside the first.*

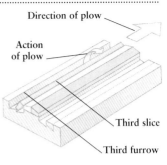

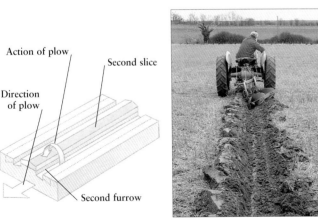

Front moldboard is raised – only the rear one is in use

1 **THE FIRST FURROW** *Decide on the direction in which to plow the field. Up- and downhill is usually better than across. Set marker sticks parallel to one edge of the field, at opposite ends, and use these to guide the first furrow. Adjust your plow so that only a shallow furrow is drawn. Draw the first furrow straight. A good, straight start is half the battle.*

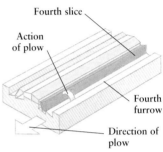

Fourth slice
Action of plow
Fourth furrow
Direction of plow

4 **THE FOURTH FURROW** *Turn again; cut a fourth furrow to complete the ridge (or crown). Continue plowing around and around the ridge, until the land reaches its full width.*

Action of plow
Second slice
Direction of plow
Second furrow

2 **THE SECOND FURROW** *At the end of the first furrow, turn around (to the right) to point back toward the end of the field you have just come from. Adjust the height of the plow so that the second furrow is a bit deeper. Position your plow so that the*

soil it throws up against the first furrow meets it, and buries any grass or stubble in between.

After completing this furrow, you will need to set the plow a little deeper at the end of each furrow until you are plowing at the desired depth.

5 **SIZE OF LAND** *A good distance between ridges on average soil might be 65 ft (20 m). Mark out the field carefully before starting, in order to avoid tiny corner pieces, called "short work," which can be frustrating.*

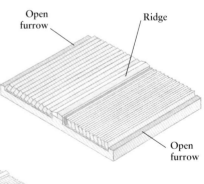

Open furrow
Ridge
Open furrow
First land
Second land
Third land
Fourth land

6 **THE FINISHED FIELD** *Your finished field will show ridges and furrows, which should be neither too high nor too deep. For the purpose of demonstration, the ridges in this drawing are closer, and the lands smaller, than would be usual in real life.*

Plows

THE FUNDAMENTALS OF PLOWING have been set out on the previous pages – what kind of implement a plow is, and how it works. Here is a small selection of the varieties of plow that have evolved on farms around the world, for use with horses or simple tractors. One obvious problem with the basic plow is that it throws its furrow in only one direction; the solution to this is the reversible plow, of which there are several types, drawing one or more furrows and pulled by horse or tractor. Another problem is that while it may be deeply satisfying to follow a horse-drawn plow, you may not wish to walk those miles, and North American farmers have cracked this one, too.

SULKY PLOW
Styles of horse-drawn plow vary around the world. In Europe it is usual to walk behind the plow, but in the United States the sit-on, or sulky, plow is more common.

The plowman can make adjustments to the plow without leaving the seat

TRACTOR-DRAWN PLOWS

TRACTOR-DRAWN PLOWS work at faster speeds than those pulled by horses, and can draw more furrows at once. If the land is quite sandy, even a smallish tractor can plow three furrows at a time. Modern farming now demands such efficiency that plows cutting as many as 14 furrows can be seen at work on the most technically advanced farms, but the home farmer would do better to revive a plow from a simpler, less intensive age. Tractor-drawn plows are hitched to the tractor by one of two methods. Early plows are simply pulled, but later plows take advantage of the tractor's hydraulic system.

MOUNTED PLOW
Here the plow and tractor are effectively one unit, the depth at which the plow cuts being controlled from the driving seat by use of the hydraulics. Ideal for the home farmer.

REVERSIBLE PLOW
The two sets of shares on this plow are used alternately; the plow is turned over after each furrow. One set "throws" (turns the soil) to the right and the other to the left.

TRAILED PLOW
All the adjustments to this plow can be made from the seat of the tractor, but as the plow is nonreversible, the field must be set out in lands (see p. 139). The wheels determine the depth of the furrow, and make it easier to turn the plow around at the end of each furrow.

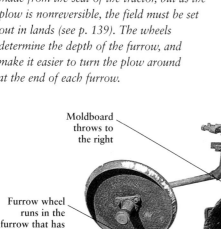

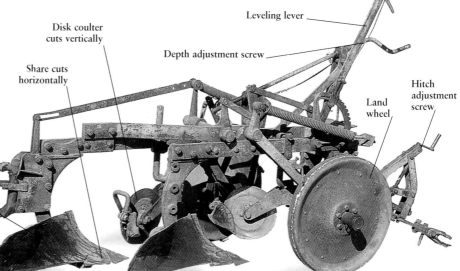

Disk coulter cuts vertically

Share cuts horizontally

Leveling lever

Depth adjustment screw

Hitch adjustment screw

Land wheel

Moldboard throws to the right

Furrow wheel runs in the furrow that has just been cut

HORSE-DRAWN PLOWS

LIGHTER THAN TRACTOR PLOWS, and usually drawing only one furrow at a time, horse-drawn plows come in a variety of designs to suit the land and the furrow to be cut. At one time, a manufacturer would offer 20 or more moldboard designs for any one plow. These days, consider yourself lucky to find a decent horse-drawn plow at all. Buy a plow you are happy with, but one that suits your horses as well – you are going to spend many hours together. Before long, your plow will feel like an extension of yourself, and you will not be able to part with it.

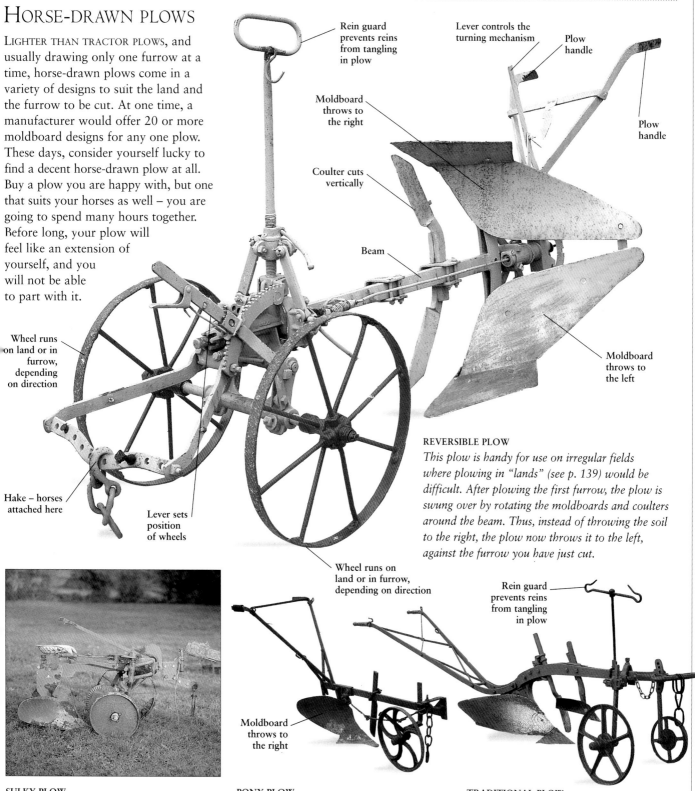

Rein guard prevents reins from tangling in plow

Lever controls the turning mechanism

Plow handle

Plow handle

Moldboard throws to the right

Coulter cuts vertically

Beam

Moldboard throws to the left

Wheel runs on land or in furrow, depending on direction

Hake – horses attached here

Lever sets position of wheels

Wheel runs on land or in furrow, depending on direction

Rein guard prevents reins from tangling in plow

REVERSIBLE PLOW

This plow is handy for use on irregular fields where plowing in "lands" (see p. 139) would be difficult. After plowing the first furrow, the plow is swung over by rotating the moldboards and coulters around the beam. Thus, instead of throwing the soil to the right, the plow now throws it to the left, against the furrow you have just cut.

Moldboard throws to the right

SULKY PLOW

This plow is much favored in the United States. The lever on top lifts the moldboard when turning at the end of a furrow. If you do not relish walking the 11 miles (18 km) it takes to plow 1 acre (0.4 ha), you should consider the sit-on, or sulky, plow.

PONY PLOW

This is a light plow, designed with a reduced draft to enable it to be pulled easily by a pony, a donkey, or a pair if they are lightly built. Do not expect to be able to plow to any great depth with a pony plow, but it is useful for working in confined areas.

TRADITIONAL PLOW

This plow is pulled by two horses, and is the most common horse-drawn plow in Europe. It is capable of deep work on a variety of soils, and in skilled hands produces high-quality results. If you contemplate acquiring only one plow, get one of these.

Making good tilth

THE ONLY SEEDS THAT will grow anywhere belong to weeds – if you want crops, you will have to put some effort into preparing the soil. Making the perfect seedbed, or tilth, is as much a matter of instinct as technique. You have to know not only *how* to do it, but also *when*. I learned this the hard way, by impatiently taking a pair of horses and a harrow to a plowed field at the end of winter, only to find the field so wet that by the time we were halfway across, the horses were up to their knees in mud. If I'd waited a week, it would have been perfect.

Here, I describe two ways of making good tilth. The first is for land that was plowed some months previously. The second is the method you will use if you wish to sow immediately after plowing – or at least within, say, two weeks. You may, of course, be farming a tiny site, where it is practical to make your tilth with spades and rakes. If you are, all this is still relevant: looking at the process on a field scale will give you a clearer understanding of what you are hoping to achieve.

Unplowed land   Freshly plowed land   Harrowed land

FIELD DEMONSTRATION
On a piece of freshly plowed land, you can see the gleam of the cut edges of the furrows; harrowed land has a duller appearance.

PREVIOUSLY PLOWED

FINISH PLOWING before winter, and in spring you will find that the frosts have shattered the big clods of earth, and the wind and the rain have softened what lumps were left. You will have saved on horse feed or tractor diesel, and let the weather do the work for you.

If your field is to lie unsown for any length of time after plowing, run a spring-tine cultivator over the field at two- or three-month intervals during this period. Your land will be in such good condition that a rotary cultivator is powerful enough to make the tilth, with a crumbler roll to finish the job.

1 **SPRING-TINE CULTIVATOR** *This device has other uses in farming, but here it is used to break up soil and remove weeds. It pulls up the underground rhizomes of perennial weeds like quack grass and creeping thistle, leaving them on the surface to wither and die*

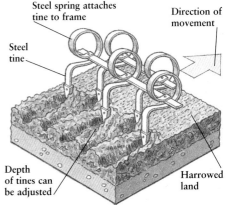

Steel spring attaches tine to frame

Direction of movement

Steel tine

Depth of tines can be adjusted

Harrowed land

in the sun. The cutting depth of the tines is adjustable, making this a versatile implement to have on your farm: in some situations, it can break stubble, for instance.

2 **ROTARY CULTIVATOR** *Some rotary cultivators are small, hand-guided appliances (see p. 114), but on a field scale you will need the tractor-driven version. This machine is powerful, and if you work at too great a depth you may bury the fertile topsoil and bring the less desirable subsoil to the surface. The blades work with a chopping, digging action, and will cut up any weeds that you may have missed in the previous step. A crumbler roller is fixed at the back to consolidate the fine soil of the seedbed, and break any larger clods the rotary cultivator may have left.*

Rotary cultivator   Direction of movement

Crumbler roll

FRESHLY PLOWED

IF CONDITIONS ARE RIGHT, land that has been freshly plowed can be worked into a seedbed almost immediately. The exceptions to this are stiff soils that contain a lot of clay. You need to leave them to stand for a week or two. Light, sandy soils, on the other hand, will succumb to the harrow right away. Again, timing is the key. If the weather is too wet, do not even try.

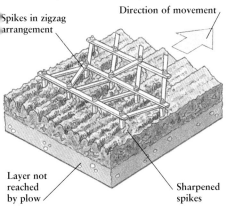

Spikes in zigzag arrangement

Direction of movement

Layer not reached by plow

Sharpened spikes

SPIKE HARROW

This is the simplest, cheapest way of making good tilth after plowing. Spikes are fixed to a frame in a zigzag pattern, so they do not follow each other's path. Each spike parts the soil it passes through, dividing it into two streams, each of which is parted in turn by the next spike. Keep the spikes sharp, and they will cut the clods and crumble them into fine soil. This harrow is ideal for light soil, but may be too small for heavy soils.

DISK HARROW

This is the equivalent of taking a kitchen knife and slicing through the clods. Disk harrows are heavy and need a lot of pulling, which can be hard work for horses.

Pulled behind a tractor, two sets of disk harrows, set one behind the other at different angles, can cut through sizable clods. The angle at which the disks are set will determine the fineness of the tilth.

Disk harrows will not bring up buried material. If you have plowed a field of grass to sow cereals, the last thing you want is the old turf back on the surface again.

Angle of disks can be adjusted

Direction of movement

Layer not reached by plow

Disks cut the soil

ROLLER

Rollers give the finishing touches to tilth. There are two types – the flat roll, shown on the right, and the ribbed roller (also called a Cambridge roll), shown far right. The ribbed roller is more suitable for making good tilth – use it if you can, as a flat roll is prone to causing "capping" (see p. 145).

Getting the timing right is crucial. You will have no success putting the roller over clods that are too wet or too dry. Do your rolling after a shower of rain, while the soil is still drying, and you will often find that the most awkward clods will crumble to dust.

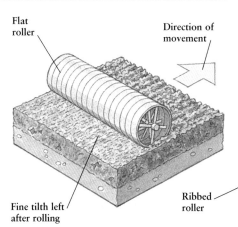

Flat roller

Direction of movement

Fine tilth left after rolling

Ribbed roller

Sowing the seed

Try using a seed fiddle as an alternative to hand sowing

SPREADING SEED ON THE LAND and expecting a crop in return is one of the greatest acts of faith in the farming year. The best you can do for your seed is to minimize the risks to its health. To be able to do that, you have to understand the needs of the seed just as it bursts into life. It needs air, moisture, and food, and it will not germinate if the soil is too cool. The traditional way of testing the soil is to remove your trousers and sit on the land: if it feels cool to you, it will be cool for the seed. Make sure that your seeds have sufficient moisture by sowing after a shower or when rain is forecast. As far as air and food are concerned, the seedbed is the key, for only by close contact with the soil will the seed flourish. If the tilth is too coarse, the gaps between the clods of soil will be large. Small seeds will not touch the soil on all sides and so will be unable to draw enough moisture from it to germinate. Big seeds, such as beans, need a coarse tilth, while tiny seeds, like clover, need crumbs. A fine tilth is well aerated, as the plow and harrows work air into the soil.

SCARING BIRDS

BIRDS ARE THE biggest enemy of newly sown seeds. They wait until the seeds are just about to sprout, when they are at their juiciest, and then strike. Scarecrows work. Construct your scarecrow so that the slightest breeze makes it move or rattle, and your seeds will survive to produce a fine crop.

BROADCAST SOWING

THE SIMPLEST WAY TO SOW your seed is to spread it by hand on a field that you have plowed in autumn and allowed to weather over the winter. The soil will have a fine tilth on top, but the furrows will still be showing. The seed will tend to drop into the furrows, where a pass with a light harrow will cover it.

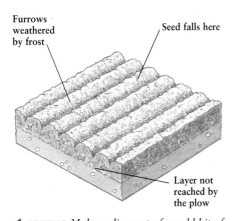

Furrows weathered by frost

Seed falls here

Layer not reached by the plow

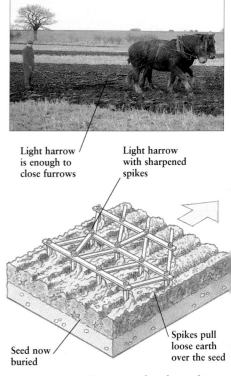

Light harrow is enough to close furrows

Light harrow with sharpened spikes

Seed now buried

Spikes pull loose earth over the seed

1 SOWING *Make a sling out of an old bit of burlap and put it over your shoulder. This will carry the seed. Pick up pinches of seed between the fingers of alternate hands and scatter them as you pace forward. Match the movement of your arms to your stride. If the seed is sown too thickly, the*

yield will be reduced, but with practice, you can achieve an even spread. Expect to take at least 40 years to perfect the technique.

The seed fiddle (shown top left) is more accurate than hand sowing. Pushing the bow back and forth turns a disk. Seeds fall on the disk from a hopper and are spun outward.

2 HARROWING *To ensure that the seed is properly covered and in contact with the soil, harrow it after sowing. A light harrow is all that is needed to pull the tops off the weathered furrow slices and cover the seed. The smaller the seed, the lighter the harrow, or the seed will be buried and lost.*

SEED DRILLING

IF YOU WANT TO SOW a precise amount of seed, in straight rows so that you can eventually hoe between them, then you must use a seed drill. This can be drawn either by a tractor or by horses. A basic, winter-weathered tilth is good enough for broadcast sowing, but seed drilling depends on a very fine, deep tilth, of a standard that can be achieved only with a harrow and rollers (see p. 142).

One person watches to see that the drill is working properly

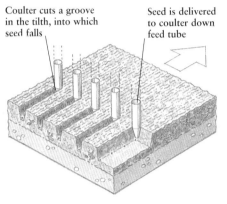

Coulter cuts a groove in the tilth, into which seed falls

Seed is delivered to coulter down feed tube

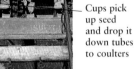

Cups pick up seed and drop it down tubes to coulters

Seed falls through the coulter into the soil

1 DRILLING *Using a seed drill calls for precision. You need to have a very even tilth if every seed is to be buried to the same depth, and you must set the drill up correctly to give the right spacing between the rows and between the seeds themselves.*

Seed drills vary in detail, but the principles are the same. As the drill moves forward, cups dip into the seed hopper, each lifting just one seed at a time. As the cups revolve *farther, each seed drops out and falls down a feed tube, to emerge at soil level through a coulter. The coulter cuts a furrow in the soil, into which the seed drops.*

Thrown-up soil can block the coulters, and if you don't watch carefully for this, you will get gaps between seeds. The greatest embarrassment is to let the drill run out of seed and not notice. Your error will be there for all to see when the seeds sprout!

Roller ensures close contact between seed and soil

Flat roller (not ribbed, see p. 143)

Deeper soil undisturbed by drilling

Lines left by drill contain seeds

2 ROLLING *The roller reduces the tilth to a finer crumb and wraps it around the seed. The danger with a flat roll is that you might "cap" the land, rolling the surface into a smooth crust. When rain falls, the water runs along this "cap" and off the field, instead of soaking in to nourish the seed.*

Cereal harvest

Ripening ears of wheat

TOWARD THE END OF SUMMER, you start to walk through your field of ripening cereal, nerving yourself for the final, but most crucial, task. *When* to harvest is one of the most difficult decisions of the farming year. Here's the way that I decide, and though crude, it works. For barley, wheat, and rye, break up an ear of grain in your hand. Split a grain with your thumbnail. If it is milky or cheesy in texture, it is not ready; if cut now, it will get moldy in storage. Wait until it is hard, like a nut. However, if oats are left to ripen for too long, the oats fall out and are lost, and the straw becomes too fibrous for stock to chew. Avoid this by cutting the oats early, and allowing the grains to ripen in the sheaves. If you want wheat straw for thatching, harvest when the straw is still quite green, at the expense of the cereal.

READY TO CUT

TAKE A FEW EARS of corn and rub them between the palms of your hands to release the grains. You can test it either with a thumbnail or with your teeth: if the grain won't split, it's ready.

CUTTING THE CROP

USING A COMBINE HARVESTER is the speediest, but also the most wasteful, way to harvest a crop. It renders the straw useless for anything other than bedding and throws away the chaff, which can provide valuable bulk in an animal's diet.

On a small plot, you can harvest by hand with a scythe or a sickle, but on large plots this is a job only for heroes. For home farmers, the binder still has virtues; if you can find one in good condition buy it, no matter how old. Mine is over 50 years old, and is as good as the day it was made. A binder is an ingenious machine that cuts the cereal, bundles it, and ties a string around it, producing a sheaf. It is gentle with the crop, but is a complex mechanism, and can try your patience.

CUTTING BY SCYTHE
If you are using a scythe or a sickle, expect to cut no more than ½ acre (0.2 ha) a day. This scythe has a cradle to catch the cut wheat, making it easier to bundle into sheaves.

HARVESTING WITH HORSES
Hauling a binder is very hard work for horses. Work them for two hours, and rest them for two hours. Keep a spare cutter knife sharpened, and change knives once an hour. At the same time, oil the machine all around. Expect both you and the horses to have trouble keeping cool.

TYING AND SHOCKING

IF IT IS CUT BY HAND, the cereal has to be gathered up into bundles, called sheaves, which are tied and shocked. Shocking involves leaning eight to ten sheaves against one another to form a tunnel. This allows air and sun to finish drying and ripening the cereal before it is taken to be stored in a stack.

1 MAKING THE ROPE *Make a rope by tightly twisting five long, strong straws together. If the straw is brittle, try watering it with a can to soften it.*

2 TYING THE SHEAF *Gather together a bundle of stalks at your feet, and tie the straw rope around it. Then twist the rope around itself and tuck in the end.*

3 STARTING A SHOCK *Carry a sheaf under each arm. Then in a swinging movement, bring the cut ends firmly down at your feet, at the same time pushing the heads together.*

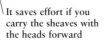
It saves effort if you carry the sheaves with the heads forward

4 FINISHING A SHOCK *Add more pairs of sheaves, pressing the heads together but ensuring that the bottoms are wide enough apart to allow the free flow of drying air.*

Occasional showers will do little damage to well-built shocks

CARTING AND STACKING

THE CUT CEREAL should stand in the field until it is fully dry and ripe before carting. Oats, by tradition, should be left to "hear the church bells three times." In other words, they should be left in the shocks for at least two weeks. Rye, wheat, and barley can be carted much sooner.

Select a site for the stack. If you plan to use a threshing machine (see p. 148), the site must be accessible to this piece of heavy equipment.

CARTING
Choose a dry day to cart, with a fresh wind if possible, to remove the final traces of moisture from the sheaves. Build the loads up carefully. It is not unusual to lose a load if the cart hits a rut.

STACKING
This is a great art. Build high at the center, with a slope to the sides for the rain to drain down. Your first stacks will look pretty shapeless. Ten harvests later, they might start to look decent.

THATCHING
Thatch the stack when it has settled into its final shape. Do not cover it with plastic sheeting, or it will sweat and get moldy. A good thatch keeps the weather out, but lets out moisture too.

After the harvest

THERE IS A TRAP into which it is easy to fall. You must not assume that because you have taken your crop all the way from seed to harvest, the work is done and you can forget about it. It is only *after* the harvest, when you have turned ears of cereal into food for yourself or for your livestock, that you can consider the work done. I write this from bitter experience. I once grew a field of oats, harvested them, and built the sheaves into a fine stack, only to find, six months later, that rats had eaten every grain. Assuming you have a harvest, you run fewer risks of disaster in the next stage – threshing and winnowing. Finally, you must mill your grain, or have it milled, if you want flour or animal feed.

HAND THRESHING AND WINNOWING

1 THRESHING *Bring the flail down firmly and repeatedly on the straw. Pause to check the ears from time to time. Thresh until all the grains have been removed. This job is best done by two people, swinging their flails alternately.*

Flail is made from hazel poles

Leather joint

2 WINNOWING *Scoop up the mixture of cereal, chaff, and broken straw. Either throw it into the air or let it run between your fingers. The breeze will take away the chaff, and the cereal will drop at your feet.*

HANG ON TO YOUR CEREALS

It is very difficult to keep rats and mice away from your harvest, especially in winter when the cereals are in storage. A stack provides an ideal home for mice and rats – it is warm and snug, with the food laid on. What more could a rodent ask for? There are poisons and there are traps, and the best of luck with them. Then there are dogs, and some brave cats, that will face a rat. Encourage owls, which will devour mice. If you are interested in natural solutions, such as owls or cats, avoid poisons, or you may kill the wrong target.

The best method of all is to keep the rats and mice out in the first place. Store your threshed cereals in rat-proof bins, or surround a stack with fine mesh *as soon as you have built it.* Word spreads quickly in the vermin world.

THRESHING THE GRAIN

For a small crop, cut by scythe or binder (see p. 146), you have a choice of ways to thresh. Find a threshing machine – an antique device that needs at least ten strong people to run it efficiently – or, if you want to develop muscles you never knew you had, make a flail and thresh your cereal that way. A flail is a simple device, as ancient as farming itself, made of two strong sticks joined by a hinge of leather or rope. Lay the unthreshed stalks on a clean sheet on a hard surface and hit, and hit, and hit. If the cereal is ripe, it will come away easily. Remove the straw, and there is your harvest.

STORING CEREALS

RIPE GRAINS have a moisture content of up to 15% by weight, so if you store your cereals where air cannot circulate, they will rot. Use a bin built of fine mesh, which allows air to pass through, but keeps out vermin. Check the temperature regularly by pushing a metal rod into the middle of the bin. Take the rod out after a few minutes: if the tip is warm, the cereal has begun to rot. You must turn the cereal with a shovel immediately, allowing fresh air to circulate through it.

WINNOWING AND SIEVING

There will be a large amount of debris, called chaff, both from the straw and from the husks that enclosed the grains. To remove this, wait for a breezy day and spread out your sheet again. Throw the results of the flailing into the air and watch the breeze blow away the light chaff, leaving clean cereal to drop to the ground. Do this several times, then sieve the cereal, and you should have a crop as clean as any machine could manage. Flailing and winnowing make excellent excuses for a party, which eases the burden considerably.

GRINDING FLOUR

To take a crop of homegrown wheat and see it all the way through from seed to a loaf of bread, having done all the intermediate stages yourself, is a source of endless satisfaction. And in these days of food additives, it is a great source of reassurance as well.

It is pleasant to do your milling in your own kitchen. With a hand grinder (see p. 168), it will take you about a quarter of an hour to get enough wheat to make a loaf of bread. You can also get electric grinders, which are faster. Whichever way you do this, there will not be the slightest doubt that what you have made is whole-meal flour: there is no part of the wheat that is not in the flour. It will make a strong, tasty loaf.

If you want a finer flour, say for cake making, then you must grind with the plates of the grinder pressing more tightly against each other, which will be much harder work. Incidentally, this is the time when you find out whether the crop was truly ripe when you harvested it. Dry, hard grains are much easier to grind than unripe ones, which will clog the grinding plates and make it a hard-won loaf of bread.

I used to take my wheat harvest to a windmill, restored by an enthusiast, and watch the huge stones, and the wind, do the work for me. Although you can make your own white flour by using fine sieves to remove the brown bran, a miller is better equipped to do this, and it will not take long. If he is an honest man, he will bag up the bran, so that you can feed it to the horses.

MILLING FOR LIVESTOCK

It was once common to fling unthreshed sheaves of oats to cattle and let them grind them with their teeth. Oat straw is almost as nutritious as hay: why bother to separate the oats from the straw, only to reunite them in the trough later?

It is, however, much easier for an animal to digest cereals if the grains have been broken open, by being rolled or ground. For cattle or sheep, a roller mill produces a first-class feed. The roller mill works on the same principle as a mangle – cereal grains are cracked or crushed, depending on the setting of the rollers between which they pass.

For some stock, rolled cereals are too coarse – they will go through untouched and be wasted. Cereals for these animals are put through a grinding mill. This is the kind of mill we are used to seeing in the form of a windmill: it grinds grain to a flour between revolving stones. Barley for pigs has to be ground finely. Chickens will peck at whole grains, but for efficient digestion they, too, need grain that has been properly ground.

GRAIN FOR GRINDING
Cereal grains have two protective layers: the husk, which is taken off in threshing, and the bran, which is kept when making whole-meal flour or removed to make white flour.

MILLING ANIMAL FEEDS

Hopper holds grain
before milling

Rollers can be
adjusted to
produce coarse
or fine feeds

ROLLING MILL
Cereals pass between rollers that crush them or lightly crack them, according to the setting of the controls. This is not the same as a grinding mill, in which the cereals are rubbed between metal plates to produce a finer, flourlike feed.

COARSE SETTING
This wheat has been milled with the rollers on a light setting. This simply cracks the grains, making them easier for animals to digest.

Growing rice

RICE WILL GROW at altitudes of up to 10,000 ft (about 3,000 m) – as it does in the Himalayas; more commonly, it grows in swampy regions at sea level, especially near river mouths. It can be grown in a wide range of different situations, but it has very specific needs. It must have high temperatures to flourish, and needs more hours of sunshine than other cereals. Famously, it also needs a lot of water: unless the rainfall is truly of rain-forest proportions, you have to flood the rice field with water. As a result, rice growing is limited to a well-defined geographic range. If you have the right location, you may be relieved to know that rice does not have to be part of a crop rotation: there are recorded examples of rice having been grown in the same field for 2,000 years.

RICE VARIETIES

RICE GROWS in many countries and in many varieties, which include long-, medium-, and short- (or round-) grain rices. Rice is milled to produce either brown rice, complete with the bran (see p.148), or white rice without it.

Long-grain rice   Short-grain rice

HOW TO GROW RICE

INVEST TIME AND LABOR in creating two paddy fields – a small nursery field, and a larger one for the crop itself. Unless you can convert a pond or another site, dig out soil to lower the surface. You will have to build up the banks and cut water channels; the result is a long-term site, so it is worth it. Start each season by plowing or digging, to clear the ground of weeds. There will be little chance to do it once the rice is planted.

JAPANESE HOME FARM RICE FIELD
These rice seedlings are growing well; soon the farmer will raise the water level – half-way up the stems is a good depth. The mature plants form a canopy, reducing heat loss from the water at night and helping to maintain the high temperatures rice needs to ripen.

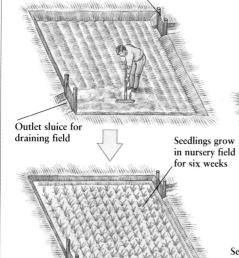

Inlet sluice for flooding field

Outlet sluice for draining field

Seedlings grow in nursery field for six weeks

Seedlings are transplanted by hand

Ripe rice ready for harvesting

1 RICE NURSERY *Work the nursery bed to a fine tilth and clear it of weeds. Plant the seed into warm soil. Then open the sluice and flood the nursery, thus providing the right conditions for the seed to germinate.*

2 TRANSPLANTING *Transplant the young plants into a field flooded to a depth of no more than 1 in (3 cm) at six weeks old. Use a stick or a finger to make the holes. Raise the water level as the plants grow.*

3 HARVESTING *Drain the field and cut the rice by hand, using a sickle. Thresh the crop by machine, by flail (see p. 148), or by striking the plants against a ladder to release the grains. Then winnow the rice (see p. 148).*

Growing corn

YOU DO NOT NEED tropical heat to grow corn. You need rich soil and warmth – corn will not germinate unless the temperature is 50°F (10°C) or above. But I have had good crops of it even in one of Britain's less favored regions. There is no greater pleasure on summer mornings than to walk between tall rows of plants that are bowed down with heavy ears of corn. I have often cut a few stalks and fed them fresh to my horses, for which it is a great treat. All farm animals eat corn; grind it and feed it to the chickens, and it will impart a vivid yellow to the yolks of the eggs.

DRYING AND STORING
A good way to store corn is to dry it in the sun, then keep the ears in a vermin-proof shelter.

Here, strings of ears dry in the sun outside a traditional corn barn in Turkey.

HOW TO GROW CORN

GIVE THE LAND lots of good manure, and the corn will love it. Don't even think about planting seeds before any danger of frost is passed, or you will lose the crop. Weeds are a threat to the newly sprouted seedlings, so you will need to hoe the field until the young plants "get away." Once they have gained a certain height, the canopy they form will suppress further weed growth.

The major threat to young corn is birds, especially crows, which work their way along the rows until the entire crop is gone. A foolproof scarecrow has yet to be invented, but a dead crow, hung from a tree, is a good deterrent.

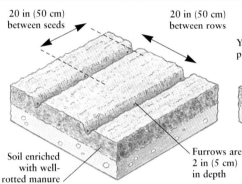

20 in (50 cm) between seeds

20 in (50 cm) between rows

Soil enriched with well-rotted manure

Furrows are 2 in (5 cm) in depth

1 SPACING *Sow the seeds 20 in (50 cm) apart in both directions, in straight rows for easy hoeing. Corn is pollinated by the wind rather than insects, and growing it in well-spaced blocks, rather than single rows, lets the wind do its work more effectively.*

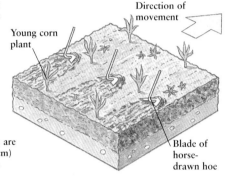

Direction of movement

Young corn plant

Blade of horse-drawn hoe

2 WEEDING *Weeds compete with young corn plants for light and food. Hoeing rows of corn is good work for a horse-drawn hoe, providing that the rows are straight. Once the plants are 12 in (30 cm) tall, weeds will pose no great threat to them.*

USES OF CORN

CORN CONTAINS plenty of protein, and apart from its value as a human food, it is excellent fodder for nearly all farm animals. I have found it especially useful at the end of the summer, when the meadows are almost bare of grass but it is too early in the year to bring the animals into winter quarters. I cut the corn, stalk and all, carry it from the field, and lay it out on the meadow. Cattle and sheep alike relish it.

CORN GROWN AS FODDER
In large-scale farming, corn is often made into silage and is sometimes fed fresh to animals. Home farmers often dry the ears and grind the grains as an animal feed for winter, or dry the stalks to make good hay.

GROWN FOR THE KITCHEN
The varieties of corn grown for human consumption are called sweet corn, and are indeed sweeter than fodder corn.

Growing potatoes

Wicker basket traditionally used by potato gatherers

IF YOU HAVE the right kind of soil, you will do well with potatoes. They need "free-working" land – in other words, land that is not too heavy and sticky. The fields must be easy to plow, harrow, and plant in spring, and in autumn they must not soak up the rain so badly that your machinery gets bogged down during the harvest. A sandy loam is perfect; anything heavier spells trouble. Potatoes also need plenty of rain in the summer if they are to produce a heavy crop. Apart from the joy of eating homegrown potatoes yourself, remember that cattle will enjoy them in winter, though you need to chop them. Poultry will eat them boiled, and sheep nibble them too, so none of the crop need go to waste.

POTATOES FOR THE SMALLHOLDER

	Early	*Maincrop*	*Specialty*
Typical varieties	'Anoka,' 'Dark Red Norland,' 'Pontiac'	'Yukon Gold,' 'R. Burbank,' 'Kennebec'	'All Blue,' 'All Red,' 'Russian Banana'
Time of planting	Potatoes of all varieties, early or maincrop, should be planted two weeks before the last frost of winter – in other words, approximately the time when the average daily soil temperature reaches 40°F (5°C).		
Time of harvesting	15 weeks after planting	Up to 20 weeks after planting	16–18 weeks after planting
Uses	Sought after by shoppers. New potatoes bring good profits if they are skillfully grown and sold.	These varieties are the mainstay of the potato business. Choose your variety to suit the market.	They can be hard to grow, but there is a good market for the more unusual types.

PLANTING SEED

TO PRODUCE GOOD crops of potatoes, plow the land deeply, and manure it heavily. Planting begins as soon as the threat of frost is over. An early harvest is a blessing, for your own table or for your customers, so it is in your interest to make your seed germinate as early as possible. This is achieved by the process of "chitting." Spread the seed potatoes on trays in winter sunlight, in a spot protected from frosts, and they soon start to sprout. When planting chitted seed, you have to be careful not to knock off these delicate new shoots.

1 PLOWING *The land is plowed with a special two-bottom plow (a potato baulking plow) that throws soil to both sides. It leaves a series of ridges and deep trenches. Some farmers plow immediately*

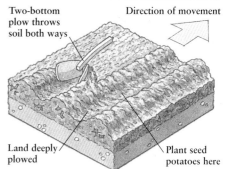

Two-bottom plow throws soil both ways

Direction of movement

Land deeply plowed

Plant seed potatoes here

after harvesting, and let winter frosts reduce the earth to a finer tilth. At the same time, they often put down fresh manure to rot in the trenches all winter, for potatoes need plenty of nourishment to give good crops.

2 PLANTING POTATOES *Planting potatoes needs no machinery. You drop the seed potatoes in, about 1 ft (30 cm) apart, while walking down the furrow. For the sake of your back, have a long, hot bath afterward.*

3 PLOWING OVER *The same plow that drew the furrows now splits the ridges, pushing the soil back and burying the seed potatoes in the process. To control weeds, harrow the field before the potato shoots*

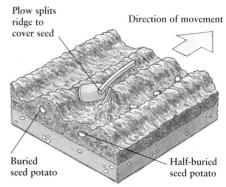

Plow splits ridge to cover seed

Direction of movement

Buried seed potato

Half-buried seed potato

appear. While the plants grow, remember to hill them up: draw up soil around the stems. Do this more than once, and you will keep light from the potatoes; if exposed to light, they become green and poisonous.

LIFTING THE CROP

THERE IS NO REASON why you should not dig up your potatoes with a fork, but you may prefer to have a machine do some of the work for you. Here it is being done with a horse-drawn potato spinner, but tractor-drawn spinners are also used. Horses have the advantage that they can still perform the work if the land becomes too sodden to support the weight of a tractor.

If you have a choice, wait until the weather has been dry for a few days, and the crop will be that much cleaner.

Board catches potatoes

1 SPINNING *As the potato spinner is pulled along the rows, it flicks the ridges over with rotating fingers and flings the crop free of the soil, to land at one side. A board stops the potatoes from flying too far.*

2 GATHERING *The rest of the harvest is carried out by hand; the potatoes are gathered up and carried away to be bagged or stored. Get as many people to help with gathering as you can – it is very heavy work.*

STORAGE CLAMPS

COLD AND VERMIN are the chief dangers to your potatoes once they have been gathered. Store them in a well-ventilated, cool, dry place. If your farm or plot is located in an area with sufficiently mild winters, you can store the crop in a traditional "clamp." A clamp is a mound formed by laying the potatoes on the ground in the open air and covering the crop with straw and earth to protect it. Do not build your clamp in a hollow in the ground, where water might collect or frost might form.

1 LAYING THE FOUNDATIONS *Build the clamp on a thick layer of dry straw, to insulate the potatoes. This should be deep enough to allow some ventilation.*

2 SHAPING AND THATCHING *Don't heap the potatoes – they should lie flat. If you have a lot of potatoes, make a long pile. Cover it with thatching straw (see p. 161).*

3 COVERING UP *Dig soil from around the clamp and use it to cover the straw in order to stop it from blowing away. Then add another layer of straw to provide further insulation.*

4 FINISHING OFF *Cover the clamp with more soil, both to keep out vermin and to weigh down the straw. Leave a straw-filled hole in the top (several for a longer clamp) to let air circulate inside.*

MEADOW MENU

RICH GRAZING
A properly sown meadow will give a milking cow like this all she needs to stay healthy and produce plenty of milk.

WHEN PLANNING A MEADOW, forget farming and think cooking. Consider this: for much of the year, the only feed your animals consume is what they get by grazing. It is you who lets them into the meadow to graze, so in effect you are their chef. It is, therefore, you who should take special care in choosing what goes on the menu. Avoid all temptations to follow the current practice of sowing a uniform field of a newly developed grass. Admittedly, such a grass will grow in abundance, but only with plenty of fertilizer. Instead, look at it from the animal's point of view: would you want a uniform diet, all day, every day? Think of this when you see cattle up to their knees in what appears to be luscious grass, but with their heads over the fence, nibbling at the verge. Variety is the spice of life, and never was this more true than in the meadow. Consult the range of recipes below, and add herbs to whichever mixture you choose. Herbs add valuable minerals to an animal's diet. If anyone thinks you are crazy for deliberately sowing "weeds," tell them to ask the livestock which they prefer.

MEADOW RECIPES

For horses and cattle, any climate

Cattle like long grass: they wrap their tongues round a tuft, pull it up, and munch the pasture by the mouthful. Horses also cope well with it, but as they make more use of their teeth, they can handle short grazing too.

11 lb (5 kg) Intermediate perennial ryegrass
11 lb (5 kg) Late perennial ryegrass
6½ lb (3 kg) Creeping red fescue
4½ lb (2 kg) Timothy grass

Sow at 33 lb/acre (37 kg/ha)

For sheep and goats, any climate

Goats like eating herbs, so add some to the mix. Sheep need their grazing short, so put cows on the pasture first if you can. White clovers are safer for sheep grazing than red – there is less chance of sheep developing bloat.

4½ lb (2 kg) Early perennial ryegrass
8¾ lb (4 kg) Intermediate perennial ryegrass
11 lb (5 kg) Late perennial ryegrass
4½ lb (2 kg) Timothy grass
2¼ lb (1 kg) Mixed white clovers

Sow at 31 lb/acre (35 kg/ha)

For poultry, any climate

This mixture is suitable for all types of poultry. Red fescue has creeping roots that enable it to survive in dry conditions, but it performs best in cool areas. The mixture will even do well in shady conditions.

22 lb (10 kg) Late perennial ryegrass
11 lb (5 kg) Creeping red fescue
6½ lb (3 kg) Smooth-stalked meadow grass

Sow at 39 lb/acre (43 kg/ha)

For all animals, cool, wet climate

Meadow fescue stands up well to harsh winters and will do well on low-lying meadows, which may be damp and slow to warm in the spring.

White clover

22 lb (10 kg) Meadow fescue
6½ lb (3 kg) Timothy grass
2¼ lb (1 kg) Mixed white clovers

Sow at 31 lb/acre (35 kg/ha)

For all animals, warm climate

Ryegrasses are the most common agricultural herbage, and are the basis of some excellent meadows. A ryegrass meadow will stand up well to trampling by cattle. This mixture offers animals a range of nutritious grasses, of different lengths and textures, maturing one by one at times that are well distributed throughout the grazing season.

8¾ lb (4 kg) Early perennial ryegrass
8¾ lb (4 kg) Intermediate perennial ryegrass
6½ lb (3 kg) Late perennial ryegrass
4½ lb (2 kg) Orchard grass
2¼ lb (1 kg) Timothy grass
2¼ lb (1 kg) Mixed white clovers

Sow at 33 lb/acre (37 kg/ha)

Seasoning

Add a selection of the following herbs to your grass mixture to improve its nutritional value and provide more interest for the stock.

7 oz (200 g) Sheep's parsley – medicinally valuable, and rich in iron and vitamins.
10½ oz (300 g) Burnet – brings calcium from deeper levels to the surface.
3½ oz (100 g) Ribwort – most mineral-rich of all the herbs; grows in prolific patches.
3½ oz (100 g) Yarrow – high in protein, but can be grown only in dry environments.
10½ oz (300 g) Chicory – contains minerals, trace elements, and vitamins. Sheep will fight for this!

Sow at 2¼ lb/acre (2½ kg/ha) of grass

ALPINE MEADOW IN SPRING
*Some of the best grazing is found where grasses, herbs, and flowers occur
naturally, such as in this meadow in the Alps. The herbs and flowers will add
flavor to the milk, and the hay will capture the heady scents of summer.*

Keeping pastures sweet

BECAUSE MEADOWS APPEAR to be tranquil places where animals graze, butterflies hover, birds sing, and wildflowers blossom, it is easy to get the impression that all this is achieved without any effort on the part of the farmer. Nothing could be farther from the truth. Keeping meadows productive takes time and effort, just as it does to grow any other crop. Pasture management entails a year-round series of activities, all tied to the themes of turf and soil care, access limitation, and weed control.

QUALITY IS EVERYTHING

GOOD AND BAD PASTURE
The meadow above has a rich variety of grasses and plants. The one on the right is riddled with docks and is useless.

The docks will soon take over if no action is taken

CARE OF TURF AND SOIL

Pasture management starts in the spring, when you take a set of chain harrows and tear away the dead grass that has become compacted over the winter. This is a hugely enjoyable job, carried out in the warm air with a scent of fresh grass rising up around you. The spikes of the chain harrow scratch open the turf, let air and warmth reach the roots, and encourage growth. They break up and spread molehills and animal droppings.

Next, get out the roller. The frosts will have opened up the ground, but the grass needs to feel the soil packed more tightly around its roots if it is to grow.

Then check the pH value of the soil (see p. 133), and if you have any doubts about your result, have a full chemical analysis done professionally.

If you find that your meadow is not too acidic, you may decide to fertilize it by spreading manure, and spring is a good time for this, just before the grass comes into its main period of growth.

If the meadow has become too acidic, which can happen as a result of long-term grazing, the remedy is lime. For this, you must wait until autumn, as the lime needs months to work into the land before the growing season begins.

The other great weapon you possess in caring for your turf is your ability to create an animal-rotation plan, in which you let one kind of stock graze a piece of land after another, bringing on the various animal species in turn.

GRAZING SUCCESSION

THIS PICTURE SHOWS a patch of pasture four times, in the four phases of an animal rotation. The succession of animals ensures the best use of the pasture. In the first phase, the grass is long and is grazed by horses. They leave the field untidy, as they eat no weeds, and they cause irregular growth with their habitual dunging areas. Then cows graze on the grass left by horses, and sheep tidy up after the cows. The short turf that sheep leave is still good for geese.

Progression in time

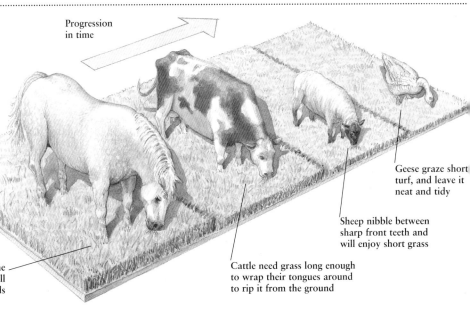

Geese graze short turf, and leave it neat and tidy

Sheep nibble between sharp front teeth and will enjoy short grass

Cattle need grass long enough to wrap their tongues around to rip it from the ground

Horses prefer the longest grass, but will not be tempted by weeds

ACCESS LIMITATION

The main benefit of animal rotation is that it makes it much more difficult for livestock parasites to multiply on the pasture. Besides this, you are setting up a succession of livestock species on any given plot, and one of the skills of stock raising is knowing how to arrange this succession to your advantage (see left).

The hygiene benefits work like this: the worms inside an infected animal lay eggs, which are passed out with the animal's droppings. These tiny eggs are eaten by other animals along with the grass, and hatch into a new generation of worms inside their new hosts. These worms then lay more eggs, which are eaten by another animal, and the cycle continues. A better way of building up worms is hard to imagine.

Parasites are rarely able to live in more than one species of animal, so the rotation seeks to break the cycle by moving out one species of livestock and bringing in another.

Intestinal worms simply must be controlled. If rotation doesn't have the required effect, find a clean site and move your animals there. They must stay there until you have rid them of the infection with veterinary wormers. After that, you will have to keep them off the infected site for several years.

WEED CONTROL

Some weeds are a bonus, some are a nuisance, and a few are poisonous. Just because a pasture has weeds does not mean it is poor grazing. Indeed, there is a growing body of opinion that a good selection of weeds supplies much-needed variety to grazing, and that some weeds are positively beneficial in supplying minerals brought up from lower down in the soil via their deep roots.

Among the pests are docks and nettles. These plants have precious little nutritional value, but are very good at spreading. You can control nettles by regular "topping" with a mower, but you will have to dig up docks.

A few weeds, such as hemlock and ragwort, are toxic. Ragwort (there are several species) becomes more toxic if it is accidentally cut and mixed into the hay. Watch for it, and get rid of it.

PASTURE MANAGEMENT

WEED CONTROL
All weeds will succumb to weed killers, but here is a more satisfactory way to deal with them. This is lethally poisonous ragwort. *Catch it before it sets seed, or it will quickly spread. Take the entire plant, roots and all, out of the field and discard it.*

GOOD SOIL, GOOD TURF
Include pastures in your crop rotation. Here, the cereal has been undersown with grasses (see p. 134) to give the pasture a head start.

ACCESS LIMITATION
With strip grazing, you get the most from a meadow. Use an electric fence (see p. 43) to confine animals to one area at a time.

Making hay

MAKING HAY IS AN ART, and often a sweat. Hay is grass that has been mown, dried, and stored, to be fed to stock when the winter meadows are bare. To make good hay, the ingredients have to be well chosen, the temperature just right, and the whole operation carried out with a lightness of touch. The grass is at its best just before flowering, so if you can, mow it then. Often, the weather will have different ideas. Listen to forecasts, scan the skies for portents, and hope for at least a week of fine, settled weather. If you are delayed long enough for the grass to bloom, all is not lost; you will have a bulkier crop, although a less nutritious one. You do not need constant, blistering sunshine to make hay. Some of the best hay I have made has been the result of long, slow drying of the grass in a fresh breeze, over several overcast days of low humidity. Bleaching in strong sunlight makes bad hay. The best hay still has the greenness of the grass about it, and has captured the warm smells of summer to cheer you through the dreary days of winter.

GROWING ALFALFA FOR HAY

CROPS SUCH AS alfalfa and clover make high-protein hay and can be cut at least twice a year. Mix an upright grass with these crops, to keep them from collapsing under their weight and becoming difficult to mow.

Orchard grass supporting alfalfa

Mowing is a swinging movement of the body, not the arms

CUTTING THE HAY

A GOOD SCYTHE HANDLER might cut as much as 1 acre (0.4 ha) of grass in a day, but only after years of practice. Each scythe has to be "set" for the individual user, depending on his or her height. The angle of the blade can usually be adjusted at the heel, and a "grass nail" between the blade and the handle (or snaith) prevents the blade from flexing when cutting. All this is a waste of time if the blade is not razor sharp. Hone it at least every 15 minutes. Alternatively, a sharp, well-oiled mowing machine, whether pulled by horses or a tractor, takes much of the anguish out of making hay.

Knife housed in side arm

USING A SCYTHE
Stand with your legs wide apart and keep the blade horizontal. Swing the scythe in a wide sweep from your hips, bringing it toward you at the end of the stroke. If you do not keep the blade level, it will dig into the ground or slip over the grass. Keep it sharp (see p. 37). The sharper it is, the less you sweat.

USING A MOWING MACHINE
A mower, whether tractor- or horse-drawn, works like a pair of scissors, slicing the grass between fixed "fingers" and a moving blade, or knife.

Fixed "finger"

Knife moves from side to side

TURNING THE HAY

GRASS NEEDS TURNING enough to dry it, and no more. Too much violence knocks off the leaves (especially from alfalfa and clover), and the best bit of your hay will be left on the field. Start turning it as soon as it has wilted. As you turn it, you will be moving it to drier ground. Unwilted grass attempts to draw any remaining moisture from the ground, so the sooner all the grass is wilted, the better. Try to keep it fluffy, so that any drying breeze will get to the heart of it.

TURNING HAY BY HAND
Hay can, of course, be turned by hand. This is best done on a windy day, when you can fling the crop into the air and let the breeze blow through it, to dry it all the faster.

SIDE-DELIVERY RAKE
Haymaking always seems to be a race against the clock, and this implement will help. Revolving spikes flip the hay and move it aside in a single movement.

Set rake to make sure that no hay is left unturned

SWATHES OF HAY
After turning, the hay is left in neat rows, called swathes, making further turning, forking, or baling much easier.

Wet-weather hay

EVENTUALLY THERE WILL arrive a haymaking season when the weather does not want to play. There is no more dispiriting sound than that of rain falling on hay that has been cut and turned and is *almost*, but not quite, ready to cart. Not only are you back to square one, but every time your hay gets a soaking it is losing nutritional value.

Don't let it get you down. There are ways of making hay that need no more than two good drying days. In latitudes where settled weather cannot be counted on, all manner of ways to save a hay crop have been developed. You can build a series of mini-stacks of hay, called haycocks, simply by raking the loose hay together. But it is a lot of work, and the haycocks have to be opened up again when the sun shines.

The best method of wet weather haymaking uses tripods. Legumes like clovers and alfalfa take a lot of drying, and tripods may be the only way to guarantee a crop of hay from them in anything other than perfect conditions. Hay tripods and haycocks are, of course, only temporary measures, and the hay will eventually have to be ricked.

HAY ON TRIPODS
The hay from this field in the Tyrolean Alps in Austria has been put on tripods. Once the hay is "on legs," it is safe from all weathers; it can be left to stand like this for as long as you like, even right through until winter.

MAKING HAY TRIPODS

A TRIPOD SHOULD STAND about 6 ft (180 cm) tall and be made of ash poles. Join three poles together at the top with wire. Staple two strands of wire around the tripod, about 2 ft (60 cm) apart. As a rough guide, you will need around 15 tripods to the acre (35 to the hectare).

The secret of success is in the careful placing of the hay around the tripod so that air can circulate freely through it. Freshly cut grass is too moist and dense to be hung on the tripod immediately; it will simply stifle the airflow. The grass needs to be well wilted before tripoding. If you are lucky enough to have two drying days, that should be enough.

1 PREPARATIONS *Rake the crop into a circle around the tripod. If you need to finish quickly – for example, because the weather may be about to break – have one person raking, one building. Make sure the tripod is on firm ground and cannot topple.*

2 COVERING THE TRIPOD *Lay forkfuls of hay lightly along the lower strand of wire, ensuring that the airway underneath the tripod is not blocked. Work around and around, maintaining a light touch. Keep the center open, to create a chimney effect.*

3 ON AND UP *Continue until the lower strand is full, and then start on the upper one. It is tempting to load as much on as you can, but you must not block the free flow of air – that is what will make your hay.*

Sides should be as steep as possible to let rain run off

4 TO TOP IT ALL *Finish off the tripod with a firm forkful on the top. Then "comb" the sides with your pitchfork to encourage the rain to run straight down.*

Storing hay

YOUR CROP OF HAY is not safe and secure until it has been stored where the weather cannot ruin it. Making hay is hardly ever without torment, and to have made good hay only to cut into the stack six months later and find that it has gone rotten through poor storage is heartbreaking. Baled hay is easier to store. Loose hay takes up more space and, unless you have a very large barn, you will want to build a haystack, or hayrick, outdoors. Think carefully about where you build it. A stack in the field reduces carting time in the summer, but makes for a long haul in the winter when you are feeding it to animals. You might think that a haystack is easy to build, but it is not. The best advice I was given was that the resulting stack should look "like a loaf of bread." What that means is that the top should be nicely rounded to allow rain to run off freely, while the base should be narrow, so that water falling off the eaves does not wet the sides. This is easy to say, but it takes years of practice to achieve.

A hay knife, for slicing the hayrick

USING A HAY BALER

STORING HAY in machine-made bales saves a lot of work, and is the best way if you do not have enough hay to make a decent-size rick. But there are drawbacks. Baled hay has to be kept drier than stacked hay. If the tightly packed hay gets damp, it will not dry easily and will be prone to rotting.

MAKING A HAYRICK

MOVE THE HAY from the field to the site of the rick. This is done with a cart or a trailer, and is called "carting." Now start to build your hayrick.

Lay down a bed of straw to keep out moisture. Then, with a pitchfork, pile forkfuls of hay on the center of the bed. Once you have made a good-sized heap in the middle, start to build around the edges. As you build, keep the center higher than the sides: do not allow the stack to sag in the middle and provide a handy place for rain to collect.

CARTING HAY
Build loads of hay carefully before carting them. Freshly forked hay is alive, and it will not take much of a jolt to have the whole load back on the ground.

Thatched top (see p. 45)

BUILDING THE RICK
Place each forkful of hay carefully so as to make the sides straight, then straighten them further by combing down with a rake. The rick will shrink to half its size in six months.

GOOD AND BAD HAY

MOISTURE IS THE ENEMY of hay. Hay can go bad either because dampness creeps into it while it is in storage or because not enough moisture was allowed to evaporate during the initial haymaking process in the field.

Good hay, well made and stored

Rotten hay, where rain has leaked in

Hay knife must be kept razor-sharp or cutting hay will be twice the work

USING THE RICK
Take hay off the rick in slices, using a hay knife to cut the slice. Cut a piece the size of a bale, and carry the hay on a fork to the animals. In wet weather, cover the exposed parts of the rick with tarpaulin.

Root and leaf crops

GROW ROOT AND LEAF CROPS in the summer in order to be able to feed them to your livestock in the winter – you will be glad you did. All these crops are remarkably easy to grow, while from the point of view of the animals they must be a welcome mouthful of luscious, juicy food in an otherwise austere winter diet of hay and cereals.

For home farming, the root crops to grow are mangels, turnips, and rutabagas, and the leaf crops are cabbages and kale. It is not just that they are cheap winter fodder. I am also convinced that they add more to the animals' general health than feed supplements ever could.

ROOT CROPS FOR WINTER FEEDING

SHEEP GRAZING ON TURNIPS
Save yourself some work by taking the stock to the crop rather than the other way around. These sheep are feeding on turnips. An electric fence is being used to limit their grazing to one area at a time. Not only are the sheep relieving the farmer of work, but they are also acting as manure spreaders, enriching the land for the next crop.

GROWING ROOT CROPS

Under the heading of roots grown for livestock feed come turnips, rutabagas, and beets, the most important of which are mangels. These are also known as mangel-wurzels or mangolds. You follow the same basic method to grow all these root crops: sow them in rows direct in the field in late spring, when the soil has warmed up sufficiently for them to germinate and start their growth quickly.

When growing turnips and rutabagas, to get the heaviest crops you must "single" the seedlings with a hand hoe – in other words, thin them to about 8 in (20 cm) apart. This is time-consuming, but gives the vegetables room to grow to a good size, and gives you a chance to swipe a weed or two in the process. Later, you can weed between the rows with a horse- or tractor-drawn hoe.

Mangels, like other beets, have seeds that each sprout several plants. Thin each clump of seedlings to leave the strongest one. When ripe, mangels contain a large proportion of water and sugar, and I have yet to meet an animal that will refuse a mangel in midwinter.

There are some modern varieties of fodder beet that set only one plant per seed. Although there are people who would try to convince you that these are better, the mangel is a terrific root crop; it is prone to hardly any diseases and can be grown almost anywhere.

STORAGE OF ROOTS

RATS AND FROST are the main enemies of stored roots. Keep frost at bay by building a clamp of earth and straw (see p. 153). Watch for rat holes appearing in its side: if you see any, perhaps you need to get a cat.

MANGELS
These can be fed whole, but here they are being chopped by hand, ready to be mixed with other winter feeds.

POTATOES
Potatoes that are not good enough for sale make good winter feed. Cows love them raw, but boil them for pigs.

RUTABAGAS
These are usually a sheep feed, but, as with turnips, they can be sliced and mixed with other feeds for cattle.

FEEDING AND STORING

Some roots may need no storing at all. Turnips are not harmed if you leave them to overwinter in ground that does not freeze very deeply. You simply give your sheep a small area at a time to clear. Most sheep nibble turnips down as far as ground level, and leave the rest, although I once had a ewe that knew how to paw out the bottom half. Failing this, it is worth walking along the rows with a stick, pulling out the leftovers for the flock to eat.

Mangels *must* be harvested, or frost will reduce them to a pulp. Pull them from the ground, and twist off the leafy tops, which are toxic. Store the mangels in a root cellar.

It is very important not to bruise mangels, or they will rot. It takes only one decaying mangel to start the rot spreading through the entire crop.

LEAF CROPS

Kale, the best known of the leafy winter crops, is a tall plant with broad, green, branching leaves. It has a remarkable resistance to frost, and will grow on all but the most acidic soils. Plant out kale seedlings in rows in spring or early summer, and they will grow into a field of dense, waving foliage.

You may not have to cut your kale. If the land is sufficiently dry, you can let your cattle graze it in the field, perhaps using an electric fence (see p. 43) to feed it to them strip by strip. If the land is wet, the animals will churn the soil with their feet ("poach" it), so you have to cut the kale and cart it to the farmyard.

If you graze kale early in the season, and then take the cows out of the field, you may get a small regrowth, which will suit sheep. The stumps can be a problem, but pigs can deal with them.

Cabbages are members of the same family – the brassicas – as kale. They tend to be grown for sheep, which are put to graze the crop in the field rather than having it cut and brought to them (most sheep are too short to graze kale).

Cabbages are best grown from young plants, dibbed into the ground by hand (see p. 98) and weeded by hoe. You may prefer to sell your best ones; the stock will be content with the rest.

KALE, A TASTY MIDWINTER MOUTHFUL

FEEDING CUT KALE
This is thousand-headed kale (the leafiest variety). Feed it to stock the same morning you cut it, when it is at its freshest and most nutritionally valuable.

FIELD GRAZING
Letting stock graze kale in the field will save the work of cutting and carting it, and livestock overwintered in a yard or cowshed will appreciate the fresh air.

HOME COMFORTS

ONE OF THE MOST CREATIVE parts of home farming takes place not

on the land, but back home in the kitchen, when the autumn

days are getting shorter and the cupboard must be stocked

for the winter. This is where your hard-won

harvests of cereals, fruits, vegetables, and meats are made into the

finest food you will ever have tasted. Bread, cheese, jam, preserves,

cider, or wine – nothing beats the taste of food and

drink over which you have labored, perhaps for

many seasons, and can now at last enjoy.

FRUIT YOGURT
A cocktail of your own produce: yogurt, strawberries, and slices of honeydew melon.

FRUITS OF YOUR LABOR

To GET THIS FAR, YOU HAVE worked hard, and you can be proud of what you have achieved. It matters not how large or small your parcel of land might be. What counts is that you took up the challenge: you decided you would farm, chose the site, bought the land, and moved in. You dug deep beds or else plowed fields. You shoveled compost or spread manure to fertilize the land. You raked the soil or, on a field scale, used a harrow and rollers to make good tilth.

You coped with drought, downpour, invasions of weeds, and the ace and deuce of pest and disease. Despite obstacles, you succeeded, overall, with crops and livestock. You suffered the ups and downs of farming life. Now you can reap your reward. Of all the experiences in home farming, the ones that happen around the

HOW MUCH WILL YOUR FARM PRODUCE?

	Small livestock	*Large livestock*
Garden farm (see p. 14) 	From a hive of bees, you may extract 30 lb (13.5 kg) of honey in a year, some of which can be made into mead. If you have a small pond with ducks, expect about 150 eggs a month from six ducks. You may choose chickens or a few rabbits instead of ducks. ***Autumn inspection of a beehive***	On a garden farm, there won't be room for the larger animals, unless you are lucky enough to live near a tract of forest or rough land and can get permission to tether a pig or a goat there. If you can fatten a pig, expect 50–80 lb (23–36 kg) of pork, depending on the breed, which you can cure into hams or bacon or make into sausages.
Small home farm (see p. 16) 	 ***Pasta with home-produced eggs*** Keeping a dozen hens and half a dozen geese would be no problem here. Hens will produce an average of 270 eggs a year. Geese can give you 20 eggs per pair a year. You could even have several types of small livestock on this farm.	This farm will support two or three goats or the same number of sheep or pigs. A good milking goat can give 3 quarts (3.5 liters) a day. She will need to kid every two years to sustain the milk flow. ***Washing homemade butter in the butter maker after churning***
Medium home farm (see p. 18) 	With 3 acres (1.2 ha), you will have to decide how much space to allocate to small livestock and choose which kinds to keep. You may decide to raise rabbits for table use. From two does (females) and one buck (male), you will have roughly 20 rabbits to sell, or kill for your own table, every year. Rabbits are ready for eating at about six months old.	A house cow now becomes possible. A good milk cow can give 4 gallons (18 liters) of milk a day. Cheese-making methods vary, but for home cheese production you will use 1 gallon (4.5 liters) to make about ¾ lb (350 g) of cheese. If you decide to make butter, expect to get about 1 lb (0.5 kg) of butter from every 2–3 gallons (roughly 10–15 liters) of milk.
Larger home farm (see p. 20) 	With a farm of this size, you may be more interested in large livestock, but don't forget that poultry, rabbits, and bees all provide good returns for a relatively small amount of work. And why should you pass up the opportunity to have fresh eggs, meat, or honey?	 ***Milking with a small-scale electric machine*** You could keep a small herd of cows for milking or for more beef than a family can eat. A cow can have one calf a year, and this can be fattened in 18 months to provide 660 lb (300 kg) of beef.

kitchen table can be the best: enjoying the matchless taste of freshly dug potatoes or cutting into a loaf that you baked, from wheat that you have sown and harvested by hand. No slice of bread will ever taste better. This is food that you have brought all the way from the earth to the table.

The skills involved in turning raw produce into desirable food can be just as difficult to learn as any farming technique. But you have come this far, so why should you not now go on and jump the final hurdle? It is this willingness to create and experiment that sets the home farmer apart from all others.

The techniques that follow have been tried and tested, more than most recipes in modern books. These methods have been used for centuries, practiced daily by people who live off the land. Countless generations of farmers, both large and small scale, have been served well by this charming, informal, and essentially wholesome style of home economics. Now it is your turn.

> **❝** *No slice of bread will ever taste better. This is food that you have brought all the way from the earth to the table.* **❞**

Fruit and vegetables	*Field crops*	*Storage*
A farm of this size can supply all the fruit and vegetables for a family of four. You will have to grow both maincrop and new potatoes, to maintain a year-round supply. Expect to harvest about 18 lb (8 kg) from a 10-ft (3-m) row. *Harvesting parsnips*	No fields – no field crops. However, if you are farming in a rural area, you can harvest plenty of wild plants from common land, roadsides, grass verges, and the like – even if to use only as feed for rabbits or chickens.	Some vegetables can last through the winter, provided you give them some protection from frost. It does not have to be elaborate – a wooden shed might have enough room to store most of your harvest from this size of farm. *Onions keep for up to nine months*
This plot is capable of producing more fruit and vegetables than you and your family can eat. For example, a mature blackcurrant bush can yield 11–15½ lb (5–7 kg) of fruit. With a few bushes, you will have fruit to make the best jam you ever tasted and, even taking into account the quantity you freeze for family use, you will still have plenty to sell.	Although this farm does not have full-size fields, you can grow a strip of wheat to supply enough cereal for bread making or poultry feeding. Yields could be as much as 1 lb of grain per sq yd (just over 0.5 kg per sq m). An alternative plan for this strip would be to grow alfalfa as livestock fodder.	There are many methods of storing soft fruits: freezing, making jams and chutneys, preserving, and drying. You can store citrus fruits, such as oranges and lemons, in boxes of sand. Wrap apples and pears in paper and place them in wooden boxes. *Pickled mixed vegetables*
You could grow some fruit and vegetables on a field scale, for selling or for feeding to your livestock. You can sell some of your harvest, such as strawberries, directly to the public as "pick-your-own." You make a bit less profit, but it saves the work of picking the fruit yourself. To grow fruit and vegetables for your own use, you have the kitchen garden.	*Wheat stack nearing completion* It is difficult to predict the quantity of hay from the acreage, as it is climate dependent, but an average bale of hay weighs some 29–48 lb (13–22 kg), and you can get 20 bales from 1 acre (0.4 ha) of good grass. One-quarter acre (0.1 ha) of wheat can supply the bread needs of a family of four.	The best, and tastiest, way to store milk is as cheese. Another excellent option is to make ice cream, especially if you have fresh fruit to use for flavoring. Any meat that cannot be eaten when fresh will have to be frozen or preserved in some other fashion. Why not try drying some of your beef or smoking some chicken? If you have pigs, you will need space to hang hams up to cure.
With this much land, you can plant a greater variety of fruit trees; consider establishing an olive grove or a vineyard if the climate permits. A row of 20 good vines will produce 110 lb (50 kg) of grapes, which could give you 5½ gallons (25 liters) of wine. *Trailer load of Chardonnay grapes*	One way or another, this farm will probably produce all the fodder your animals need. Whether you live in a warmer climate and grow corn and rice, or in a cooler region and grow leaf and root crops, a prodigious amount can be produced in this area. For example, well-fertilized mangels can yield up to 20 tons from 1 acre (0.4 ha)!	All crops need proper winter storage areas. You must keep your cereals dry and safe from vermin. You also have to keep your hay dry – if wet, it will soon become moldy. *Barn built on stone supports to deter rats*

Making bread

YOU START OFF THINKING you are learning a craft, and then discover that it is an art. In one form or another, bread has been baked for millennia. It has been made from the simplest of ingredients, in the humblest of surroundings, and no one need have any difficulty baking an ideal loaf. The secret lies in practice. As you get to know the feel of the dough, you will come to recognize precisely the texture it should be to form the sort of bread you prefer. Experiment with a range of flours for different textures and flavors, or stick to a traditional whole meal – home-ground if you're lucky. You can use a food mixer, but you will miss out on half the fun and on the learning experience. Your bread making should be a hands-on business.

BREAD INGREDIENTS

FOR A BASIC LOAF, you need only three ingredients: flour, water, and yeast. You can also add spices, seeds, fruits, nuts, and herbs. Put in a little oil if you want to make the loaf easier to slice. Tired flour that has sat in a bag for months, prone to moisture or heat or any of the other things that destroy its quality, will never make a good loaf. Yeast, too, has to be alive to work. If fresh yeast has not been kept cool or has been allowed to dry out, it will be dead, and expecting your loaf to rise is asking for a miracle.

PLAIN WHOLE-MEAL LOAF

1 MILLING FLOUR *Having grown your own cereal, you might like to mill it by hand. It takes 15 minutes to grind the 3 cups (340 g) of flour needed to bake a large loaf. The drier the cereal, the easier it is to mill.*

2 ACTIVATING YEAST *Use fresh or dried yeast. Fresh yeast gives a firmer loaf. Dried yeast (shown) is activated by adding lukewarm water and sugar. When it froths, it is ready.*

BREAD FLOURS

MOST FLOURS WILL MAKE some form of loaf, and it is fun to experiment with mixtures of flours. Remember that it is the gluten content of the flour that makes the most important difference. Gluten combines with water to make an elastic, sticky substance that makes bread rise. When you knead the dough, you activate the gluten. Flours low in gluten will always make flat loaves, however much yeast you add to them.

| Rye flour makes a chewy loaf | Mixed-grain flour adds texture | Whole-meal, hand-milled wheat flour | White flour has the bran removed |

3 MIXING DOUGH *Add the activated yeast mixture to the flour and oil in the bowl; start mixing, gradually adding water until you have a dough that can be grasped but does not stick to your hands. Getting the texture just right comes with practice.*

4 KNEADING *This process ensures that bread will rise. Insufficient kneading gives flat, dense bread. Too much gives a loaf with large holes in it. Using your fingers, thumbs, and palms, work the dough rhythmically until it has changed from a soggy mass into a stretchy one. This takes about eight minutes.*

5 LEAVING TO RISE *Do not put the dough in too warm a place to rise. If you do, it may not rise at all. Cover the bowl with a cloth to keep the dough clean, and find a cozy place where drafts will not chill it. It should rise to no more than twice its original volume, or it might collapse while baking.*

6 THE FINISHED LOAF *"Knock back" the risen dough to flatten it. Then give it a second, lighter kneading, and roll it into shape by hand or place it in a bread pan. Let it rise again before baking. The loaf is done when tapping its base produces a hollow sound.*

RAISED BREADS

NOT ALL BREADS are made to rise with yeast. Soda bread uses baking soda to produce instant gas. Some breads can be made to rise with neither yeast nor soda – naturally occurring bacteria cause the dough to ferment and rise. These are called sourdough breads.

Soda bread

Rye bread

Mixed-grain bread

White bread with sun-dried tomato

FLAT BREADS

SOME FLAT BREADS, such as pita, contain yeast and are flat as the result of very fast baking, which causes the bread to rise quickly and then collapse. Others, such as chapati, contain no yeast and never rise.

Whole-meal and white pita breads

Chapati made with whole-meal flour

Other cereal foods

IN THE WESTERN WORLD as a whole, the most common way to eat cereals is to turn wheat into bread. The next most common cereal food is pasta, another wheat product; and wheat is also the main ingredient in pancakes, dumplings, cookies, couscous, wheat beer, and various other drinks. But there is no reason why an imaginative cook, with a knowledge of traditional cuisines, cannot turn all manner of cereals into nutritious food. It is only in recent time, historically, that bread has been made principally with wheat. Before the farming innovations of recent centuries, bread used to be made mostly with barley. As a home farmer you may find it rewarding to try out a range of different cereals on your land to determine which are the ones that will grow best for you. Do not underestimate traditional methods for turning them into food.

OTHER GRAINS

IF YOU ARE GROWING cereals for your own consumption, remember that some need more processing than they would as a livestock feed. Cattle can eat barley still in its husk; but as a human food, barley is usually very lightly milled in such a way as to remove the husk. This is what is known as "pearled" barley.

Oats, too, need to be cleaned of their spiky, indigestible husks. This is difficult to achieve, so making your own oatmeal or porridge oats is not an easy process. Buckwheat is either ground in the same way as wheat or cooked whole like rice. It is sometimes included in stews.

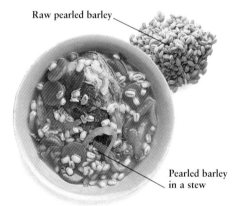

Raw pearled barley

Pearled barley in a stew

PEARLED BARLEY
Pearled barley can be used to thicken soups and stews, as it is good to eat when cooked slowly. Barley can also be made into bread, though it tends to be thick and heavy.

Raw long-grain rice

Cooked long-grain rice

PILAU RICE
Pilau rice is boiled, colored with saffron or other agents, and seasoned. Rice can also be fried, often with chopped foods, ground and made into cakes, or eaten in desserts.

Raw whole corn kernels

Grilled polenta

POLENTA: CORN PASTE
Polenta is ground corn. In northern Italy it is cooked slowly with water, stirring all the time, to produce a paste. This is served with sauce or a stew. Once made, the paste can be cut into squares and grilled, as here.

Rolled oats

Oatmeal

OATS
Oat flour is the most finely ground product of oats and is used to make some breads. Coarser milling gives rolled oats, used to make oatmeal and cookies. Still more coarsely milled oats are used in granola.

Raw kasha

Kasha boiled in stock

KASHA AND BUCKWHEAT
Buckwheat can be grown on poorer-quality land. The so-called green variety is known as kasha, and it can be substituted for rice in most dishes. Buckwheat flour, mixed with molasses, makes a tasty, dark brown bread.

MAKING PASTA

1 SIEVING FLOUR *Sieve 2½ cups (250 g) of flour to remove lumps. The usual flour for making pasta is milled from durum wheat, but you can get good results with all-purpose flour.*

2 EGGS AND OIL *For this much flour, you will need 3 eggs and 1 tablespoon of oil. Make a well in the center of the sieved flour and add the eggs, then the oil and 1 teaspoon of salt.*

3 MIXING DOUGH *Traditionally, this is done with the fingertips, to work the eggs and oil into the flour. It is easy, at this stage, to spill the eggs and oil out onto the table!*

4 KNEADING *Pasta dough can be tougher than bread dough. Use fingers and hands to work it thoroughly. It is ready when it is elastic. Let it stand for an hour.*

5 ROLLING OUT *Flour table and rolling pin to prevent sticking. While rolling, keep turning the dough to get an even consistency. Use an even pressure on the rolling pin.*

6 CUTTING STRIPS *This is just one way to finish pasta: roll it out into a sheet, then roll the floured sheet up and cut it into slices. Unroll these slices, and you have fettucine.*

7 DRYING *A broom handle is being used here. The pasta strips are draped across it for 5–10 minutes until they are leathery. To make firmer pasta, lay the strips on a towel to dry for up to two hours.*

READY TO EAT

Tomatoes, olives, and basil have been added

Fresh fettucine needs to be boiled for 3–5 minutes

Simple dairying

BUTTER, YOGURT, AND ice cream are the easiest dairy foods to make, and they are often produced in the home for family use. In all such cases, the kitchen makes an adequate dairy. If you have grander plans, you must invest in a separate area that meets public-health standards. Raw milk is a perfect home for bacteria, and you should take this into account at all times. Even in a kitchen, all surfaces and utensils must be kept scrupulously clean, or you will not be producing butter, you will be getting a bellyache.

DAIRY HYGIENE

OLD DAIRY utensils may look attractive, but stainless-steel ones are much easier to keep clean and hygienic. Ordinary washing will not be enough for dairy equipment. You must sterilize utensils either by immersing them in *boiling* water (as shown) or by using a solution of hypochlorite. Your nose will soon detect when dairy utensils are not being sterilized sufficiently.

5 minutes in boiling water is adequate

BUTTER

1 RIPENING *Skim the cream off the milk; only the cream is used to make butter. The cream first has to "ripen" – a process in which bacterial activity makes the cream more acid. To achieve this, a starter is usually added. Cultured buttermilk contains the right bacteria, and that is what is being added here.*

2 CHURNING *In this process, the fat in the cream is forced to come together. At first, tiny globules form. When you see whitish lumps like this on the paddles, the butter is churned.*

3 DRAINING *Sometimes the butter will "come" quickly. At other times, you seem to be churning forever, but the butter will appear. Drain off the watery buttermilk it leaves behind.*

4 WASHING *Add cool water to the churn and turn the handle to wash the butter. It will need several rinses. If you do not remove every trace of the buttermilk, the butter will quickly sour.*

5 WORKING *Turn the butter onto a board and "work" it to get rid of all the water. Flat, hand-held boards called Scotch hands are used. Press the butter flat, wipe away any moisture that appears, and repeat.*

6 SHAPING *Finally, use the Scotch hands to shape the butter. It can be pressed into molds carved with patterns or shaped into a block. Shaping gives an opportunity to remove the last traces of moisture.*

YOGURT

1 TESTING THE TEMPERATURE
Yogurt is milk soured by bacteria. For these organisms to do their work, the milk must be kept at body temperature.

2 ADDING MILK TO CULTURE
Add the warm milk to a culture of the right bacteria to start the process. The best place to get the culture is from your last batch of yogurt. If buying yogurt to use as a culture, make sure that it is "live" yogurt.

3 OVERNIGHT MAGIC
For the bacteria to be able to turn all the milk into yogurt, you will have to keep the mixture at a constant temperature. Either pour the warm milk and culture into a vacuum flask (as shown) or insulate the pan with cloths and leave it in a warm room. Leave the mixture overnight for the magic to happen. If all goes well, next morning you will have yogurt.

4 THE RESULT *Flavor your yogurt with whatever fruit is available. You can eat it fresh (adding honey if preferred), freeze it, or use it in cooking.*

ICE CREAM

1 CUSTARD *Take 1 pint (570 ml) milk, two eggs, ½ cup (100 g) sugar, and 1¼ cups (280 ml) heavy cream. Bring the milk to a boil. Add to the mixed egg yolks and sugar. Warm the custard until it coats the spoon.*

2 WHIPPED CREAM *Take the custard off the heat and let it cool. Whip the egg whites and cream, and fold them into the custard. The result is a basic ice cream mixture; if you aren't going to flavor it, freeze it now.*

3 FLAVORING *Make use of whatever fruits are in season. Here fresh raspberries, mashed through a sieve to form a purée, are being used as the flavoring. Chocolate, coffee, maple syrup, or vanilla could be used instead.*

4 FREEZING *Now transfer the mixture to a shallow dish, and place it in the freezer. Allow it to freeze partially, until it is slushy, then remove it from the tray, whisk it, and return it to the freezer until fully frozen.*

Making cheese

IT IS PART OF the tradition of small-scale farming that produce has to be preserved, and this is where the craft of cheese making has its beginnings. By making your milk into cheese, you are turning a food that lasts for a few days into one that can last for months. The principle is simple: you are separating the proteins you want to keep from the rest of the milk. The agents you add – starter and rennet – cause the proteins to collect in the form of curds, the basic ingredient of all cheeses. But it is where you go from here that makes cheese so interesting. Give two cheese makers milk from the same animal, and it is highly unlikely they would ever make the same cheese. There are too many variables.

SOFT CHEESE SELECTION

SOFT CHEESES ARE EASIER to make than hard cheeses, so you might want to try making them first. All milk, whether from cows, sheep, or goats, makes superb soft cheeses, and flavorings such as herbs and spices can be added. It is well worth experimenting once you have mastered the basics.

Ewes' milk cheese with nuts

Cows' milk cheese with garlic

Goats' milk cheese

Ewes' milk cheese rolled in herbs

HARD CHEESE

1 TESTING THE TEMPERATURE
Warm cows' milk to 90°F (32°C), or goats' milk to 84°F (29°C). Use about 1 gallon (4.5 liters) of milk.

2 STARTER *Stir in the starter, a bacterial culture that creates the necessary acidity. You can buy starter or make it: the basic method consists of leaving some unpasteurized milk to curdle.*

3 RENNET *Let stand for 45 minutes, then add rennet that has been diluted with boiled water. Rennet is the curdling agent, and it can be derived from either animal or plant sources.*

4 FORMING CURDS *Stir the top of the milk for at least ten minutes until you start to feel resistance to the whisk. This is the curds forming. Cover, and leave in a warm room for 45 minutes until the curds are firm.*

5 CUTTING CURDS *Use a stainless-steel knife to cut the curds into small pieces, and stir the curds and whey together. Heat very gently to a temperature of 100°F (38°C) for cows', or 95°F (35°C) for goats', milk.*

6 STRAINING *Test the curds by pinching between thumb and finger – they should separate easily. Strain them through scalded cheesecloth. Gather up the ends of the cloth, tie them together, and hang the curds up.*

SOFT CHEESE

1 STRAINING *Begin the process in exactly the same way as if you are making hard cheese. Once the rennet is added, the curds may take 12 hours to coagulate fully. When the curds split easily if a finger is pushed through them, they are ready. Strain them through scalded cheesecloth.*

Cloth must be scalded to prevent cheese from going bad

2 HANGING *Tie the corners of the cloth together and hang the curds up to drain overnight. By morning, the curds will be well drained. You can now add a little salt and any herbs or other flavorings you might want in your cheese. For a different taste, why not try adding fruit, such as apricots?*

3 MOLDING *Now shape your cheese. The simplest way to do this is to press it into rounds with your hands (they are, of course, clean), but Scotch hands (see p. 172) are very good for making blocks. Otherwise, you can use molds, as here. Roll the shaped cheeses in herbs or nuts, or wrap them in leaves.*

7 CRUMBLING CURDS *Hang the curds for about an hour, until they have drained and settled. Turn them into a large bowl and crumble them into smaller pieces. Salt can be added at this stage. Add 2 teaspoons (10 g) of salt for every 1 gallon (4.5 liters) of milk.*

8 READY FOR THE PRESS *Line the cheese press with scalded cheesecloth. Spoon the crumbled curds into the press, making sure they are well packed into the sides. Put the circular plate over the curds; if necessary, pack the press with a spacing block.*

PLOUGHMAN'S LUNCH

9 PRESSING *Press the curds for eight hours, take the cheese out of the mold, turn it, wrap it in clean cloth, and press at greater pressure for 24 hours. If you can resist it, let it mature for six weeks.*

Whey runs out at base of press

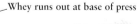

Curing bacon and hams

TRADITIONALLY, EVERY SCRAP of meat a pig produced was preserved in one way or another. Nowadays, we have the luxury of freezers, but some of the ways of preserving meat practiced by earlier generations are still well worth trying out for yourself. You can cure pig meat to make hams and bacon, which, kept in the right conditions, will last for years. There is no other meat that can be preserved for so long. Of all meats, ham and bacon have been devalued the most by modern food-manufacturing techniques. For example, many hams now have brine pumped into them to ensure rapid curing, and an increased water content. It all makes for a miserable product. If you keep pigs, you *must* cure your own hams and bacon to recapture a flavor that has been lost, as well as to keep alive one of the great home-farming traditions.

MEAT HYGIENE

IT WAS FOR VERY GOOD reasons that the traditional curing season began in late autumn and continued only until the end of winter. There are many enemies, both inside and outside the meat, that will try to ruin your preserving ambitions. Because curing is a lengthy process, bacteria have time to flourish, so you *must* start off with properly sterilized equipment (see p. 172 for sterilizing techniques). Another "must" is to keep everything cool and in the shade. An ideal place is the back of a chilly pantry, where the curing ham will not be disturbed.

SIDE OF PORK

AS A GENERAL RULE, the farther you go toward the rear end of a pig, the better the meat. That is why the finest hams are made from the top half of the rear legs. The shoulders can also be cured into hams, but the meat is coarser. Hams made from shoulder meat are often pressed to make slicing easier.

The central trunk of the pig is usually made into bacon; the meat nearest the back makes the meatiest bacon, called Canadian bacon, while the meat from lower down is fattier and only streaked with meat.

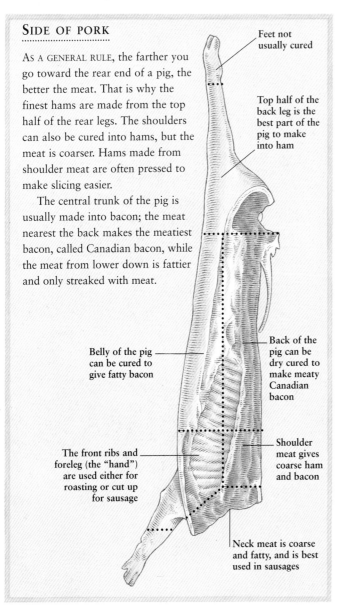

Feet not usually cured

Top half of the back leg is the best part of the pig to make into ham

Belly of the pig can be cured to give fatty bacon

Back of the pig can be dry cured to make meaty Canadian bacon

The front ribs and foreleg (the "hand") are used either for roasting or cut up for sausage

Shoulder meat gives coarse ham and bacon

Neck meat is coarse and fatty, and is best used in sausages

DRY CURING

1 SALTING *Rub salt into all surfaces of the meat. Salt is the basis of curing. It draws moisture out of the meat, preserving it and killing bacteria.*

2 BROWN SUGAR *You can also rub other flavorings, such as brown sugar, into the bacon. When the salt becomes wet from the water drawn out of the meat, brush the salt off the meat, wash the dish, and rub in fresh salt.*

3 WASHED CLEAN *After two weeks or so, the bacon will be cured. Wash it to remove surface salt. Then wrap the meat in a cheesecloth and allow it to dry in a cool place, where it will not be attacked by flies.*

BRINE CURING

1 STRAINING *Strain the remnants of the herbs and spices out of the brine (see panel on right) as you ladle the brine into a crock.*

2 IMMERSING *Wash the ham to make sure that it is clean. Then slip it into the crock containing the brine. The crock should be of a sufficient size for you to be able to immerse the whole ham.*

MAKING BRINE

ADD SALT TO a large pan of water until a fresh egg floats in it. The brine will then be strong enough. Add herbs, spices, molasses, brown ale, or cider for interestingly flavored hams. Simmer the ingredients together for five minutes, and the brine is ready.

3 WEIGHTING *The ham will tend to float, leaving part of it exposed to the air – and to bacteria! Place a clean wooden board on top of the ham, and weight it in such a way that the ham is totally submerged and the weights cannot fall into the brine.*

Replace the brine if it thickens or becomes opaque

4 COMPLETE CURE *Turn the ham often to ensure an even cure. Use your nose to check for any hint of the ham going bad. It will quickly become apparent: a good ham always smells fresh and salty. There is no fixed time for the cure. A week will be enough for a small ham.*

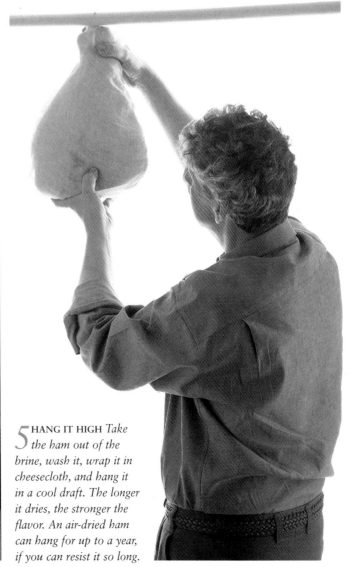

5 HANG IT HIGH *Take the ham out of the brine, wash it, wrap it in cheesecloth, and hang it in a cool draft. The longer it dries, the stronger the flavor. An air-dried ham can hang for up to a year, if you can resist it so long.*

Sausages and smoking

THERE IS HARDLY a meat-eating culture in the world where the sausage does not feature in the national or regional cuisine. There is a very good reason for this. Sausages are the best way of using those parts of an animal that are too coarse or fatty to be used for anything else, or of using scraps of meat left over when a carcass has been stripped of its best cuts. They also provide a way of marrying different meats into one dish.

Smoked and dried meats are also traditional foods, eaten all over the world. Smoking has long been used to flavor meat and go some way toward preserving it, and people have been preserving meat by drying it, in the sun or over fires, for centuries.

DRYING MEAT

DEHYDRATION has a strong preservative effect: without water, bacteria in meat are unable to multiply. The two main types of dried meat are biltong, which is South African, and jerky, which is North American. Biltong is shown here, being dried in an oven. Both can be sun- or oven-dried, but biltong is dry cured with salt beforehand. You can also dry sausages.

MAKING SAUSAGES

1 **GRINDING** *Grind the meat, using a hand or an electric grinder. Although you can use less useful cuts of meat to make sausages, there is no excuse to use rubbish. Sausages need fat for flavor. Up to half the meat can be back fat.*

2 **SAUSAGE MIX** *You will have to add salt and pepper to the ground meat, but you can also add a wide range of herbs and other flavorings, such as onions. To produce a sausage that is less meaty, add bread crumbs.*

3 **WASHING CASINGS** *Natural casings are animal intestines. Wash them thoroughly to remove the salt solution in which they are stored. Artificial casings are now available.*

4 **WASHING THE INSIDES** *It is as important to wash the insides of the casings as the outsides. Run fresh water through the casings until they are absolutely free of salt.*

5 **FILLING** *You can buy a sausage maker to fill the casings, but a funnel or an icing bag will do. Hold the casing over the end of the funnel, and press the meat evenly into it.*

CLOSING THE CASING
6 *Twist at intervals to make sausages of the length you would like. Finally, knot the ends to keep the sausages stuffed.*

Beef and bacon sausage hanging to dry

Chili salami hanging to dry

Garlic and herb salami wrapped for storage after drying is complete

DRIED SAUSAGES
To dry sausages, hang them in a cool, dark, dry, airy place. Check them every few days. If they smell bad, throw them out. After 5 or 6 weeks, they should have lost 50–60 percent of their original weight and are perfect for eating raw.

SMOKING MEAT

MEAT IS USUALLY smoked to give it flavor, but smoking slowly removes moisture too, helping to preserve the meat. A smoker needs a lid to keep the smoke in, something to hold the meat, and a basket in which the fire can sit. It also needs to be tall so that the fire in the bottom will not cook the meat. You can buy a smoker or simply make one from a metal trash can. Use hardwood, not softwood, sawdust to make the smoke.

CHECKING PROGRESS
Don't be tempted to check too often – every time you lift the lid, the smoking time increases.

Fresh sawdust ready to light

Add some smoldering sawdust to ignite the rest

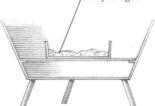

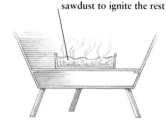

1 FRESH SAWDUST *Take off the upper part of the smoker. Put some hardwood sawdust in the fire tray. Sprinkle the sawdust with water so that it will not burn, but smolder.*

2 HEATED SAWDUST *Put a few ounces of sawdust in a pan. Heat this sawdust on a stove until it smolders. Spread it over the fresh sawdust – this will start to smolder as well.*

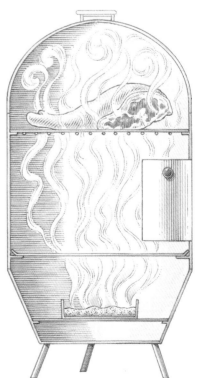

Stir sawdust every two or three hours, and add more if necessary

3 SMOKING *Now put the upper section of the smoker in position, and lay the meat on the top grill. You can smoke a whole range of meats, including sausages, ham, and bacon. Keep turning the meat so as to smoke it evenly, and stir up the sawdust regularly.*

Jams and canning

FRESHLY PICKED FRUIT has a desperately short life. Of course, there are quite a few fruits that you can dry in the sun, if you live in a place where sunshine is no rarity. In the past, before freezers were common, there were only two ways to preserve fruit without sunshine: cook it with sugar to make a jam or conserve, or can it. When you make jam you fundamentally alter the fruit, but when you can fruit, you retain much of its original taste and texture. You can can vegetables too, but it works better with fruit, which contains more acid and is less likely to go bad. Canned vegetables also tend to look dull, but canned fruit can be a cheering sight on the pantry shelf in the middle of winter.

TESTING FOR THE SETTING POINT

THERE ARE THREE WAYS to test whether jam will set. (1) Use a thermometer: most jam will set at 220°F (105°C). (2) Drop a blob of jam on a cold saucer: the jam should form a skin that wrinkles when you push it with your finger. (3) Cool jam on a spoon: instead of running off, it should fall off in large flakes.

Thermometer – heat to 220°F (105°C)

Wrinkle test – a blob of jam should wrinkle

Flake test – the jam should fall in flakes

MAKING JAM

1 WASHING FRUIT *Firm fruit is better than overripe fruit. Remove any leaflike attachments ("hulls") from berries. Wash the fruit several times in cold water.*

2 COOKING THE FRUIT *Put the fruit (with water if needed) in a large preserving pan. Simmer until the fruit breaks down to a pulp.*

3 ADDING SUGAR *Add the sugar to the fruit pulp. The quantity will depend on which fruit you use. This raspberry jam used equal weights of sugar and fruit.*

4 SKIMMING *Keep the jam from boiling rapidly until it reaches the setting point (see above). Skim off any froth that collects on the surface.*

5 FILLING JARS *When the jam reaches the setting point, remove the pan from the heat and let the jam sit for 15 minutes. Then pour the jam into warm, sterilized jars.*

CANNING FRUIT

1 PREPARING FRUIT *Reject any fruit that is damaged or even slightly rotten. One bad fruit can spoil an entire jar. Wash fruit and prepare as appropriate. These figs need only be halved.*

2 MAKING SUGAR SYRUP *Syrup gives extra flavor to canned fruits. Add 1 cup (225 g) of sugar to 1 pint (600 ml) of water and boil. For figs, low in acid, add a little citric acid.*

3 FILLING THE JAR *Pack the fruit into wet, sterilized jars as tightly as you can. Be careful not to damage fruit. Strain the sugar syrup and pour it over the fruit, either hot or cold.*

4 RELEASING AIR *Gently push a sterilized knife blade down the side of the jar to release any air bubbles. Another way is to tap the jar gently on the table. Top up with syrup if necessary.*

Jar sealed with cellophane cover

Waxed-paper disk

6 SEALING *Seal the jars right away, while the jam is still hot, to ensure they are airtight. Place a disk of waxed paper on the top of the jam and press lightly to remove any air bubbles. Then seal with a cellophane cover held on by a rubber band.*

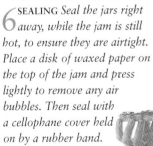

THE BEST BIT
Avoid all temptations to eat your jams before winter has even started. Store them with care, and they will last you until the fresh fruit is in season again.

5 STERILIZING *This method of sterilizing requires the syrup in the jars to be hot. Place the jars in a pan with a false base (a wire grill or a layer of cloths). Separate the jars of fruit with* cloths, so that the jars will not knock against each other. Pour warm water to cover the jars and heat slowly. Simmering sterilizes the fruit. Time taken depends on the fruit and the size of the jars.

Pickles and chutney

THE PRESERVING OF VEGETABLES or fruit in vinegar is called pickling. The strongly acidic nature of the vinegar ensures that bacteria cannot survive. Pickled vegetables can have a considerable shelf life and this is a good way of preserving, although, unlike canning, the flavor of the vegetables is heavily overladen with that of the vinegar. For the best-looking pickles, you should use white vinegar, but brown malt vinegar will give more flavor. There is also scope in pickling for adding spices such as cinnamon, cloves, and peppercorns to create interesting flavors.

Chutneys are also a useful way of converting vegetables or fruit into a form in which they can be stored and used at a later date – and they're delicious too. As well as vinegar, sugar is used in chutneys, both as part of the preserving process and to make the chutney tastier. Chutneys are halfway between jams and pickles.

RAW VEGETABLE PICKLES

NOT ALL VEGETABLES have to be cooked before pickling. Onions, for example, pickle well if merely left for sufficient time in vinegar. Cabbage does not need to be cooked before pickling, nor does cauliflower. Immature, green walnuts can also be pickled raw.

COOKED VEGETABLE PICKLES

1 **INGREDIENTS** *The basic ingredients are vegetables (or fruit), washed and in perfect condition, and vinegar, with spices if you like. Most vegetables need to be salted and rinsed before pickling, but beets do not.*

2 **PREPARING VINEGAR** *Prepare the spiced vinegar in advance – it is best left to mature for a month or two before use. Tie your chosen spices in a piece of cheesecloth. Boil the spices in the vinegar, or leave the spices to steep for longer in cold vinegar.*

3 **COOKING VEGETABLES** *Cook the washed vegetables according to the pickle recipe you are using, and slice if necessary. Boil beets for 1½ hours until tender and then top and tail, peel, and slice them.*

4 **FILLING** *Pack the vegetables into hot jars as tightly as possible, but not right to the top. Fill the jar with the vinegar until all the vegetables are covered, then add a bit more. Seal with tops of glass or vinegar-proof metal.*

HOME CHUTNEY

1 CHOPPING UP *Wash, peel, and chop the vegetables or fruit in the recipe for the chutney you are making. The various squashes for this chutney are being peeled, deseeded, and chopped.*

2 ADDING SPICES *All chutneys contain spices. This squash chutney includes finely shredded ginger, red chilies, and black and white mustard seeds. Put the spices and vegetables in a pan.*

As well as the squashes and spices, this recipe includes apples

3 ADDING VINEGAR *Add the vinegar to the other ingredients in the pan. Any vinegar will do, but cider vinegar is often preferred for its fruitier flavor. Bring the mixture to a boil and simmer for about 25 minutes until the vegetables are tender (not mushy).*

4 ADDING SUGAR *Add the sugar to the hot mixture, and stir until it dissolves. Soft brown sugar is being used in this case. Bring the chutney back to a boil, and simmer for about 1 hour until the mixture thickens.*

5 FILLING JARS *Sterilize the empty jars by boiling them in water for ten minutes or placing them on a baking tray and heating in an oven preheated to 325°F (160°C) for ten minutes. Ladle the chutney into the hot jars right away, while it is still hot, and seal them immediately. Chutneys improve with time – those you keep until the end of the winter will be even better than the earlier ones you couldn't resist.*

This chutney goes well with a simple meal of bread and cheese

Making wine and mead

IT IS A GREAT country tradition to take fruits or flowers, or even some vegetables, and capture their flavors and scents by making them into wine. Wine making is more widespread today than in past times, for sugar is much easier to obtain; in earlier centuries, farmers would have made ale or mead, which is a honey wine. You can be as scientific about wine making as you wish to be, and much of the specialized equipment that can be bought will rival anything a chemistry laboratory could offer, but the principles are simple. You are inviting yeasts to turn sugars (whether added or occurring naturally in the produce) into alcohol by fermentation, and if you give them the right conditions in which to work, they will usually be happy to oblige.

NOT JUST GRAPES

ALMOST ANY FRUIT or vegetable can impart its flavor to wine. You might try carrots, parsnips, elderberries, or even mangels. Do not be too hasty to drink them. Many of these are subtle flavors that take time to develop.

MAKING WINE

1 FILLING THE PRESS *Tip the grapes into a suitable press. This is a cider press, but it will work just as well with grapes. Alternatively, you can improvise and wrap your grapes in cheesecloth and crush them by hand.*

Pressed juice will run out between wooden slats

2 PRESSING *You need a fair amount of pressure to extract all the juice from the grapes. Collect the juice in a sterilized bowl. Clean equipment is essential, or you will end up producing vinegar instead of wine.*

3 STERILIZING TABLETS *Pour the juice into a fermenter. Crush a sterilizing tablet and add it to the juice, along with 1 teaspoon of pectin-destroying enzyme. If the grapes are sweet, you won't need to add any sugar.*

4 YEAST *Allow the sterilizer several hours to exhaust its potency. Put wine-making yeast in a jug with sweetened grape juice. When the mixture froths, pour it into the grape juice, which should be at 75°F (24°C).*

Air lock keeps out airborne bacteria and wild yeasts, but lets carbon dioxide escape

5 FERMENTATION *Fit an air lock onto the fermenter. The fermentation will take a day or two to get going. It will be vigorous for a week or so, before settling to a steady rate. Keep the wine at 70–80°F (21–26°C).*

6 RACKING *When no more bubbles rise through the wine, fermentation is over. In all, it may take two to three weeks – it varies with conditions and ingredients. Siphon the wine into another fermenter, leaving the sediment behind. Leave the wine until a new layer of sediment settles, then rack again. Repeat this process until the wine is clear.*

7 BOTTLING *Sterilize the bottles and a flexible tube (see p. 172). Stand the fermenter on a higher level than the bottles. Suck some wine from the fermenter into the tube, stop the end of the tube, and insert it into the bottle. The wine will flow of its own accord.*

Use a plastic tube that can be easily sterilized (see p. 172)

Corking tool for forcing corks into the bottles

8 CORKING *You can use brute force to cork your bottles, but a corking tool makes the process much easier. Store wine on its side to keep the corks* *moist. Any air creeping into the bottle will spoil the wine. Wines mature slowly, and some may not reach their best until a year or more has passed.*

MAKING MEAD

MEAD IS SWEET WINE made from honey, and was one of the earliest of alcoholic drinks. Today, besides the wine, a liqueur form of mead is often produced. The making of mead is part of a very ancient tradition. If you have a hive of bees, then set aside some of the honey to make mead. Many health-giving virtues are claimed for mead, as are aphrodisiac properties!

1 HONEY SOLUTION *Use 3 lb (1.4 kg) honey to 3½ quarts (4 liters) water. Boil the water to sterilize it, let it cool to hand hot, then dissolve the honey in it. Pour it into a fermenter.*

2 YEAST AND LEMONS *Add yeast (see facing page) and some lemon juice or powdered citric acid. Fermentation needs acid, and there may not be enough in the honey.*

HONEY WINE *Ferment, rack, and bottle the mead as for wine. It may take three years for the bottled mead to reach its best.*

Making cider

IF YOU HAVE a good supply of apples from your orchard, then when the first cold mornings of late autumn arrive, you will want to start thinking of making your winter cider. There are special varieties of cider apple – indeed, special orchards filled with them – but you can make decent cider with all kinds of apples. Do not worry if your apples are a little overripe or bruised – that makes them easier to press – but avoid underripe fruit. Here is my way to make a *fine* cider. Rougher, sharper ciders can be made simply by piling the pressed juice into clean barrels and leaving it.

APPLE JUICE

INSTEAD OF FERMENTING all your apple juice to make cider, why not keep some of it as juice? It tastes better than any you can buy. The juice will not keep for long before it starts to ferment, unless you freeze or pasteurize it. A clearer apple juice can be made by straining.

Unstrained apple juice

HOME FARM CIDER

1 CRUSHING *Roughly chop the apples and then crush them. If you try to press them whole, you will get a lot less juice. I now use a specialized crusher like this – it reduces the apples to just the right consistency to press the maximum juice out of them. In the past, I've had as much success with the more strenuous method of placing the apples in a strong tub and pounding them with a wooden cudgel.*

Crusher has rotating blades that pulp apples

Press holds 2½ gallons (12 liters) of apple pulp

2 THE PRESS *My crusher comes complete with its own cider press. A specialized press is the only practical way to extract the juice from the pulp. Roughly, 20 lb (9 kg) of pulp give you 1 gallon (4.5 liters) of juice.*

Juice flows down the spout into a collecting bowl

3 PRESSING *Apply pressure to the pulp and gradually increase it as the juice runs out. When juice stops flowing, let the pulp settle, then try again – more juice will come out.*

4 THE REMAINDER *Once you have pressed all the juice out of the apples, you will be left with a cake of apple pulp. If there is a pig on your farm, it will be interested. If not, put the pulp on the compost pile.*

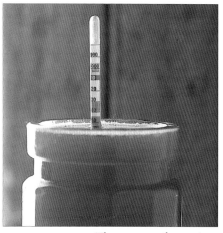

5 HYDROMETER *The amount of sugar in the juice determines the strength of the cider. Use a hydrometer to test the specific gravity (an indication of the sugar content). If the gravity is less than 1.040, add sugar.*

6 ADDING YEAST *Pour the juice into a fermenter. Traditionally, yeasts naturally in the juice are left to ferment the cider. I do it the modern way – add a sterilizing tablet, then (after several hours) a wine yeast.*

7 FERMENTATION *Fit an air lock. Ideally, the fermenter should not be more than three-quarters full, to allow enough space for fermentation. This will take anything up to two weeks. Keep the cider at 59°F (15°C).*

8 RACKING *Rack the cider as many times as necessary (see p. 185). It is important to keep exposure to air to a minimum, so do not leave the fermenter open or half full.*

9 BOTTOMS UP *When your cider is as clear as it's going to get, siphon it into bottles (see p. 185). Cider will improve with age and may not be at its very best until three years after bottling. For a sweeter cider, add some sugar just before drinking. Don't put sugared cider in a sealed bottle – it might explode!*

INDEX

Page numbers in bold type indicate a reference to an illustration or a caption to an illustration.

ACKNOWLEDGMENTS

VALE FARM Rose and Nicholas Heiney for help with potato planting; Derek Filby, horseman; Robert White for demonstrating farming skills; Alan Hubbard for hedging demonstration; Michael Spink for demonstrations of use and maintenance of Ferguson tractor; Martin Harvey for help with Ferguson tractor; Richard Jones for demonstration of hay baling and for permission to photograph Dutch barn; Juliet Hawkins for conservation report; Beth Wilson and family for catering and hospitality.

PEAK HILL FARM Richard and Margaret White for permission to take photographs and for demonstrating farming skills; Robert White for demonstrating farming skills and for general assistance; Donald Mitchell and Sarah Sacharczuk for sheep-shearing demonstration.

ASHURST FARM Peter Haynes and Collette Pavledis for permission to take photographs and for demonstrating farm skills, assisted by Alex White, Topsy Jewell, Michi Mathias, Rebecca Doy, Camille Gry Smenge, Paul Andrews, Jordan Haynes, and Jacob Frizell.

UNION FARM AND NORFOLK RURAL LIFE MUSEUM Andrew Mackay for arranging permission to take photographs; Richard Dalton for consultation, supervision, and demonstrations; Chris Queen, Matthew Perkins, Martin Cooper for help with cereal harvest; Helen Whiteleg for livestock handling; June Hill for help with manure pile; June Ross for spinning display; Mick Massey, blacksmith; Mike Crisp and Leslie Rose for their help on several occasions; Joe Godderidge for permission to photograph sulky plough.

SPR POULTRY CENTRE David Bland (author of Practical Poultry Keeping, Ducks and Geese for Pleasure, and, with Alexandra Bastedo, of Poultry Matters video) for permission to take photographs at SPR Poultry Centre and for subsequent consultancy on poultry keeping; Denise Betsworth for goat-milking demonstration.

ALEXANDRA BASTEDO ANIMAL SANCTUARY for Alexandra Bastedo's assistance and permission to take photographs at the sanctuary.

SHEILA BERRETT for permission to photograph beekeeping demonstration and equipment, and for much help and advice.

VANA HAGERTY for permission to photograph rabbits and their housing, and for much help and advice.

LYNN AND CHRISTOPHER BEADLE for permission to photograph goats and their housing, and for much help and advice.

JULIE WHITELAW for loan of cheese-making equipment and demonstration of deep-bed digging.

SPECIALIST ADVICE AND EQUIPMENT Michael Devenish for advice on cider making; Vigo Vineyard Supplies, Hemyock, Devon, for use of cider press and for valued advice; Ian Wilkinson of Cotswold Grass Seeds, who supplied the meadow menus; Debbie Pain at RSPB for information on farmland birds; Peter Jackson and Brian Marson at Burgon & Ball Ltd, Sheffield, and Paul Bates at Spear & Jackson Garden Products Ltd, Wednesbury, for help with "Blades and sharpening"; Anna Malos and BTCV London staff for advice on "Hedging"; Liz Wright of Smallholder magazine, Bailey Newspaper Group Ltd, Dursley, Glos, UK; tel. (management) 01453 544000, (editorial) 01345 741182, for suggesting sources of information.

EDITORIAL CONSULTANTS Katie Thear of Country Garden & Smallholding magazine (Station Road, Newport, Saffron Walden, Essex, UK; tel. 01799 540922; fax 01799 541367; e-mail cgs@broadleys.com) for general review of the text; Joshua Nelson of Beaver River Associates, Rhode Island, consultant on North American and warm-climate farming; Ray Fordham of Wye College, University of London, for advice on "Fruits of the earth" chapter; Poppy Body, home economist for "Home comforts" chapter; Barbara Ellis; Ray Rogers.

PUBLICATIONS acknowledged by the author as highly valued sources: Anna Pavord, The New Kitchen Garden, and Geoff Hamilton, Successful Organic Gardening (both Dorling Kindersley books).

INDEX by Julie Rimington.

PHOTO CREDITS
t = top, l = left, r = right, c = center, b = bottom
J. Allan Cash Ltd: 53tl. Cephas Picture Library: E. Burt 117crb; F. B. Higham 2tl; L.-O. Nilsson 92bc; M. Rock 20br, 130tl. Bruce Coleman Ltd: J. Jurka 8Ocl; G. McCarthy 126t; J. McDonald 92bl; H. Reinhard 84t, 116tl; Dr. E. Pott 85cl (ii), 122BR; K. Taylor 92br. Ecoscene: 10cl; F. Blackburn 18bcl; A. Brown 124b; A. Cooper 80bl; C. Gryniewicz 151bl; A. Hampton 66t, 69c, 151br, 156t; A. Towse 131bc; D. Walker 116bcr. Jeremy Evans 83clb. Eye Ubiquitous: G. Redmayne 53tr. FLPA: 119t; J. C. Allen 132t; R. Austing 124tr; L. Batten 124tl; R. F. Bird 40cr; T. Davidson 82l; E. & D. Hosking 143b, 167br; I. Rose 85cr (i); M. Rose 59bl; Silvestris 161cl; R. Tidman 161cr; T. Whittaker 87br; R. Wilmshurst 154b. Robert Harding Picture Library: 42bl, 73, 80tl, 83tr, 111cra, 145b; W.H. Black 136cr; N. Blythe 143c, 150cr; F. Friberg 160t; /Odyssey/Chicago: R. Frerck 151tr. Heritage and Natural History Photography: Dr. J. B. Free 83clb, 83bl. Holt Studios International: J. Adams 184tl; N. Cattlin 1c, 13l, 20bc, 43cr, 54b, 58tr, 63, 69br, 70t, 72b, 74cr, 80br, 86t, 86b, 87t, 87cl, 87cr, 102t, 137bl, 155, 162t, 163b, 170tl; W. Harinck 167bl; P. Mitchell 42br; A. Morant 70b; P. Peacock 68br, 90, 166br; G. Roberts 59cl, 59br; D. Smith 118br; I. Spence 2c, 12l, 106tr; P. Wilson 137br. David Lamb 147br. NHPA: 68cr, 85cl (i); G.I. Bernard 80bcr, 162bcr; V.G. Canseco 20bl; M. Garwood 85cr (ii); S. Kraseman 14bcr; M. Leach 71c; E. Soder 87bl; R. Tidman 68tr; D. Woodfall 14br, 16bcr, 88. Museum of English Rural Life: G. Brightling 8tr; G. Dann 56tl. Norfolk Rural Life Museum: G. Brightling 60c, 60bl, 60br, 60/1, 61cl, 61bl, 116bl. A. Oakford: 2cr. Oxford Scientific Films: R. Blythe 20bcr, 22br; D. Bown 10cr; M. Chillmaid 71t, 71b; T. Heathcote 14t; G. A. Maclean 129cr; R. Toms 118bl; /Animals Animals: C. Palek 140t; /Okapia: H. Reinhard 12r. Photos Horticultural: 97tl, 104tr. RSPCA: C. Seddon 154t. South of England Rare Breeds Centre: G. Brightling 66b. Tony Stone Images: P. Cade 144tr; P.H. Coblentz 115tr; J. & E. Forder 13r. Wild Images: M. Busselle 82tr. Wildlife Matters: 14bl. Woodfin Camp & Associates, Inc: P. Solomon 114tl.

Additional photography by G. Brightling, Dave King, David Murray, Philip Dowell, A. Einsiedel, Ian O'Leary, Roger Phillips, Jacqui Hurst, Philip Dowell, Steve Gorton, Steven Wooster, Linda Whitwam, Max Alexander, and Robert Purnell.